HEMA MALINI

Beyond the Dream Girl

An Authorized Biography

RAM KAMAL MUKHERJEE

Foreword by Prime Minister Narendra Modi

Edited by

NOOSHIN MOWLA

HarperCollins *Publishers* India

First published in hardback in India in 2017 by
HarperCollins *Publishers* India
A-75, Sector 57, Noida, Uttar Pradesh 201301, India
www.harpercollins.co.in

2 4 6 8 10 9 7 5 3 1

P-ISBN: 978-93-5277-322-0
E-ISBN: 978-93-5277-323-7

COVER PHOTO CREDITS
Make-up: Billy
Hair: Jaya Surve
Location: Advitiya

Typeset in 12/14.5 Arno Pro at
SÜRYA, New Delhi

Printed and bound at
Thomson Press (India) Ltd

Baba ... for allowing me to chase my 'dream' and 'beyond'.
Maa ... for showing me *Seeta Aur Geeta, Sholay* and *Meera*.
And the rest was destiny.

Hema Malini Family Tree

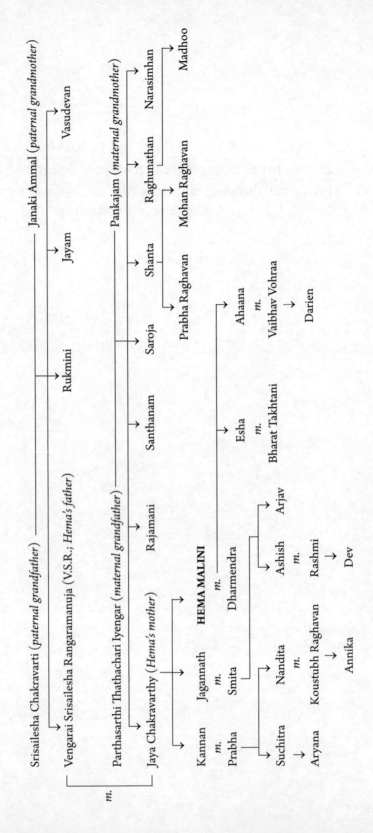

Contents

Foreword by Prime Minister Narendra Modi ix

Introduction xi

Prologue: The Story of Sujata 1

1. No Ordinary Childhood 5

2. The Dream Girl Is Born 18

3. Flight to Freedom 26

4. A Taste of Stardom 33

5. Double Whammy 42

6. The Colours of Spring 50

7. Tryst with a Poet ... and Poetic Cinema 57

8. Colleagues Extraordinaire 65

9. An Eternal Love Story 74

10. 'Hunterwali' Hema 82

11. 'Amma' Malini 94

12. In and Out of the Box 101

13. The Debut of King Khan 110

14. Taking a Different Direction 118

15. Dancing Diva 131

16. 'Abhi-netri': Hema's Political Journey 141

17. Experiments with Spirituality 160

18. Still at the Top 169

19. Esha's Tale 175

20. Dawn and Darien 186

21. An Accident on the Highway 194

22. Playback Time 200

23. Bliss 210

Afterword by Ramesh Sippy 218

Filmography 220

Index 231

About the Author 241

Foreword

I am delighted to know that the book *Beyond the Dream Girl* is being published on the life of noted actor and political leader, Hema Malini-ji.

Hema-ji has distinguished herself as one of the leading Indian actors of our times. Her cinematic brilliance has spanned several films through the various decades. Her many roles have connected and endeared her to a wide range of cinema lovers. The efforts of Hema-ji to popularize Indian classical dances, particularly among youngsters, are deeply commendable.

It is gladdening to note that the biography on Hema-ji also covers her early years and how she gained a foothold in the film industry through hard work and dedication.

Hema-ji has also been an active BJP member for many years. She has served diligently in the Rajya Sabha and is currently serving in the Lok Sabha. I have found her extremely sensitive towards the development aspirations of the people of Mathura, her constituency.

Once again, congratulations on the book and may it further connect Hema-ji to the lakhs of well-wishers she has in India and the world.

(Narendra Modi)

New Delhi
18 September 2017

Introduction

Dreams don't work out, unless you work.

If I was asked to choose the one enduring lesson Hema Malini left me with, it would be the above. Her aura had been described perfectly by Sanjeev Kumar when the late actor, after having worked in half a dozen films with her, declared, 'Hema Malini is neither a goddess nor a saint, but she is someone who is worshipped for both qualities.'

When I decided to write my second book on her – this time, an authorized biography – I was keen on exploring the person beyond the superstar. I was equally aware that I had my work cut out. Hema is an introvert and barely talks about her personal life. What added to the challenge was venturing into the same territory after nearly two decades.

My first book on Hema Malini, *Diva Unveiled*, published in 2003, was a pictorial depiction of the actor's life. A cub reporter at that time, I remember how she had told me I was too young to take up the project. Moreover, veteran journalist and editor of *Screen Weekly*, Bhawana Somaaya, was already writing her biography. I stuck to my resolve nonetheless.

Although well received by film aficionados, *Diva Unveiled*, because of its pricing, ended up more a collectors' item. But I have no regrets. The book helped me find a new lease of life in Bollywood, as well as recognition as an author.

Over the last fifteen years, I have had the opportunity to observe Hema's life from close quarters. From *Seeta Aur Geeta* to *Baghban*, from campaigning for Vinod Khanna in Gurdaspur to becoming an MP from Mathura, from being the Dream Girl to becoming the flag-bearer for liberated, independent women – it has been a phenomenal life. Her transition from actress to director to politician to playback singer has been commendable. All the while, she has also been playing the role of a cultural ambassador through her immensely popular dance ballets. She continues to be one of the strongest proponents of classical dance and music in the country.

However, in a career span of five decades, she has won the Filmfare Award just once. That says a lot about her PR skills. 'I never had a PR person, I never partied and I had to never ask for work. But now things have changed,' she says.

While interviewing her, I realized that there is a lot that has not been written about her, and now, as she turns seventy, she is probably in a position to drop her guard. Hema has always called a spade a spade. Apart from her mind-boggling capacity to master new terrains, in this book she opens up, for the first time, on her childhood years, her unpredictable career graph, her unconventional life choices and the steep, hard climb she has endured to get to where she is today – in complete harmony with herself.

Hema's journey as a politician is probably one of the most interesting chapters in this book. From the Rajya Sabha to an elected BJP MP from Mathura, she has had a great run. 'I want to serve the nation. Whatever I am today is because of the public. It's now my turn to do something for society,' she says. She continues to be a well-loved name in political circles. From Sonia Gandhi to Atal Bihari Vajpayee, from Laloo Prasad Yadav to Narendra Modi, her popularity cuts across party lines. MP and Trinamool Congress minister Derek O'Brien shared in jest an incident that took place at the silver-jubilee celebration of HarperCollins India, 'Once, Hema-ji's earring fell on the carpet of the Parliament corridor, and every minister, from the ruling party to the Opposition, immediately fell on his knees to look for it!' It shows her aura even in politics.

Each time anyone asks me why I was writing another book on Hema, I ask back, 'Why not?' I had just taken a break from my editorial job at *Stardust* and had been working on my first fiction book, *Long Island Iced Tea*. It was also around this time that Swarup Nanda, my friend and founder of Leadstart Publishing, connected me with Shantanu

Ray Chaudhuri, executive editor at HarperCollins India. 'There is so much more than just being a "Dream Girl" to Hema-ji's life. I am sure there are readers who want to know her story,' he said when I broached the topic. In all my years in the industry, I have rarely come across as passionate an editor as Shantanu – the man who walked me through this journey.

Call it a miracle or divine intervention, things started falling into place. I came across Nooshin Mowla, a young and talented girl from the City of Joy, who was of great help in making this book a possibility. Formerly a producer of a hugely popular television series on Hindi cinema, she was just the editor I was looking for. To review the same subject but through a new lens is never easy, and that's where Nooshin played the part of staunch critic and sounding board. 'Don't be so possessive about your text, you need to tell a story, and ideally an interesting one,' she kept saying.

Many others played their part. Prabha Chakravarti – Hema's sister-in-law – helped me put together the facts painstakingly, despite her pressing schedule. Hema's cousin, 'superwoman' Prabha Raghavan, helped me with the images, allowing me access to some rare and exclusive collections.

Esha Deol Takhtani and Ahaana Deol Vohraa – Hema's lovely daughters – shared some previously untold stories on their relationship with their mother. I was also fortunate enough to interview Hema's colleagues, directors, producers, friends and extended family members who were only too happy to talk about her.

The only person missing in this picture was Hema Malini herself! Her political commitments and, later, a major road accident on the Jaipur highway made her virtually inaccessible. But I was willing to wait. When she realized how adamant I was, she finally relented.

'You think people still want to read about me?' she asked.

'This is for the new generation – those who have perhaps never watched your films,' I told her. For the rest, it had been over ten years since they last read about her. This time I wanted the world to know how much more there was to India's first female superstar. Moreover, this wouldn't be an ode – it would include the controversies, the challenges and all that had made her journey thus far so inspiring.

During the same conversation, I asked her, 'Do you have a Facebook or Instagram account, Hema-ji?'

She looked at me and said, 'No, why?'

I replied, 'This is exactly why I want to write a book on you.'

Every wall stands on bricks of faith; for this book, I too have had my fair share. I thank my mentor Nari Hira, the founder of Magna Publishing, for granting me access to the archives of *Stardust, Showtime, Society, Savvy* and *Diva Unveiled*. Sonali Jaffar Kotnis – my colleague and ex-editor of *Stardust* – thank you for suggesting my name to Mr Hira for the coffee-table book on Hema Malini. Vickky Idnaani and his entire team – thank you for creating the cover image for this book. Bonita – thank you for being so clear in your vision. And Amrita and Bidisha in the editorial team at Harper for your meticulous work on the text – I could not have asked for more.

My baba (late) Jaydeb Mukherjee and my maa Roma Mukherjee for giving me a pair of wings to fly – I am eternally grateful. My wife Sarbani Mukherjee, who stood by me like the Rock of Gibraltar and also played the role of co-researcher in this mammoth task – I couldn't have done this without you. My brother, Krishna Kamal, for being my inner strength; my colleague Chandrima Pal, for playing the role of an agony aunt; my four-year-old son Rian, the perfect stressbuster in the middle of mayhem – thank you all, eternally.

I would also like to thank Sukumar Pramanik, secretary to Hema Malini, for his contribution to the book. He has been associated with Hema-ji for the last fifteen years and has witnessed my journey too.

And of course, Hema Malini, who believed in me till the end.

PROLOGUE

The Story of Sujata

'She is going to be called "Sujata" from today. Her current name is not good enough,' declared the film producer to the stunned mother and daughter standing before him. As he languidly got up from the easy chair, their looks of astonishment didn't escape him. In fact, he smiled inwardly at their ignorance. It had been seven years since Bimal Roy's *Sujata* had released. A powerful comment on the caste system, the film had moved its audience in unprecedented ways. The producer, who had watched the film eighteen times, had been on the lookout for a face that would match the intensity of the film's titular character. His protégée would take off from where Nutan had left.

C.V. Sridhar, both mother and daughter had heard, was a formidable name in the Tamil, Hindi and Telugu film industries. The man had spotted, handpicked and offered to launch the career of young Hema Malini, an accomplished Bharatanatyam dancer who was making quite a splash across the country with her stage performances. He met her orthodox Iyengar family and offered to launch their beloved daughter in a Tamil film. With just one caveat – her name would have to be changed.

For Hema and her mother, Jaya Chakravarthy, the fog of bewilderment took some time to lift. As they stared blankly, first at him, then at each other and back again at him, they realized that his statement wasn't made to initiate debate. The decision had already been taken within the first three minutes of their meeting. Hema would be called 'Sujata' from that day.

The offer from Sridhar hadn't surprised them. Hema's concerts were receiving rave reviews and film offers had been pouring in from both the Hindi and Tamil film industries. Back home in Madras, however, the situation caused considerable strife. Her parents were divided on the matter and had stopped talking to each other. In all their married years, Ranga Ramanuja Chakravarti (better known by his official name Vengarai Srisailesha Rangaramanuja – V.S.R. – Chakravarti) and Jaya had never had such a huge disagreement. A deadlock of this kind was unheard-of in the family.

For the shy and intensely reserved Hema, the decision to take up Sridhar's offer had caused much distress. Films held no excitement for her. Dance had always been her one true love and that's all she had really wanted to do. For someone who could barely introduce herself to strangers, the thought of facing the camera, performing with unknown men and being pushed into a world of ostentation and glamour was nightmarish. 'I wasn't keen on joining films at all. Being shy, I was always petrified of exploring new avenues ... and films – I didn't even want to think about them,' she says. But it wasn't a decision for her to take.

'If you don't like the first film, you can opt out of this career. But you have to give it a shot,' Jaya Chakravarthy said. For her, the temptation was hard to resist. An accomplished artist herself, specializing in painting and classical singing, she was a strong-willed lady of considerable dignity and pride. A woman who ran the house with an iron hand and brought up her children almost single-handedly while her husband was busy at work, Jaya had a natural propensity towards wielding power. For Hema, she was a mother, a mentor and her closest friend – a relationship that used to surprise many because it involved two equally strong, fiercely independent women.

'I kept telling myself, this would be my first and last movie,' Hema reminisces. '*Mujhe actress nahin banna hai!*'

If getting used to a new name overnight wasn't hard enough, the following day was kept aside for a photo shoot. Forced to wear a sari – a first for her – Hema's thin and lanky frame didn't make for a very pretty picture. 'I was looking thin and ugly as hell in that sari. But Sridhar insisted that I do the photo shoot in a sari and nothing else. Though my mother tried her best, the pleats kept coming undone. I looked clumsy. I wish they had asked me to wear a pavada, a half-sari. But nobody cared about me or my choices at that point,' she recalls.

Over time, however, as days rolled into months and work on the film began, things began to look up. While the young star-to-be was getting groomed, the publicity team worked double time to create the necessary buzz. 'Sujata', by now, had already generated a good amount of curiosity amongst people. To add to it all, Sridhar had made an official announcement in the local newspapers about how he was all set to launch a new girl along with J. Jayalalithaa (the Tamil superstar who went on to become a popular political leader and chief minister of Tamil Nadu). The magnitude of the situation was slowly beginning to dawn on Hema. But as is the way of the world, just when things seemed to finally come together, they fell disastrously apart.

Shooting for the film had begun soon after Sridhar's announcement. Deep inside, Hema still didn't have her heart in the film-making process. She felt acutely out of place. And then suddenly, without any warning or consideration, one day Sridhar announced that he was dropping Hema from the project. Each time Hema Malini recounts this episode, she talks about the frozen silence that had followed Sridhar's words on the sets that day.

While mother and daughter were still coming to terms with the unceremonious expulsion, the producer wasted no time in signing on a replacement. What made matters worse was that Sridhar went to the press to tell them that 'Sujata' hadn't been able to deliver and lacked the skills to become a star.

To be at the receiving end of such unwarranted vitriol would have crushed any spirit. But even at sixteen, Hema was clearly made of something else. The Sridhar episode still reminds Hema of the immense relief she had felt; the relief of being released from the world of films and of getting her name back. But what stayed with her more intensely was the humiliation and heartbreak on her mother's face. For Jaya Chakravarthy, it was too big a shock to forget.

'For me it was a blessing in disguise,' Hema says. 'For a while I was extremely happy. It was like winning a liberation movement. But for my mother it was an ego issue. I knew that she went into depression. Later, I also realized that Sridhar played dirty and humiliated us.'

The sight of her mother that day, sitting in a daze, chin on her palm, was enough to drive Hema to her decision. 'Amma, I am going to be an actress.'

I wouldn't have believed in destiny if I hadn't met Hema Malini – a woman with profound faith in the divinity of the universe, but also someone who has played an active part in shaping her destiny. You are not what happened to you in the past, nor what you anticipate for the times ahead. You are what you focus on today. 'Now' alone determines your final story.

From being summarily dropped from her first attempt at acting, Hema Malini went on to become the uncrowned queen of Hindi cinema, playing the romantic lead in well over a hundred films. From being rejected to reigning as the heartthrob of an entire generation, she is the only Dream Girl this country has known, with a face that mesmerized fans and a screen presence the spotlight worshipped. Doe-eyed with alabaster skin and a smile that could light up a whole town, Hema's bewitching looks are talked about till date.

But that isn't her only claim to fame. In an industry where the word superstar is synonymous with the ubiquitous 'hero', where films still sell by the name of the male lead, Hema Malini tore through the patriarchy – as deep-seated as time itself – to build a name and reputation that could hold its own vis-à-vis her male co-stars. Her life has been a series of unconventional choices – many controversial. Her spectrum has been diverse – from films to television, actor to director, stage performances to public office. And through every choice she made, she has displayed a strength of character. Hers hasn't been an easy life, but one she has led with stupendous courage and integrity, helping her earn a rare kind of respect. In the chimerical world of filmdom, fickle as stardust, Hema Malini has prevailed.

1

No Ordinary Childhood

On the midnight of 15 October 1948, while most of the country was celebrating Goddess Durga's victory over the demon Mahisasura, Jaya Chakravarthy was bracing herself for her third delivery. After bearing two sons, she was certain that her next child would be a girl. When she was seven months pregnant, she had set off for her parents' house in Ammankudi village near Tiruchirapalli, Tamil Nadu, for the delivery, with her sons Kannan and Jagannath. Her husband, V.S.R. Chakravarti, worked as regional director in the Employees' State Insurance Corporation (ESIC), Ministry of Labour and Employment, and was posted in New Delhi. 'He had a transferable job, so we used to shift from one place to another. As per our family tradition, I came to my mother's place near Tiruchirapalli when I was seven months pregnant,' Jaya recalled.

Coming from a traditional Iyengar family, Jaya's father was a religious man who had ensured that his daughter was proficient in every Hindu religious ritual. Apart from being well versed in the aartis and the shlokas, Jaya used to spend a lot of time doing up the puja room with paintings and portraits of gods and goddesses. Talented as she was, Jaya was a loner – most of her early pregnancy days were spent in her room, taking singing and violin lessons.

A devout follower of Goddess Lakshmi, she went through all her 108 names and finally settled on 'Hema Malini' for her newborn. 'Hema' comes from the Sanskrit word 'hem' which means 'gold'. Hema Malini refers to 'the garland of gold that is used to adorn Lord Vishnu'. 'The name had a rhythm to it and I intuitively knew that my daughter would one day become a renowned dancer,' she said. For someone who would go on to change the fortunes of her family, there couldn't have been a name better suited.

Many years later, Jaya shared with Hema another reason behind choosing to name her after Goddess Lakshmi. While she was pregnant, Jaya would often dream of the goddess and paint her images.

Hema Malini was born on 16 October 1948. Her childhood was spent in a government colony near Gole Market, New Delhi. The colony had small cottages with patches of lawns and colonial-style verandas. Kannan, Jagannath and Hema studied at the Madras Educational Society School (MES). 'It was a cosy life; nothing earth-shattering happened in the Delhi of those days. Life was quite peaceful,' Kannan remembers.

The three siblings got along well, except for the preference Hema got from her parents. Being the youngest, and the much-awaited daughter of the family, she was showered with constant attention and care while the boys were left to fend for themselves.

'I call her Hemu, and she addresses me as Chila and my younger brother as Jaggu,' the eldest brother Kannan tells me. 'There is a six-year gap between Hema and me and two years between Jagannath and Hema. So, if there was any sibling rivalry, it was between the two of them!'

Radiant even when she was little, efforts were made during Hema's growing-up years to ensure that she didn't get self-conscious about her looks. 'As a child, I was never told that I was a pretty-looking girl,' she says with typical earnestness. 'I wasn't even aware that people found me beautiful. My exposure to the world was minimal because I hardly stepped out of the house, so I hardly got any compliments.'

Even though Hema was a strikingly good-looking child, her schoolmates at least weren't made aware of it. 'As children, you do not really pay much attention to looks,' K. Anuradha, who passed out from another branch of Hema's school and has now taken over as the principal of the Gole Market branch, says. 'I only remember Hema because she used to participate in all the functions as she was a good dancer, and the students of all the branches used to attend these school functions together. But she wasn't famous then, so there is no particular memory of her in my mind.'

A neighbour from Gole Market, who doesn't want to be named, recollects, 'I just remember that we both went to DTEA, Mandir Marg branch. Yes, when I look back and try to remember her face, I can say that she was a good-looking child. But at that time, it was not her extreme good looks that had impressed us kids. I remember her because she was the only one in our group to possess a bicycle and that is my most lingering memory of her! She was also a very good dancer, even at that age.'

The only hints about her looks that came Hema's way were through her mother's friends whom she frequently entertained. 'My mother's guests were generally from the world of art and culture, while my father's guests were more his work friends – two completely different sets of people. Sometimes I would overhear them praising me. I used to invariably hang around my mother, stuck to her pallu while they all sipped coffee in the veranda. Every time I would ask her who they were talking about, she would say, "Not you. They are talking about someone else!"'

New Delhi in the 1960s was very different from what it is today. Known for its quiet, tree-lined neighbourhoods, this was also when the city was revelling in a cultural resurgence. Indian classical music, dance and performing arts were beginning to flourish. The 1950s and '60s saw the establishment of several top-class auditoriums and institutions in Delhi, paving the way for the city to take over as the country's cultural capital.

Hema had an unusual childhood. While her classmates and contemporaries spent their free time in play and frolic, she led a strictly disciplined life away from all of it. After school, she was packed off to dance class at the Triveni Kala Sangam, one of Delhi's most prestigious dance academies, post a quick rest.

'Till she was about four or five years old, she was quite plump and cuddly,' Kannan recalls. 'But after her sixth year, my mother said that Hema had a bout of diarrhoea and lost weight, after which she became very thin. That was one of the reasons why she was put into rigorous dancing classes, so that the physical exercise could bring her back to good health.'

'I guess I was just five years old, or maybe younger, when I started learning Bharatanatyam under the tutelage of my first guru, Ramaswamy Pillai,' Hema recalls. 'My mother used to take me there and watch my performance. The ghungroos used to hurt my ankles whenever my feet thumped the floor because they were heavy and hard. I cried often, looking at my mother, hoping she would allow me to rest. But it never happened! She used to say: "There is purpose in pain, otherwise it would have been devilish. Pain and pleasure, like light and darkness, succeed each other. The rewards for those who persevere far exceed the pain that precedes the victory." Naturally, I couldn't understand a word of that then! But today I realize it was her austere nature that turned me into a perfectionist. Everything I have achieved in life is to her credit.'

In fact, Jaya took Hema completely under her wings. She remained, to the end, Hema's staunchest critic. Whether it was dance, her looks, her posture or later, her films, Jaya felt there was always room for improvement. 'Am I really pretty, Amma?' Hema would ask her sometimes with genuine interest. 'You are ok,' she would say.

'She was never rude. Rather, she used to pamper me a lot. I was after all her dream child! Sometimes at night she would gently come to my room and apply coconut oil on my feet while I would be fast asleep because of all the pain from dance practice,' Hema recollects. 'I think she was right in being that way. Kids tend to lose their concentration if they get caught up in all the praise. They start taking things for granted. I am a mother of two daughters and now a grandmother and though I was more lenient with my kids, I have inculcated in them all the values that were taught to me by my parents.'

Jaya had been married at the age of thirteen and had hardly had any time to pursue her passions. Over the years, V.S.R. Chakravarti had made it a point to help her revive her interests, while also ensuring that she completed her matriculation and her Prabhakar degree in the Hindi language.

'People call me a multitasking woman, but I think that no one can beat Amma when it came to multitasking. Apart from her domestic responsibilities she would sing, teach, cook, supervise my dance lessons and even give private tuition to local kids. I barely remember Amma sitting and gossiping with others,' Hema says.

Not many know that Jaya Chakravarthy had always secretly dreamed of becoming a dancer. Trained in classical music, she went on to become a skilled vocalist, but had to give up on her dreams of taking up dance as a full-time occupation. It wouldn't be entirely incorrect to say that through her daughter she had found a way to vicariously live out her aspirations. In fact, Jaya's ambitions for Hema far outweighed any the young girl may have had for herself. But Hema willingly surrendered to every demand her mother made. And so Hema's grooming had started even before the toddler could say her own name! For Jaya, life had handed her a second chance. With time, as Hema's proficiency as a dancer became more and more apparent, Jaya spent all her waking hours in channelizing her talent.

Hema was six years old when she performed before Pandit Jawaharlal Nehru. All she remembers is how her mother seemed more nervous than usual that day. 'Give your best today!' she said to a slightly perplexed Hema, for whom the name of the chief guest rang no bell. After the performance, Jaya took her daughter to meet the prime minister. Hema says, 'I was too young to remember what exactly happened in that situation, but I clearly remember Panditji. I touched his feet and looked at him. While Amma was talking to him I was staring at his face and the rose that was stuck in the buttonhole of his cream sherwani. He was such a handsome man! After the conversation, he told me, "*Bahut sundar performance diya hai tumne. Kaha se itna kuch seekha?*" I remember blushing and smilingly looking at my mother. I guess that was one of my biggest days as a young dancer.'

The following year, Hema got a chance to perform before President Rajendra Prasad and Queen Elizabeth. 'Before the curtain rose I could feel a thousand butterflies in my stomach, even though I wasn't aware of who these dignitaries were or their importance. But just my Amma instructing me from behind the wings and softly murmuring the guru mantra in my ear before the start of any performance used to give me all the confidence I needed. I knew I would never go wrong,' she says.

As a child, Hema woke up every morning to the sounds of her mother's violin and her father's recitation of Sanskrit shlokas. While she got ready for school every day, she was put into the habit of reciting her dance lessons out loud to herself. That way she would never forget her adavus, mudras and abhinayas.

Perhaps it was Hema's upbringing that made her shy and introverted by nature. A quiet child who hardly ever fought with anyone, she mostly kept to herself – dance, classical music and painting filling up her days. 'She is excellent at drawing sketches even today,' Kannan reveals. 'But she led a very secluded life. That is her only regret.'

'In school, I barely interacted with my classmates. Amma would keep me occupied with something or the other,' Hema recollects. 'I used to often stare out of my room's window and wonder what all those kids were laughing at and what was so funny about life! They screamed, they played, they ran all over the park and were a big group of happy children. I just couldn't relate to them and I'm sure they couldn't to me. But in my heart of hearts I was dying to do all that they did ... play, gossip, run around trees ... but I never had the guts to do these things.'

Peeping through the window, there were days when she felt let down and angry. But strangely, the feeling never lasted. Even as a young girl, Hema always had an unusual maturity about her. 'I used to hate practising all day. At times, I used to get angry with my mother, but I never raised my voice at her. I wasn't scared of her, but I respected her for what she was. She could understand that I wanted to play like the other kids, but she never asked me herself. She knew that if she asked I would compel her to set me free from practice! But I guess that hardship finally paid off.'

In all her school years, Hema Malini considered only one person her close friend. Nandita Bhattacharya (later Ahlavar) studied in the same school and lived in the same neighbourhood. 'Apart from Tamil and Hindi, Bengali has been my third exposure to regional languages because of my friend Nandita. She was the same age as me and I liked spending time with her, but even then, Mom would drag me out and enrol me in additional music classes so I could learn the surs and taal, which would further help my dance,' she remembers.

The mothers of both the girls had struck up a deep friendship and while they caught up with each other after picking their girls up from school, the young girls too got a chance to spend time and play together. 'I call her (Nandita) Dillo,' says Hema, adoration plain on her face. 'I have spent some of the best moments of my life with Nandita when we were together in Delhi. When we were nine, one day we confessed to each other that we both had a crush on Lord Krishna! During our free time, we used to buy posters of Krishna from Birla Mandir. We had learnt that he was the ultimate symbol of love and we both secretly wanted to marry him!' Hema bursts into laughter. Hema and Nandita remain dear friends even today.

Till she was thirteen, Hema used to sleep with her mother in her room. Theirs had always been an unusually strong attachment, despite the tight control she exercised on her daughter's life. Every bit of Hema's life was micromanaged by Jaya – from handling her dance schedules to later choosing her films and accompanying her every day to the film sets. In fact, when Hema joined the industry, producers and film directors had to first meet Jaya before getting access to the actor, even for something like a script narration. In the world of Hindi cinema, this extent of dominance was insufferable and names like 'Thandi Malini' and 'Hima Malini' cropped up, scornful of the actor and her mother's overprotectiveness. Forever the doting and obedient child, Hema, however, was only too happy to be so utterly dependent on her mother. 'She was my amma, my guru and my saheli,' she says lovingly.

Hema recalls how her mother used to spend a considerable portion of the day cooking in the kitchen, while it was the kids' duty to lay the plates. 'After dinner, we would run out to play hide-and-seek while my father would help Amma do the dishes. We had a part-time maid who helped Amma in things like coconut-grinding and basic house cleaning. Strangely, Appa never forced me to learn any housework or cooking. Household work like carrying mattresses and folding the cot were Appa's duties, which my brothers picked up later.'

Hema has many fond memories of her father too. 'Delhi's scalding summer used to be really exasperating,' she says. 'Every night during the summer, my father used to arrange our beds on the terrace because the rooms used to get hot and stuffy. He was a very caring man. When my mother used to be ill or sometimes wake up late, he would make the morning tea and nashta for her and boil milk for all of us. Though he was away from the house most of the time on work, he used to keep track of every small detail. I guess it was during those conversations they had over dinner every night that Amma used to update him. They shared a lovely relationship. In all those years, I had never seen my parents fighting or arguing over silly issues. Maybe that's the reason why we all have such strong family values, learning from them.'

One of Hema's most vivid memories is of her father taking her to school and dance classes. 'During the monsoons, he would protectively hold an umbrella over my head while riding me to my class on his bicycle.' That cycle often gave trouble and on such days V.S.R. Chakravarti would walk his daughter to the bus stop, her little hand firmly in his grip. 'Appa and I hardly ever exchanged any words in those days but we shared a strong bond. He was never physically demonstrative of his love and affection, but his firm grip on my hand gave me the courage to fight against all odds in life.'

Living in Delhi meant that Jaya got ample opportunities to enrol Hema in competitions and stage performances. The young dancer was slowly gaining ground and one day the actress Vyjayanthimala dropped in to watch her performance. 'I particularly remember her fingers ... they were so artistic. After the show, she shook hands with me and complimented me for my performance. I had always considered her a role model. In fact, so did my mother. It was a hugely memorable day,' says Hema. In another decade, as she prepared to ride the waves of stardom, Hema Malini would be touted as a worthy successor to Vyjayanthimala – both southern beauties who brought in a new dimension of classical virtuosity to Hindi cinema.

Incidentally, the first time the Chakravartis saw Vyjayanthimala was at Delhi's Sapru House where she gave a Bharatanatyam performance. The family, which usually avoided social gatherings, had made an exception in this case. 'I still remember her Kanjeevaram sari, bright kohl-lined eyes and charming smile,' Hema – a little girl then – recalls her first memory of meeting her onscreen idol. Both V.S.R. Chakravarti and Jaya were so moved by the performance that they took the decision of training their daughter in the same dance form, so that one day she could grow up to be India's finest Bharatanatyam exponent.

Over time, as the number and scale of Hema's performances grew, she came to be known as 'Dilli ki Hema Malini'. Madras (now Chennai) already had a Bharatanatyam dancer by the same name – a promising young girl whom Jaya had always admired and hoped her daughter would one day succeed. In a matter of years, Hema would not just succeed but far outshine her namesake, and there would no longer be a need for a prefix to her name.

Despite the success and recognition, however, it wasn't all rainbows and sunshine for young Hema. She enjoyed performing on stage – the few hours she relished thoroughly – but the drudgery of practice was taking a toll on her young spirit. By the time she was ten, a mild defiance sometimes took over.

'It happened once I started performing regularly on stage. I was frequently punished for it. Whenever I used to disobey her, she would force me to practice the "alarippu, jatiswaram and shabdam", which were the basic steps of Bharatanatyam and which I knew backwards. I could perform them in my sleep! But that was the punishment. Once, to protest against Amma, I remember singing loudly and thumping my feet on the floor, trying to fake an impression of rehearsing! It was a great achievement as a kid to cheat on my Amma,' Hema says, smiling.

What made matters more difficult for Hema was the constant changing of dance schools and teachers. It seemed Jaya was never satisfied with the kind of training that was imparted to her daughter. Hema was first put in a general dance class where, Jaya learnt, the little girl would often hide behind other dancers to save herself from being pulled up for making mistakes. A year later, she was put under the tutelage of Srimati Indira. Finally, as mentioned earlier, it was at Triveni Kala Sangam, under the famous Sikkil Ramaswamy Pillai, that Hema received most of her early training.

'He was my first guru … a kind, old man,' Hema recollects. 'The Miss India of the era, Indrani Rehman, was also his student. I watched Indrani practise with Guruji on many an evening.'

Things were going well with Guru Pillai until, Hema tells me, one day he decided to sing onstage during her performance. Apparently, he wasn't the best of singers and that was reason enough for Jaya to seek out someone else. Thereafter, Hema trained under a string of other names, including Thiruvalaputhur Swaminatha Pillai, Mylapore Gauri Ammal, Arunachalam Pillai, Vempatti Chinna Satyam and Guru Natanam Gopalakrishnan. 'I remember one of my gurujis (she doesn't want to give the name) was so aggressive that we all were petrified of him. While I would perform on stage, he would invariably hit out at the mridangam player or the vocalist with his kartal. Out of fear they used to sit at a distance from Guruji. Those days we didn't have recorded music, so it used to be live performances. I would get distracted with all the drama unfolding before me and those poor fellows would be paranoid. It might sound funny when I narrate this now after so many years, but back then it was a nightmare for a dancer to concentrate on her steps and also be a part of this circus. Often, the audience would find my guruji's "throwing fits" more entertaining than my dance,' Hema laughs.

In the midst of all this, the only respite Hema had was her brother, Jagannath. Closer to her in age, he never missed a chance to play pranks on his sister; the two were always at each other's throats in happy horseplay.

'Whenever I used to practise my dance, he would come into my room and make funny faces. I would lose my concentration, burst into laughter and run after him,' Hema remembers. 'We used to fight all the time over the silliest of issues. Jagan would always provoke me when Amma was around and I would invariably react. So, I would end up getting scolded! Not only that, each time I would be out of the city, Jagan would come to my room and tear the pages of my notebook in which I used to write my jathis (dance lessons). It used to make me so angry. So many times I ended up throwing ink all over his face! If Kannan bhaiya was like a protective father figure, Jagan was more like a friend.'

In 1962, V.S.R. Chakravarti moved to Madras with a transfer from ESIC. In fact, the decision to move out of Delhi had been taken by Jaya. By then, Kannan was studying science at Hansraj College while Jagannath was about to finish school. Both V.S.R. Chakravarti and Jaya realized that it would be unfair to uproot them at this stage. After a lot of deliberation, the parents decided to let the boys stay in Delhi with their maternal grandmother, while they moved to Madras with their daughter.

In Madras, Hema went on to join Rosary Matriculation. Although a keen student, she was finding it increasingly difficult to cope with both dance and academics. Moreover, due to her dance performances, she had to travel a lot by now, and that was taking a toll on her studies. By twelve, she had already received invitations from across the country, travelling as far as Punjab and Uttar Pradesh for her performances. This punishing schedule drove her parents to a decision. Dance was what she was meant for, so she would have to drop out of academics. Eventually, Hema completed her matriculation through a correspondence course under the Andhra Pradesh board.

By the time Hema turned fourteen, she was inundated with film offers. Calls started pouring in, particularly from Tamil film producers, who would often scope for a 'new face' from stage performances. Her first-ever film offer was for a dance performance in the song 'Singara' in *Idhu Sathiyam* (1963), and then 'Naa chandamama' in Kamalakara Kameshwara Rao's *Pandava Vanavasam* (1965). Reminded of 'Singara', Hema covers her face with her palms. 'Aiyyo, that was so funny, and I think I was almost like those extras dancing around the hero and heroine.'

'I vividly remember that Appa would take us to AIFACS Hall in Connaught Place once in a while and we would watch a Hindi film at Regal Cinema. The first film I remember watching as a kid was Vyjayanthimala's *Nagin*. A few years later, when I saw the poster of *Hariyali Aur Raasta*, I forced my Amma to buy me a ticket for the movie. She sent me and my brother to watch the film. All I remember about the movie was that the heroine was weeping throughout. It was so depressing that I decided not to watch any Hindi film ever,' she laughs.

Meanwhile, the standoff between Jaya and V.S.R. Chakravarti on Hema making her foray into films continued. Like many, he had his reservations about the industry and refused to allow his daughter to get anywhere close to it. It was the first time Hema had witnessed her parents so polarized and distant. 'It was not my decision,' she says. 'My mother decided that I should try my luck in films as well and she was adamant. My father had stopped talking to her. He simply couldn't believe that his daughter would be acting in films. Now when I look back on those incidents, they seem like nightmares.'

After the family moved to Madras, Hema's training too geared up for its next phase. She was now taken under the wing of Guru Kittapa Pillai for Bharatanatyam, Guru Vempatti Chinna Satyam for Kuchipudi and Guru Natanam Gopalakrishnan for Mohiniattam. Guru Kittapa Pillai, a recipient of the Sangeet Natak Akademi Award (1988), was the fifth-generation descendant of the Thanjavur Quartet family, possibly one of the biggest proponents of Bharatanatyam. He had also been Vyjayanthimala's guru. It was under his impeccable training that Hema perfected her talent.

After completing her training with Guru Kittapa Pillai, Hema took up a special course in abhinaya from the legendary Gowri Amma – yet another name amongst the all-time greats in Bharatanatyam. Belonging to a family of traditional temple dancers, she was the last devadasi of the renowned Kapaleeshwarar temple in Madras.

Finally, to leave no stone unturned, Jaya ensured that Hema undertook a course in the theory and practice of Carnatic music to gain a comprehensive and thorough understanding of the medium.

'Dance is my first love,' Hema tells me. 'People often remark that I am ungrateful to the film industry, but that's unfair. I have never demeaned Hindi cinema; in fact, it is thanks to films that people know me outside India. They come to see my classical shows because of Hema Malini the star. But I must also say that my love for Bharatanatyam comes before everything else and I have never cashed in on my stardom to promote what has been my truest passion.'

It is a promise she had made to her mother and one she stands by till today. You will never see Hema Malini perform on stage at an awards' night or at social functions. Unless performing for a strictly classical platform, you will find her donning her ghungroos only at the Natya Vihar Kala Kendra – the dance academy she runs in Mumbai. For Hema, dance has always been an act of devotion, a sadhana, a purpose linked intrinsically with the divine.

As she explains the dearest aspect of her life, her dedication shines through. 'Bharatanatyam is a symbol of beauty and aesthetic perfection. As a philosophy, it is a search of the human soul for the ideal. As a religion, it is man's quest for the Supreme and the desire to unite with the Ultimate. As a science, it is about attaining the perfection of body, technique and corporeal movement; and as poetry, it is the symbol of rhythmic lyricism.'

Apart from her mother, if there was one person who was thrilled about Hema's dedication towards Bharatanatyam, it was her father. Being an orthodox Iyengar Brahmin who started and ended his days with prayer, he loved the bhajans and shlokas that were so intrinsic to any Bharatanatyam recital. In fact, after his retirement, V.S.R. Chakravarti accompanied his daughter to all her shows, volunteering to introduce her on stage. 'I could see his happiness in announcing the name of his daughter on stage,' Hema says, beaming. 'He was really proud of me as a classical performer. It is so unfortunate that I got to know my father so late in life. Till 1970, my father used to accompany me everywhere. But after he fell ill, my brother Kannan replaced him.'

2

The Dream Girl Is Born

After the initial setback, the C.V. Sridhar episode left both Jaya and Hema more resolute in their decision to make Hema an actress. The focus was now back on dance recitals, but they also quietly bided their time, waiting for the next good film offer to come their way.

At one such dance show – organized by K. Subrahmanyam, one of the biggest directors of Tamil cinema – the wheels of providence jerked into motion. The evening was presided over by Suddhananda Bharathi, the great Tamil poet. Over a hundred prominent dancers and musicians were to perform before a discerning audience. Hema's thirty-minute recital was just what she needed – a take-off of sorts, it ended up giving her the perfect opportunity to break into the city's cultural circuit. Hereon, as concerts followed concerts, Madras slowly warmed up to this bundle of talent.

One of those impressed by this young, beautiful dancer was B. Ananthaswami, a Tamil producer who was making a Hindi film with none other than Raj Kapoor. The schedule was ready, but they were waiting for a fresh new face to cast opposite the showman. If Hema was in need of a godfather, here he was, with an offer of a lifetime.

'Ananthaswami had made it very clear to us right from the start that all the decisions for the film would be taken by Raj Kapoor. The film was being produced by a south Indian producer who had blocked bulk dates for Raj saab, right after *Sangam*. They were now very keen on casting a fresh south Indian face who could also dance well and match up to the status of Vyjayanthimala,' Hema recollects.

When Ananthaswami offered to cast Hema as the lead, the sixteen-year-old promptly sat up and said, 'Yes, I am ready.' Jaya was still recovering from the rejection by C.V. Sridhar in Madras and was sceptical. Both V.S.R. Chakravarti and Jaya were, in fact, wary of this producer who had come to them with a Raj Kapoor film. They were quite certain he was another movie mogul who couldn't be trusted.

'I couldn't get over the insult that Sridhar had inflicted on my mother and me,' Hema says. 'It was still fresh in my mind. I was also worried about my mother and I had already decided to act in at least one film to make her happy. I also wanted to prove to Amma that I could make it in films, apart from the fact that it would be an apt answer to Sridhar. I signed Ananthaswami's film blindly – I didn't even give myself time to think. But I clearly remember seeing satisfaction and calm almost immediately on Amma's face.'

But not everyone was elated. The news of Hema this time going as far as signing a film as the female lead left her father fuming. He stopped eating at home and his arguments with Jaya only worsened. 'My brothers and I were not included in the details, for we were trained not to ask questions,' Hema remembers. 'In short, we continued to feel frightened and uneasy. On the fourth day, finally, my father gave up. He agreed to eat his meal and for the time being at least there was a truce! I still don't know how they resolved the problem but I was given the green signal. One thing I was certain about was that my father wasn't against my classical dances at sabhas and festival functions ... but my acting in films somehow made him uncomfortable. I think he was very conscious of what his office colleagues would say.'

As it happens, there were many who played their part in sealing Hema's tryst with destiny. K. Subrahmanyam was one. A producer and director from the silent-film era and one who had gone on to make the first Tamil talkie, the great man also had an eye for talent (he had spotted and promoted Bharat Ratna M.S. Subbulakshmi). His daughter, legendary classical dancer Padma Bhushan Dr Padma Subrahmanyam, recollects, 'I was already a fairly established dancer and by the age of fourteen, I was teaching dance. My father had launched the Nrithyodaya School as my forum. That was the time Hema came to Madras. I remember Mami (Jaya) used to write very well and had published many books and articles. She was a very talented lady and that explains where Hema's talent comes from. When my father saw her, he immediately recognized her talent. It was in our dance school in Madras that her first performance was organized. My father had invited all the VIPs in town, including the sabha secretaries, art connoisseurs and the who's who from the world of performing arts.'

Incidentally, K. Subrahmanyam and Raj Kapoor's father Prithviraj Kapoor were close friends, going back a long way. Padma tells me, 'Raj Kapoor was planning his next film and knew my father's credibility and standing. When he came home for lunch one day, he told my father that he wanted me to act in his next film. My father passed the buck to me, despite knowing that I had already declined offers from MGR (actor-film-maker M.G. Ramachandran) and Satyajit Ray. I did the same with Raj Kapoor, but he insisted on waiting for a week for my mind to change. That's when my father told him, "Look, I know a girl who resembles Paddu, or is perhaps more beautiful than her, very talented and is willing to act." He introduced Hema to him. But then there was a problem. Director C.V. Sridhar had booked Hema and somehow something had gone wrong and he had dropped her from the project. Apparently, he thought she couldn't act well. This confused Raj Kapoor and he called up my father to clarify. "I am told that Sridhar pulled her out of his film," he said. My father, who in those days used to be called Director K. Subrahmanyam, told him, "If this girl does not hit the headlines right from the start I will sacrifice the prefix of Director from my name."'

Padma adds, smiling, 'She was a Dream Girl from day one!'

To make her debut in cinema opposite Raj Kapoor – it was as if the cosmos was making an announcement. Many said Hema's role had first been offered to Vyjayanthimala who hadn't shown much interest. But it is also a fact that the thespian himself was keen on starring opposite a debutante. Either way, for Hema Malini, this was the greatest start she could have imagined. For the second time in her life, her grooming for films was under way. From costume trials to diction classes, nothing was spared. In fact, when the director Mahesh

Kaul realized how strong Hema's Tamil accent was, he had to hire a professional to help modify it. Lakshmi Sharma, the announcer and newsreader from All India Radio, Bombay, was a well-known name, popular for her chaste Hindi and perfect diction. She trained Hema in language and dialogue delivery.

As the day of the screen test drew close, Hema found herself fighting an almost paralysing nervousness. The Sridhar episode kept haunting her and she had knots in her stomach. This time, things couldn't afford to go wrong, she kept telling herself.

When Jaya and Hema reached the legendary RK Studios, they were asked to make their way to the make-up room. Raj Kapoor had appointed Madhav Pai as Hema's make-up artist, Vishnu as her 'dress man' and Hanuman as her spot-boy. On entering the massive room, Hema noticed a costume of a 'banjaran' or a gypsy girl laid out carefully for her. It looked remarkably similar to the one worn by Padmini for the film *Jis Desh Mein Ganga Behti Hai* (1960). She was instructed to wear the costume and prepare herself for the screen test. 'I remember Vishnu and Madhav-dada telling me that I should not get intimidated by the legends. If I could pass the test today, one day even my costumes would be displayed with these legends at RK Studios,' Hema remembers.

Once ready, Hema was asked to perform a few scenes. 'They were solo scenes,' she recalls. 'I could see Raj Kapoor-ji, director K. Asif-ji and Shanker-ji of Shanker-Jaikishan fame looking at me. Raj-ji himself directed the screen test. He was just like a prince. I still remember his eyes and his complexion. He's one of the best-looking men I have ever worked with. My mother was also there and she was looking extremely tense. By then, Raj-ji had already made me so comfortable that during the screen test I didn't even notice where the camera was. I somehow managed to execute the scene, after which Raj-ji said, "CUT!" and I waited breathlessly for a response. I looked at my mother and then at the rest. Raj-ji was still looking at me through the camera lens. Then he looked at K. Asif-ji and Shanker-ji and said, "This girl will be the next superstar of Indian cinema!" It was a moment of complete joy but even more than that, it was one of my biggest achievements as a teenager – to be able to live up to Amma's dream of me being an actor! While the stalwarts were praising me, I had tears in my eyes and could see my mother standing in a corner, beaming! That still remains one of the best moments of my life!' Hema's face lights up at the memory even today.

Prophetic words from the eternal showman, today, one can only guess whether Raj Kapoor realized the weight his words carried. But what they did do, more importantly, was restore lost confidence and help a young girl regain belief in herself.

Once back in Madras, as days went by and the daily routine set in, life went back to its old rhythm for Hema. Everyone stopped talking about the screen test. But even though things appeared normal on the surface, they really weren't. The family was slowly coming to terms with the fact that their youngest was on the threshold of a monumental change – her new life was waiting in the wings and nothing would ever be quite the same. V.S.R. Chakravarti started spending longer hours in office – perhaps his way of coming to terms with inevitability. Time, all of a sudden, seemed to be racing against all of them.

Soon Hema and Jaya would move to Bombay. Director Mahesh Kaul's *Sapno Ka Saudagar* with Raj Kapoor and Hema Malini as leads was finally under way. After shooting for the first schedule, Hema tells me how the first thing she did after coming home was run to her room. 'I ran to see if my jathi (rhythm) notebooks were intact or if Jagan had torn them! They were untouched. That's when I realized that things had changed.'

For the first eight months in Bombay, while *Sapno Ka Saudagar* was being shot, Jaya and Hema stayed at B. Ananthaswami's house. Almost a mentor to the young actor, he made them feel at home and only after the release of the film, once other film offers started pouring in, did they move out and take up a place on rent. 'For a very short period, I stayed in Shanmukhananda Guest House at Matunga with Amma. It was a small room and I used to feel claustrophobic after shooting in a studio the whole day. When Appa came to know that we didn't have a place to stay, he decided to rent an apartment in Khar,' says Hema.

A couple of years after that, while shooting for *Johny Mera Naam* (1970), she shifted to Manvendra Apartment on 16th Road, Bandra. 'That was a one-bedroom apartment and soon we realized that we needed a bigger place, because most of the time either producers, directors or my dance teachers would be sitting in the hall. So, we shifted to a bungalow in Juhu, before I bought my own house at Vile Parle Scheme in 1973,' says Hema. Incidentally, much later, when Hema met legendary music composer Ravindra Jain at his residence, he jokingly asked if anything seemed familiar to her. 'I realized that it was the same apartment where I had started my journey as an actress. Dada (Jain) lived in that apartment his entire life, because he felt that the house was lucky,' Hema says.

Apart from being her mentor, it was Ananthaswami who was responsible for the famous tag line that went on to classify Hema Malini as the embodiment of all things sublime and ethereal ... a celestial beauty, an embodiment of divinity and grace.

When the producer was designing the posters for the film, Ananthaswami added the words 'Raj Kapoor's Dream Girl' just below Hema's face. Months before the release, the bigger cities had life-size cutouts of the debutante, a never-before-seen experience.

'It was Mr Ananthaswami who came up with this idea,' Hema recollects. 'We thought that it was a publicity stunt and people would forget about it after the film released. A few of the posters were really funny. They had things like "forty-four-year-old Raj Kapoor in love with sixteen-year-old Hema Malini" written on them! I was enjoying the entire publicity gimmick. After *Sapno Ka Saudagar* released, the press and people started calling me "Dream Girl". I could see how the name had caught on. People often asked me if I made an effort to live up to the name. I didn't! The tag came as a surprise to me. I guess my face and my personality went well with the general image of an Indian woman. Anybody could relate to my face – it's a typical Indian face. Yes, the only thing I did do was never accept roles that would embarrass or hurt my family or my fans in any way. So, the name stuck on. Distributors and producers continued using it. But nowadays I feel embarrassed when people call me "Dream Girl". I am hardly a girl anymore!'

Sapno Ka Saudagar is the story of a kidnapped princess who grows up as a gypsy girl. In the film, the character, played by Hema, falls in love with Raj Kapoor – a messiah of love, out to cleanse the world. While the songs were a hit, the film received a tepid response. Hema's skills as an actor were nothing to write home about, but she wasn't completely dismissed either. Her screen presence and dancing skills were enough to make audiences and producers go weak in the knees. She already had them enthralled.

'I didn't enjoy the acting bit at all,' Hema complains. 'Every day I used to go to my make-up room and cry by myself. I used to feel very uncomfortable doing the emotional scenes. The only things I enjoyed in my first film were the dance numbers. For those, I used to be charged throughout the day. Now when I look back I feel I was too loud in *Sapno Ka Saudagar*. It wasn't my fault. I was from the stage and had a background in dance, where one requires loud expressions. I have always been a director's actor and I did exactly what Mahesh-ji showed me,' she says before adding excitedly, 'But I will always cherish the fact that my first film was with Raj Kapoor saab! That I will never forget!'

From day one, Hema got a taste of what it was to work with someone like Raj Kapoor. She recalls, 'On the first day of the shoot I was supposed to deliver this line: *"Pyaar aise nahin hota hai, Raja."* I was playing the role of a gypsy girl who falls in love with Raj saab and I was blindly following whatever my director Mahesh Kaul was saying. But somehow, he was not happy with the shot and I kept trying. I could see my mother standing behind the camera, waiting for Mahesh-ji to okay the shot, and all that was getting me extremely nervous. To add to that, I had to deliver a Hindi dialogue in front of strangers! It was then that Raj saab called me aside and told me, "If you become conscious today, you will never be able to overcome it in your life." I went back, gave the take and, needless to say, it was immediately okayed. That became my life's mantra from that moment. No wonder he was the showman of Indian cinema!'

Even before *Sapno Ka Saudagar* reached the theatres, Hema received five new film offers. She signed them all – *Sharafat* and *Tum Haseen Main Jawan* with Dharmendra, *Abhinetri* and *Jahan Pyar Mile* with Shashi Kapoor and *Johny Mera Naam* with Dev Anand (1970).

Apart from Hema's obvious strengths, the industry was on the lookout for someone who could fill the enormous void Vyjayanthimala's retirement would create. The great actress of Indian cinema, now married to Dr Chamanlal Bali (incidentally, Raj Kapoor's personal physician), was planning to bring down the curtain on what had been an illustrious run. These would be large shoes to fill and the industry saw promise in Hema Malini – the perfect 'southern beauty' with tremendous talent.

Hema Malini has always denied the comparison. For her, there has been no greater role model than Vyjayanthimala and she shakes her head in embarrassment every time the subject is broached.

'The comparison was created by the media, nothing else,' she tells me. 'If you see her films, Vyjayanthimala-ji has always had the mandatory dance sequence in practically every film of hers, evoking "classical art" associations. That was the main reason why I fell in love with her films. I adored her in *Bahar* (1951), *Nagin* (1954), *Devdas* (1955), *Amrapali* (1966), *Naya Daur* (1957) and, of course, *Madhumati* (1958). I still remember my dance performance and meeting her after the show when I was a kid. Her dance numbers were like gospel to me. I wanted to be another Vyjayanthimala. Undoubtedly, she is my role model. Whatever I am today, it's because of her blessings. I can't even think of replacing or substituting her in any manner. She is a living legend.'

I still remember the Stardust Awards in 2004. Vyjayanthimala had arrived late, and Hema was the only one constantly asking about her and waiting eagerly. When she finally walked in, Hema sprung up and gave her a long hug. Years later, during Esha Deol's wedding, Vyjayanthimala came all the way from Chennai with her son Suchindra Bali to attend it. Hema made sure that she always kept in touch with her idol.

Both leading ladies share a special kind of camaraderie – one that can't really be explained. Perhaps it was their common roots or their love for dance ... or maybe the fact that both would rule Hindi cinema as the greatest southern stars this industry had witnessed. Neither Vyjayanthimala nor Hema Malini ever ventured into regional cinema. As national sensations, they had much bigger roles to play.

3

Flight to Freedom

If there was one thing Hema loved about Bombay, it was the sea. A quiet, commanding presence, a refuge for the soul and, for the great city, an abiding friend – like many, she was irresistibly drawn to it.

By now, Hema was only one film old and already the lure of showbiz was too strong. But despite the thrill and promise of a new world, the sixteen-year-old desperately missed both Delhi and Madras – the cities she had spent most of her childhood in. The peaceful government colony in Delhi, the sun-drenched pillared verandah, her father, her brothers and the comfortable familiarity of home – she missed it all.

Initially, only Jaya Chakravarthy and Hema shifted to Bombay. V.S.R. Chakravarti stayed in Madras because of work commitments and would visit them often. Kannan was already an officer by now in State Bank of India, eastern circle, and was later posted to the bank's foreign department in Calcutta.

'I used to miss them a lot,' Hema tells me. 'But over time and with the increasing work pressure, I slowly got used to it. My schedule during those days was crazy. It left me little time to think. It was only much later, once my father retired, that all of them joined me in Bombay. Till then it was only Amma and me.'

It is true that Hema never really had to go through the proverbial struggle associated with anyone considered an 'outsider' to the industry. She had debuted opposite one of the greatest legends Indian cinema has known. For many, it seemed like the stars had been impeccably aligned, well in advance, for this young woman. But that was only one part of the story.

Of the five films that Hema took up after *Sapno Ka Saudagar*, two – *Sharafat* and *Johny Mera Naam* – turned out to be blockbusters. The others, even if not as big, also managed to make the box office ring. In no time producers started lining up outside Hema's door. That's when Hema realized, however, that things weren't quite as easy or straightforward as they were made to seem.

It so happened that during the final stages of *Sapno Ka Saudagar*, Jaya and Hema were made to sign several contracts. Being novices, they had left it to the man who had discovered Hema in the first place, B. Ananthaswami, to take charge of the paperwork. They had implicit faith in him and didn't think it necessary to go over the fine print before signing on any of those documents. Now, as film offers started to pour in, they stumbled upon a clause that they had had no idea existed. From now on, Hema would need to seek Ananthaswami's consent before signing on any film. He would be the ultimate decision-maker. If she was indeed his protégée, this would be his way of exercising his right as her mentor while also controlling the direction her career would take.

If Jaya and Hema were stunned, producers and directors keen on signing Hema were left fuming at the blatant manipulation. But Ananthaswami remained adamant. He insisted on having a say at every stage of discussion, making it impossible for others to get past him. Apart from the bad blood it created in the industry, this was also rendering Hema unapproachable as a star and working against her reputation.

'My mother was tense,' Hema recalls. 'She couldn't handle all the complications he was creating. I vividly remember one incident. Amma was having a heated argument with Ananthaswami on this contract issue. Finally, disgusted with Ananthaswami, she tore up the contract sheet! For a second I couldn't believe that my mother could do this. I guess she was surprised too. But that was it. Ananthaswami was shocked. He never thought that my mother would be able to raise her voice against him. He was an experienced person and my mother was still not familiar with the business of Hindi films. But it happened, and it happened at the spur of the moment.'

It wasn't the ideal way to resolve a conflict, but it did put an end to what clearly was an unfair bargain. The incident left a bitter taste in everyone. Even today Hema feels uncomfortable discussing it.

'I think it was only because of Mr Ananthaswami that I am a star today. He spotted me and introduced me in *Sapno Ka Saudagar*. I shall always be grateful to him. He was not a bad human being. In fact, he was kind and generous. We stayed in his house and he was a perfect host. I also feel that it was Ananthaswami who guided me on the right track. Soon after *Sapno Ka Saudagar*, I was offered several films and it was he who did the selection. I think he meant well. But the contract that he had made us sign was not safe, for me or for my career. In fact, my mother had signed it unknowingly and it almost seemed like a trap. So though I am fortunate that I had found a guide in him, it was sad how things had to end.'

If the industry heaved a sigh of relief at Ananthaswami's abrupt exit from the scene, it was perhaps still too early to celebrate. Technically, Hema was now free from bindings, but she was far from being the master of her fate. It was Jaya Chakravarthy's turn to take over the reins.

Around this time came along Subodh Mukherji's film *Abhinetri* (1970). Cast opposite the charming Shashi Kapoor, this was the first film where Hema would be the principal protagonist. The story revolved around the lives of a young married couple – a dancer and a scientist – caught in the throes of a discord when the wife decides to take up dance as a profession. Subodh Mukherji, known for launching glorious names like Saira Banu in *Junglee* and Rakhee in *Sharmeelee*, had watched Hema in *Sapno Ka Saudagar* and was convinced about casting her in this film. In an interview to a magazine in 1970, he had said, 'Hema is like a "mome ki gudiya" (wax doll). She is a pure and classic beauty. I have treated her like a doll in this film. She looked stunning in each and every frame. In fact, in her debut film, she was playing a character which was absolutely not "Hema" in reality.'

'Hema was only twenty when she played the role of a married woman in *Abhinetri*,' Hema's sister-in-law Prabha Chakravarti tells me. 'It was a completely new experience for her but she took it in her stride and delivered a great performance. Her fresh, innocent face left an indelible mark with the audiences while her dancing skills impressed everyone. After *Abhinetri* she never had to look back.'

For Hema, *Abhinetri* was a subject after her heart. 'I loved the film, because I got a chance to play the character of a dancer,' she tells me. 'Shashi-ji and my director Subodh-ji were extremely cooperative. I was just one film old, but they treated me with respect, like any other professional in the unit. I was acting with Nirupa-ji (Roy) for the first time. She is such a brilliant performer. She has played the maximum number of mother-oriented roles in Indian cinema. The film's songs like "*Sa re ga ma*", "*O ghaata savri*" and "*Sajna o sajna*" were extremely popular,' she recollects.

Talking about her co-star, the debonair Shashi Kapoor, Hema adds fondly, 'Shashi-ji was like a ball of energy, jumping all around the set! Unlike other co-actors, whenever he reached the sets he would come and ask, "*Aur Hema, kya khabar hai, aaj kaunsa scene kar rahe hain hum?*" We have worked in a couple of movies and I admire him for his energy and profound knowledge of world cinema. I remember when he turned producer for the first time, he had invited us for the special screening of *36 Chowringhee Lane* (1981). I was pleasantly surprised to see his vision as a film-maker. Recently, when I met him at the Dadasaheb Phalke Award ceremony at Prithvi Theatre, he looked at me and smiled. Shashi-ji is now on a wheelchair and can barely talk. It's really sad to see someone so energetic bound to a wheelchair.'

On camera, Hema was getting all the adoration she deserved. Audiences too were warming up to this charming face. But behind the scenes, Hema Malini's reputation continued to draw flak. It was reported that most of her co-actors, including Shashi Kapoor (surprisingly) and Rajesh Khanna, felt uncomfortable working with her. Always a reserved person, Hema didn't make any efforts at socializing or breaking the ice with her crew or fellow actors. She preferred keeping to herself. For an industry that thrives on personal rapport and congeniality, Hema's aloofness was often mistaken as arrogance. Other actors used to find her haughty and proud and tagged her an ice maiden. Moreover, being the strong-headed woman that she was, she didn't bother to issue any clarifications.

'People misunderstood me,' she confesses. 'I too wanted to compliment my co-actors but used to feel shy. Weird questions used to come to my mind, like "What would they feel?" or "How should I compliment them?" and while thinking about these things I used to miss the opportunity of expressing myself. So people used to think that I was snooty and arrogant. I don't blame them because they didn't know me personally, so it's not surprising that they would feel that way. Moreover, my mother always used to be on the sets.'

In Jaya's presence, Hema was like a puppet. If Ananthaswami was considered interfering, Jaya was even more of an impediment. From the dialogues Hema delivered to how revealing her costume was, from whom she would be cast opposite to how the story would unfold on screen, Jaya demanded a say in every possible department. Interestingly, she never interfered while the shoot was on. She would send in a 'request list' of what was acceptable and what clearly wasn't right at the beginning. That way, every director was aware of the boundaries. Even more significantly, Jaya ensured that her daughter didn't spend an extra waking minute on the sets once the crew had packed up. Forget socializing, there was no question of even a casual tête-à-tête.

'I used to feel really uncomfortable doing intimate scenes in front of my mother,' Hema says. 'As a performer, I could understand that my concentration would deviate from the character. It was obvious. I am sure that my directors also must have felt bad about these incidents, but they never created an issue. But gradually I understood that I was compromising with my profession and not giving it my best. It wasn't as if I was dying to do intimate scenes with my co-actors, but even when the script demanded such scenes I used to turn cold and behave differently.'

If Jaya realized her daughter's predicament, she did nothing to help. If anything, her overprotectiveness only got worse. Till one day, when it drove her daughter to the point of despair. 'I think I should quit acting,' she told her mother. 'I can't continue this way. I know that I am not giving my best to my profession. I am cheating myself and my viewers.'

Hema's words were enough to drive home the point. Jaya finally decided that she would stop chaperoning her daughter. Instead, Hema's aunt Shanta was now put in charge. Talking about those days, Hema says, 'Those were crazy days. Ultimately, Amma decided that she would stop escorting me to shootings. She stayed at home and Shanta aunty accompanied me instead. But it was not that simple. My mother's heart was not at home. She would call at the studios at regular intervals or drop by during lunch breaks.' Those were the days before mobile phones, so each time Jaya called, Hema had to leave her shot and walk up to the studio office.

'The days she didn't call, she would insist that I come home for lunch. But I used to get very tense about delaying the shoot, keeping the producer, the hero and the director waiting for me. The loss of an hour during the lunch break would also lead to a delay in pack-up. This would worry my mother. She would ask me, "Why are they keeping you back? Where are you going after pack-up?" Once or twice we even had a small flare-up. My mother's main worry was that the director would make me do intimate scenes with my heroes. I never did those kinds of scenes; I mean nothing compared to what today's actresses do! She shouldn't have worried herself. But she did...'

The situation soon became fodder for the tabloids. Several stories and cover-page articles were dedicated to this complex mother–daughter relationship. For Hema, who by now was working three shifts a day and already dealing with an unforgiving schedule, it was all getting too much to cope with. But cope she did – or at least learned to. The first few years in the industry prepared her for the battles she would have to face ahead.

'People misunderstood my relationship with my mother. I don't blame them,' she says. 'It won't be possible for everyone to understand or believe the kind of relationship that existed between my mother and me. To me, she was not just a mother, she was more like my friend. I was her only daughter, so it's natural that we were attached to each other. It's true that we fought and argued a lot. Differences in opinion are natural. I'm very stubborn; I like to think that I am always right. But I could never be angry with her for long. I was dependent on her. I couldn't imagine life without her. When we used to go for some party and if she used to talk to somebody else for even five minutes, I used to feel restless and uneasy until she came back. I know it's juvenile, but that's how I was.'

During the trying times, if there was one thing that kept Hema going it was her work – which she was beginning to thoroughly enjoy – and her unflinching dedication towards it. With every film she took up, her popularity soared. In 1970, she had two major releases – Asit Sen's *Sharafat* and Bhappi Sonie's *Tum Haseen Main Jawan* – both huge box-office hits. The latter was a light-hearted film revolving around a child-inheritor of a mammoth empire. Audiences lapped up the comic relief it provided. But it was *Sharafat*, where Hema played a nautch girl in love with a professor, that became a runaway hit. According to Box Office India, the film had a collection of Rs 35,80,70,198 – almost a fortune for those times. Hema points out, 'It was a difficult role, but Asit-da used to explain each and every shot with a lot of patience. He was a perfect gentleman. He was technically competent but never took recourse to gimmicks to score a point. The story was the main thing for him, just as it had been for a director like Bimal Roy. The technique was always married to the content and never stood out like a sore thumb. Most of Asit Sen's films were taken from popular Bengali literature and always had a story to tell and emotions to bear. Like Bimal Roy, Asit Sen too was influenced by the neo-realistic wave.'

Incidentally, both these films starred Dharmendra – already a raging name and quite the He-Man of Hindi films by now. When it came to this on-screen pair, it was love at first sight for the audience. What they didn't suspect, however, was that a slow flame that would go on to burn eternally was being kindled off-screen as well.

4

A Taste of Stardom

The year 1970 was significant for Hema Malini; not in the least because it saw the release of a film that would change both its protagonists' fortunes dramatically. Vijay Anand's *Johny Mera Naam*, a rollicking story about the escapades of a group of smugglers, replete with all the frills of a romantic thriller and, of course, a delightful Kalyanji–Anandji score, was nothing short of a riot. More importantly, it gave audiences the on-screen pair of Dev Anand and Hema Malini – one that would go on to work its irresistible charm in several other blockbusters.

'Working with Dev Saab was always a pleasure,' Hema tells me. 'He was such an interesting person. Fans adored him and called him India's Gregory Peck. His dramatic dialogue delivery, puffed hair falling lightly over his forehead, buttoned-up shirts, large collars and corduroy pants, with a yellow scarf and a jacket over his shoulder – he created a fashion statement that lasted decades. I personally always respected him for his evergreen attitude, not just on- but off-screen as well. He was so charming and a thoroughly lovable personality.'

If *Johny Mera Naam* catapulted Hema to the top of the popularity charts, it proved a bigger boon for Dev Anand. At the age of forty-seven, the evergreen star's career was beginning to flounder. His last couple of films like *Duniya* (1968) and *Mahal* (1969) had tanked and most critics were ready to write him off. But this offering from his younger brother's stable was almost like a resurrection. Of all the films Dev saab had worked in over the last twenty-four years, *Johny Mera Naam* was the most successful.

One of the first things Hema recounts while talking about *Johny Mera Naam* is an incident she still can't forget. 'Vijay Anand-ji was shooting the song "*O mere raja*" with Dev and me. We were at Rajgir in Bihar. There is a Buddhist temple on the other side of the mountain where we had to go. To reach that temple, one had to take the cable car. It was a very risky ride because this was quite an old-fashioned ropeway. I was very nervous, even though it was going to take just a few minutes to reach the temple. We were shooting a scene on that cable car. I was sitting on Dev saab's lap. Suddenly the cable car stopped midway and I got very tense. For a while I thought this would be my last shot ever! There were hordes of people waiting downstairs to get a glimpse of us. They screamed, but I didn't look down. I was so nervous. Dev saab understood my state and started talking about funny things just to keep my mind off it. He spoke non-stop until the cable car started functioning again. Later, we were informed that some fan had played a prank because he wanted to see both of us! Now I laugh about this incident, but it was really scary then! And I'll never forget how Dev saab tried to pacify me!'

Post *Johny Mera Naam*'s success, Dev Anand and Hema went on to work in films like *Tere Mere Sapne* (1971), *Shareef Budmaash* (1973), *Amir Garib* (1974), *Jaaneman* (1976), *Chhupa Rustam* (1973), *Joshila* (1973), *Sachche Ka Bolbala* (1989) and *Censor* (2001). Unlike his contemporaries, Raj Kapoor and Dilip Kumar, who slowed down considerably in the 1970s, Dev Anand continued playing the romantic hero opposite Hema. The two of them also shared a wonderful personal rapport that remained till the end.

About Hema, Dev Anand had once said, 'Dream Girl Hema Malini is just Hema to me. I haven't seen a more charming personality like Hema ever in my life. I remember her from the days of *Johny Mera Naam*, when she was an introvert. Hema has fought her own destiny. Recently I was invited to some felicitation show for Hema. I was stunned to see that Hema looks prettier than she used to look in the early days. If the media considers me an evergreen actor, Hema would be the evergreen actress, hands down. I would also like to mention about her political sojourn. Hema is slowly and steadily heading towards the right track. One might never know, but one day she might become the Prime Minister of India!'

A year after *Johny Mera Naam*, Hema was offered the role of a scheming mistress for the Hindi remake of Sushil Majumdar's blockbuster Bengali film, *Lal Pathar* (1971). The original film starred Uttam Kumar and Supriya Choudhury in the lead. Hema was still fairly new in the industry and only beginning her run as a contender for the top spot amongst the leading ladies. For most, to take up a negative role at this stage would qualify as a gross misstep. But Hema said yes. Not just that, the Hindi film starred seasoned actors like Raaj Kumar and Rakhee, and Hema was pitted against them with a character that was largely unsympathetic. Before the film's release, the vernacular press was already preparing to sound the death knell on Hema's career. *'Rakhee toh Hema ko kachcha kha jayegi!'* many papers speculated. But despite the scorn and derision, and through the hellfire her character raised, Hema held her own remarkably. When no other actress was willing to come anywhere close to a role like this one, Hema took up the challenge – a risk that paid off and led to a paradigm shift in her career. *Lal Patthar*, as veteran journalist Dinesh Raheja would say, was 'an underrated achievement' – one that is still considered by many as one of her best.

'I admit that it was a challenging role for me,' Hema says. 'In fact, hardly any mainstream actress would accept such a role. I wanted to give it a shot. But the only problems that I faced during this film were the emotional scenes. I never liked crying on screen. In my first few films, whenever there was a crying scene, I used to be very upset. *"Yeh rona dhona mujhse nahin hota,"* I would say! I was too young to react in such scenes. I hardly had any personal experience to draw from. When I was doing *Sapno Ka Saudagar*, I had no idea how I should cry in front of the camera, and the film had a lengthy sobbing scene. My director used to shout at me, saying, *'Ro na!'* Even later, whenever there was a crying scene, I used to be tense from the morning. This went on for a very long time.'

If one really thinks about it, the trajectory of mainstream actors and actresses is pretty straightforward and predictable. Once they climb the popularity charts, the formula is simple – stick to what has worked for you and try and consolidate your position. If one looks back at the history of Indian cinema, it is those who have had the nerve to play out-of-the-box roles – whether successful at the box office or not – are the ones who have emerged as the real heroes.

Lal Patthar was a hit and Hema witnessed stardom, quite literally, overnight. Though a certain section of the media wanted to take the credit from Hema and hand over the film's success to Rakhee and Raaj Kumar, the audience's reaction to her role was sufficient proof. Veteran film journalist Udaya Tara Nayar said, 'Hema emerged as a powerful performer in that role, she portrayed various moods and probably was one of the first commercial heroines to play a grey shade in her early career.'

If *Lal Patthar* was proof enough of Hema being no wallflower but a woman with gumption and an unusual certitude about her choices, with *Andaz* (1971), it seemed as if she was beginning to enjoy surprising her fans and shocking her critics.

When Ramesh Sippy – then a young and enthusiastic director – was planning his first film, he decided to approach Hema. Till then, he hadn't watched a single film of hers. But he had heard good things about her skills as a dancer and an actor. So, when he chanced upon some photographs he had received from Ananthaswami, Sippy took a gamble and marched straight to Hema's house. But the job, he realized, wouldn't be easy.

Andaz was the story of two single parents, eventually enacted by Hema Malini and Shammi Kapoor. In the film, she plays a schoolteacher who loses her husband (Rajesh Khanna) in an accident. When she meets Shammi – a widower – they fall in love and decide to get married. Naturally, there are objections from several quarters.

It was an unconventional subject but the passionate director was adamant that the audiences were ready for it. Ramesh Sippy recalls, 'When I was narrating the script to her, I could see that her facial expressions were changing. She asked me, "A widow with a child, falling in love with a married man ... will people accept it?" I told her, "If you trust me and my script, I could at least try to make it possible." Hema-ji accepted the offer. She was willing to do good roles, so I guess that made our relationship very comfortable.'

While Hema shared a cordial equation with most of her co-actors, there were exceptions. Though she has never said it in so many words, working with Rajesh Khanna was almost always unpleasant. In *Andaz*, he played the role of Hema's first husband and apparently his starry tantrums and unprofessional attitude used to enrage her. For a long time, Rajesh Khanna was hailed as the greatest-ever superstar of Indian cinema. In fact, his legions of fans treated him as nothing less than a demigod. Letters in blood, women committing suicide – the Rajesh Khanna craze reached manic proportions during his heydays. It is a known fact that sometimes he would make a film unit wait for eight to ten hours before showing up for his shot. But no one dared to complain. For Hema Malini – always a no-nonsense person and by now a rising star herself – Kaka's high-handedness was unbearable. In fact, after *Andaz*, no producer was willing to cast them together again.

Hema shares, 'I don't know what the issue was but something was amiss with Rajesh Khanna. He would behave strangely with me in the initial days. No doubt he was the reigning superstar and women would adore him for his charm. But I didn't give him any special "bhaav" as a co-actor. People around him would often tell him false stories about me. And the same set of people would come to me and tell me stories about him. Rajesh thought that I was arrogant while I thought that he was too full of himself. But eventually we broke the ice when we started working together in back-to-back movies.'

Neither Hema or Kaka, however, have ever been vocal about their differences. In fact, Hema was one of the chosen few to be invited to the Rajesh Khanna–Dimple Kapadia wedding. Ironically, despite starting off on the wrong foot, the two went on to do about thirteen films together – one of which, *Prem Nagar* (1974), helped Rajesh Khanna get back on his feet at a time when he was losing shine and the Amitabh Bachchan era was threatening to take over. It was also rumoured that when Kaka was planning a comeback with the film *Babu* (1985), Hema readily agreed to play his love interest, despite knowing that it wasn't a leading role. All she did was request for a few more scenes and a dance number. Kaka was seemingly thrilled. Hema was not the kind of person who would take any undue advantage or favours from anyone, be it her own family or friends in this industry.

After Rajesh's demise, Hema spoke openly about her feelings for the superstar. 'It's very sad that Rajesh Khanna is no more. I think he was always alone. Of course, we all have to go one day, but I think he went too soon,' rues Hema. 'He could have easily lived another twenty years. I had the opportunity to work with him in many films, and the audience too loved our pairing. *Mehbooba* (1976) remains one of my favourite films with Rajesh, while my last film with him was *Paap Ka Ant* (1989), where he played a cameo. He was not just a superstar, he was a phenomenon. He was an encouraging co-actor. He had an aura, a huge fan following. Though people used to feel he was a little arrogant, I think he was a wonderful person. When we started working together, he was arrogant. So, we were not really comfortable with each other. With time, we became friends. But during *Prem Nagar* we stopped talking to each other and, to be honest, till the end both of us didn't quite know why. I always thought he would come back (from the hospital). The last time I met him was during the Apsara Awards, at the celebration of hundred years of cinema. He looked fine when he spoke to us.'

If you ask me why Hema Malini still went ahead and helped Kaka on so many occasions despite everything, it was because of someone else.

When Hema Malini talks about Dimple Kapadia, her face lights up. The first time she ever saw her, Dimple was a teenager. Over the years, the two struck up a rare camaraderie that blossomed into a warm and loving friendship. If Dimple treated Hema as the ultimate symbol of respect, for Hema, Dimple was the only true and real friend she ever made in the industry.

Hema vividly remembers the first time the two of them met. 'Raj-ji (Kapoor) had invited me to the first song recording of *Bobby* (1973). And you know how it is when a film star attends such functions. All these fans come for autographs. In the crowd was this very young attractive kid, I don't know what it was about her, but I liked her at first sight. She was very sweet, flitting about like a butterfly in a dress, so young. Later on, I came to know that she was the heroine of the film. I think Krishna-ji (Raj Kapoor's wife) introduced me to Dimple.' She adds, 'After *Bobby*, Dimple attained that fantastic success and everybody said that she was now in competition with me, but I never felt that way. I just had a warm feeling towards her, like one has for a kid sister. Suddenly, I got to know she was married – so young – and this kid was all wrapped up in a big sari, with a jooda and bangles covering her arms. Then she had a baby soon after.'

Every time Hema had a location shoot with Rajesh Khanna, she looked forward to spending time with Dimple. 'At least I'd have company,' she says. 'I remember when I was shooting for *Amir Garib* on the beach and I suddenly felt like visiting this girl. So I just took a chance and walked into her bungalow. And there she was – this kid – again wrapped up in a sari, this time holding a baby!'

In an interview to *CineBlitz* magazine, Dimple spoke warmly of Hema. 'She has a fantastic memory; I don't remember the *Bobby* incident. I was so young at that time ... but I had always been fascinated by her. The first distinct memory I have of Hema-ji was when she came to see Twinkle while she was shooting at Juhu Beach. I was zapped, totally taken by surprise. And I was very touched that this great woman made a gesture like this, it was so natural and warm. Of course, after that, since she was my husband's co-star, we met on most of the outdoor locations where we grew very close. It was her total contrast on- and off-screen that got me. I mean behind the camera, she was such a down-to-earth person, so raw ... completely unaffected by the success or by anything. I loved that quality about her. Also, I feel she's one of the most trusting human beings I've met. She wants to believe the best about anybody and trust them. She's truly a good woman. And, she's also one of the biggest romantics I've ever come across! I mean she's almost story-bookish in her idea of romance! But the thing that got me most was her regal bearing. You know they used to shoot in all those palaces for films like *Mehbooba*, etc., and she seemed so much a part of the palace. I felt she must have been as majestic in all her previous seven lives. And strangely enough, even she used to tell me she felt some connection with these places.'

In an industry where secrets are hard to share, Hema and Dimple went on to become each other's greatest confidantes. 'Yes, I used to confide all my problems to her,' Dimple confesses. 'I somehow felt myself with her, there were no pretensions. And she never judged.

She was just somebody who was there and understood what I was saying. I must have really shocked her those days. I used to be this rebel with no cause at all and she was my husband's co-star and yet she understood everything. But she also came to me for advice. And I probably gave her all the wrong advice as well! You see, I was such a hot-headed person in those days that I'd get all worked up about her problems. I'd tell her things like – "This man (Dharmendra) is never going to marry you. You better sit up and do something about it." And if she had listened to me…' Dimple bursts into laughter.

Both of them were going through trying times when it came to their relationships, and that is perhaps one of the biggest reasons they could relate to each other so well. Hema says, 'With Dimple, I used to feel that everything in life had happened to her too soon … her success, her marriage, her babies. I found her a very frank and honest person. She said exactly what she felt and I liked that quality. She was very natural and so different from the way I had been brought up, but somehow I could tell her anything. A very genuine person. I have never got close to any heroine other than this girl. During the outdoor locations, she would sit there smoking and drinking, but I never felt it looked wrong or indecent. I know she was going through a lot of tension and she was such a lonely girl. Rajesh used to shoot all day, and in the evenings, he would sit with his friends and chat late into the night and drink. She had no company. Whereas my father, mother, aunt … everyone used to be with me. I think she liked that family atmosphere. So she would spend a lot of time with us. Yes, it's true that even though she was much younger, I used to take her advice. I was going through a lot of tension in my personal life those days and used to discuss it with her. You see, I was not married then, while she was. So there were certain things or advice she could give me.'

In the middle of all the worries and heartache, the two also shared some genuinely good times. Dimple recalls one impulsive day. 'I think I used to give her heart attacks! Once, I fetched her and Dharam-ji from her house in my Lotus, and zipped down the road with them to my house. By the time we arrived, neither of them knew what had hit them. They were totally zapped and shaking in the seat,' she says with a mischievous grin.

Hema talks about another time when they were in Shimla. 'We did all sorts of weird things. Once, when we were on location in Shimla, we heard of this Brighu-ji "jyotish" in Hoshiyarpur and we were determined to go to him. The best part was that we made up our minds at 10 o'clock at night and wanted to leave that minute. Everybody advised us against it, saying it was too dangerous. But we bravely got into a car and started driving down. But halfway, the driver himself stopped and turned the car around, saying he wouldn't risk it. So we just had to come back!'

Years later, when Hema launched her first directorial venture, *Dil Aashna Hai* (1992), she signed on her good friend as the mother of the female protagonist. Incidentally, it was during the shooting of this film that the ice finally broke between Hema and Sunny Deol.

'I wanted to shoot a paragliding scene with Mithun (Chakraborty) in *Dil Aashna Hai*, and there was an aeroplane scene which was required for a song sequence,' Hema tells me. 'A few days before the shoot, a pilot had met with an accident and Dimple was very scared to do the shoot. She informed Sunny, and out of concern, Sunny came and met me. I assured Sunny that she would be safe, and that's when I started talking to him.'

It brought an end to what had been a bitter and long feud. Sunny and Hema have shared a cordial relationship ever since, bringing about the long-awaited peace she had been craving for in her personal space.

5

Double Whammy

Soon after the whirlwind success of his debut film, *Andaz*, Ramesh Sippy, charged with a new kind of vigour, was already halfway through his next. This time it would be an out-and-out entertainer about twins separated at birth. The story had been attempted before, with veterans like Kishore Kumar and Dilip Kumar showcasing some compelling skills. But Ramesh believed that the subject was more suited to a woman actor, and his first choice for the coveted double role had been the sweetheart of the masses, Mumtaz.

For reasons as varied as they were vague, Mumtaz refused the film. Some say she quoted an exorbitant fee, while others say the offer was sabotaged and someone played a dirty trick. Whatever the reason, the director was now on the lookout for somebody new. This was also the time when *Andaz* was in its final stages and Ramesh was busy with the dubbing. One day, while in the dubbing studio with Hema, the director asked her if she would like to take up his next film.

'She was taken aback. She asked me, "You think I can carry off two diverse characters convincingly?" It was a complex role,' Ramesh recalls. 'I told her that if she tried hard enough, she definitely would. "You might even win an award," I remember telling her.' She eventually did!

Seeta Aur Geeta (1972) quite easily is Hema Malini's most popular film. It is also her most career-defining. In her thirty-five-year-long career in the industry, this was the one film that fetched her a Filmfare Best Actress award. 'It was a great feeling,' she remembers. 'I was nominated with Meena Kumari-ji for *Pakeezah* and Rakhee for

Aankhon Aankhon Mein. Winning an award has always been special. Till date people talk about *Seeta Aur Geeta*. It's a landmark film in my career.'

Her first double role was rip-roaring from word go. It is the story of millionaire twins separated at birth – one servile and scared, brought up by a nasty aunt and her family, the other fearless and fancy-free, a motormouth brought up a gypsy mother. When their paths cross and they swap lives, what follows is a riot of hilarious scenes and delightful revenge sequences. With a plethora of character actors and superstars Sanjeev Kumar and Dharmendra lending support, *Seeta Aur Geeta* was lapped up by audiences.

Written at a time when the scriptwriter duo Salim–Javed enjoyed almost alchemic powers, the script for *Seeta Aur Geeta* was completed in fifteen days. Ramesh recalls, 'Once you have a particular artiste in mind, you adapt the script to suit his or her potential or even limitations. Surprisingly, Hema responded exceedingly well to what I had in mind. More than that, she worked very hard. With *Seeta Aur Geeta* she showed that she was capable of carrying off any type of role. Her part as Geeta was particularly demanding. Comedy always is. I remember the very first sequence we shot was where she creates havoc inside the police station and swings up to sit on the ceiling fan. Now, climbing up and sitting on a fan was no laughing matter for Hema. I remember her looking up rather hesitatingly. To put her at ease I asked for a ladder, climbed up and sat on the fan myself. I even asked for the ladder to be removed and swung around a bit on the blades. There was no problem after that. Hema climbed up and did as was expected.'

Hema's range was truly tested with this film. Apart from playing two contrasting characters, she threw herself into terrains she'd never attempted before. From climbing onto a fan (a scene still loved for its sheer comic timing) to shooting an entire song on skateboards to taking up action sequences, she gave it her all.

'Each day Ramesh-ji would come and ask me to do something or the other. *Kabhi bolenge pankhe ke upar chad jao, toh kabhi high jump lagao, toh kabhi hunter le ke maar peet karo* (Sometimes he would tell me to climb onto a fan, sometimes he would ask me to do a high jump, and at others to beat someone with a whip). I used to always ask him, *Aap pehele mujhe karke dikhaiye toh hi main karoongi* (You do it and show me first, then I will). He was so sweet; in fact, he used to always demonstrate the risky shots to me. My daughters still laugh when they watch that police station scene where I am hanging onto a ceiling fan!' she says, laughing.

This wasn't a simple film to make, though. Ramesh points out, 'The challenge of *Seeta Aur Geeta* was that there was so much to deal with. Besides these comic parts, there was the problem of coming up with a male cast. With a female in the lead it was not easy, for heroes do not generally like to be sidelined. Fortunately, Dharmendra and Sanjeev Kumar were both very sporting. At first, they did express their doubts about fitting into a film with a heroine in a double role. I convinced them that their characters were equally important. And not being in the frame all the time didn't mean they wouldn't have the audience with them, which was proved when the film was released. For even as Hema thrilled them with her antics, Dharmendra enjoyed equal popularity as Raka the tamashewala. And Sanjeev Kumar as Ravi the doctor carried the audience with him. There was an instant chemistry that the trio effectively established. I don't think with a pair of ordinary artistes I could have achieved what I did with them. I remember that Dharmendra had his own style of functioning at that time. He was known as a macho man – all muscle and brawn – and used to expressing more with his fists. I hadn't expected the light scenes to be easy for him. I thought I might encounter some problem. But he surprised me. The scene where he haggles with Geeta for his share of the booty they earned after their tamasha is an example of his brilliance. I knew I could count on him.'

He adds, 'On the other hand, Sanjeev Kumar was best known to the audience for light scenes. And there were so many to deal with. Remember the scene where he walks into the room in his inimitable style, is mesmerized by Geeta who is looking gorgeous in a blue sari, and slips on the roller skate? I have never worked with an actor whose sense of timing was as exact as Sanjeev's for comedy. And he always appeared to be so effortless ... so perfect.'

This was one film where there apparently was almost as much drama happening behind the scenes. Ramesh recalls shooting the hugely popular song, '*Hawa ke saath saath*', where Sanjeev Kumar and Hema Malini romance each other on roller skates along winding mountain roads. 'I remember we were location-shooting in Mahabaleshwar for it. It was a difficult shot. The artistes had to concentrate on the song whilst skating down the slopes, never knowing when there would be a "khud" (ditch) around the corner. Even for us, following the camera became a difficult task. We had attached a board we were sitting on to the camera with a coupling, for better fluidity. And at one point the coupling came off. As everyone was concentrating on the artistes, no one noticed that we were drifting, till we suddenly felt that the distance between us and the camera had widened. Luckily, we had rolled towards the mountainside and not the deep valley. Otherwise, there would have been a major disaster that day!'

With *Seeta Aur Geeta*, Hema's popularity soared. From a star to a sensation – it was a dramatic transition. Jeetendra remembers the time he was shooting for *Gehri Chaal* with Hema (produced by the same C.V. Sridhar who had rejected Hema all those years ago). It was 1973 and *Seeta Aur Geeta* was creating waves across the country. Having watched the film, the director of *Gehri Chaal* quickly changed his script to add scenes where Hema could bash up the goons. Suddenly Jeetendra and Amitabh Bachchan (who played Hema's brother in the film) were made to stand on the sidelines and watch while Hema got her hands dirty! 'All of a sudden, she was now the hero!' Jeetendra recollects with a smile.

But that wasn't the only kind of drama that was unfolding. Rumour mills proclaim that it was during the making of *Seeta Aur Geeta* that both Sanjeev Kumar and Dharmendra developed feelings for their leading lady. In fact, Hari Bhai (as Sanjeev Kumar was popularly called) was the first to profess his love and express his desire to marry Hema. 'Hema Malini is neither a goddess nor a saint, but she is still worshipped' – telling lines from a man not known for wearing his heart on his sleeve or for being vocal about his feelings

Seeta Aur Geeta was their first film together. What really happened on the sets is unclear, but friends close to Hema say that Sanjeev Kumar was too vociferous in expressing his feelings to her. It left her uncomfortable. In the next film where they were paired together, *Dhoop Chaon* (1977), the two barely spoke. In fact, the situation was such that in other films that followed *Seeta Aur Geeta*, like *Sholay* (1975) and *Trishul* (1978), they shared no screen time together at all.

'Don't ask me about these things now. I am a mother of two daughters and a grandmother; it is embarrassing.' Hema emphatically seals the topic whenever it is broached.

It is believed that being turned down by Hema left Sanjeev Kumar completely broken. He never really recovered from the heartbreak. In fact, the blow proved lethal. He took to drinking, and coupled with his love for good food, ended up with a weight problem and finally a heart condition. When he died in 1985, at the age of forty-seven, he was still unmarried.

There's an interesting story from the making of *Sholay*. It is said that Dharmendra initially wanted to take up the role of Gabbar. Ramesh Sippy then pointed out to him that in such a scenario, Hari Bhai would have to play Veeru and all the romantic scenes with Hema would go to him. Dharmendra, who by now was as interested in Hema as Sanjeev Kumar was, quickly withdrew the suggestion. Ramesh confirms, 'Yes, it was really funny. I didn't use any personal relationship, but stated the fact. I can't change my script ... so they had to interchange the characters.'

Hema's love life has been fraught with controversies. This might not be unusual for an industry where the tabloid media leaves stars no space to breathe. From Sanjeev Kumar and Jeetendra to Girish Karnad and Dharmendra, a lot has been said about her affairs. But what really is astounding is that no amount of headline-grabbing scandals or screaming speculations about her penchant for ditching men at the altar ever managed to taint Hema's image as the 'ideal woman'. While Vyjayanthimala, Waheeda Rehman and Nargis, as well as Hema's contemporaries like Parveen Babi, Shabana Azmi and Rekha were all condemned for falling in love with married men, Hema actually went ahead and married an already married man – and yet she wasn't hated or ostracized. On the contrary, and quite inexplicably, admiration for her only grew. In fact, if anything, Hema went on to pretty much define the spirit of feminism – someone who lived life on her own terms, independent, fearless and her own person.

'She commands respect,' says Jeetendra. 'You just have to give it to her. She has an aura around her which you are just forced to respect.'

When I ask Hema, she attributes it to her upbringing. 'Today I am happy that I was brought up strictly by my parents. I really thank them for being stern with me.' What adds to her persona is the kind of person she inherently is, as well as the lifestyle she is known to follow. 'I am quite a traditional and religious person,' she continues. 'Till today there is no non-vegetarian food allowed at my place. I even follow my father's practice of having only an Iyengar cook. I do puja every day before I leave the house. And till recently, no alcoholic drinks were allowed at my place. Only of late have I been offering drinks on special occasions at home. Otherwise, it was strictly prohibited.'

Before I can bring up her marriage and point out how it contradicted every stricture, she insists that it was her orthodox upbringing that drove her to marry the man she loved, instead of living with him outside of wedlock. 'It was a one-on-one decision,' she says. 'Religion has nothing to do with it. We just realized that we are in love and nothing else mattered. He (Dharmendra) knew no one in this world could stop us if we really wanted to get married. So we were honest with each other and got married. And I think I was accepted and given a lot of respect by everybody because I loved only one man and got married only to him.'

When Hema turned twenty-three, her father started the groom hunt. Jaya wasn't very happy about this – she wanted Hema to focus on her career – but V.S.R. Chakravarti was adamant. It became almost a daily ritual – showing Hema photographs of 'eligible men' and asking for her opinion. Inevitably, he was met with silence. What he didn't know was that his daughter was perhaps already in love. Hema recalls, 'The truth was that I didn't know what I wanted. I knew that I was attracted to him (Dharmendra) but the relationship had no future. In the beginning, we were just good friends. I enjoyed his company. We were paired opposite each other in so many films ... there came a time when we were shooting together not just for days or weeks but for months. Soon, it became a habit to be with each other all the time...

'As time passed, it became more and more impossible to describe what I felt for him, or better still define the relationship. To be honest, I never thought of marrying him. My only argument is that I didn't fall in love consciously. It's funny, but I always used to think that whenever I marry, it would be with someone like him. I never thought of it being him, though. It's destiny and my fortune.

'The magazines were full of stories of my affair. Journalists were writing something or the other all the time that rocked the peace at home and led to mounting tension. At that point in time I stopped entertaining film journalists as things were getting worse. My father, suddenly panic-stricken, began summoning astrologers and pundits. He wanted to know what was in my kundali. The delay in my marriage began to worry him, and this tension made him accompany me for my shootings, something which he had never done in his life. In 1975, during the outdoor shooting of Ramanand Sagar's *Charas* (1976), we were to be in Malta for weeks. And since I was to be shooting with him (Dharmendra), my father insisted on coming along with me. Often, the cast and crew had to travel together in a car. My father was not happy with this at all. He would order me in Tamil – so that Dharam-ji would not understand what he was saying – to sit in one corner while he would try and sit in the middle. But Dharam-ji would make up some clever excuse or the other to get in from my side, so that I would end up sitting in the middle and he would be beside me!

'Today we can laugh over it, but at that time it wasn't funny. Strangely, my father had no problems with Dharam-ji other than the one related to me. In fact, they got along so well whenever I wasn't around. They would always be laughing and I would want to freeze the moment. If only they could be like that forever. Everyone in my family adored him ... just not as a prospective son-in-law. It's difficult for me to describe what I went through in those days. I liked him – I couldn't deny that he was attractive and strong and there was an air of serenity about him. I tried turning away from him. But I couldn't. There was something inherently good about him. One day, while we were shooting, he suddenly asked me if I loved him. I began to blush and replied indirectly "I will only marry the person I love." That was my only answer...'

It was at the premier of a K.A. Abbas film, *Asmaan Mahal*, that Hema Malini met Dharmendra. 'I remember Ananthaswami had told my mother that I should start attending premiere shows of big films to gain visibility. I had just completed my first film and I had no idea what premiere shows were all about. My mother made me drape a traditional Kanjeevaram sari, put kaajal and wear a gajra. During the interval of the film, they called some of the artists and producers on stage for their feedback – as they usually do at premieres. When I was called on stage, I had to walk alone, and I remember being so shy. I had just finished my film with Raj Kapoor but the film had not yet released. While walking towards the stage I heard Dharam-ji tell Shashi Kapoor in Punjabi, "*Kudi badi changi hai*" (The girl is quite pretty) but I chose to ignore it. Then they introduced me as Raj Kapoor's Dream Girl. How nervous I was to be sharing the stage with Dharam-ji and Shashi Kapoor!'

The Hema Malini–Dharmendra relationship and eventually their marriage would go on to become a hot subject for the industry, with support and criticism in equal measure from all possible quarters. But neither the storm nor the sensationalism would ever manage to touch the foundations of this relationship. The way the couple maintained their silence and dignity through years of media frenzy has been a lesson for the ages. What had started as a friendly and light-hearted association as co-actors on the sets of *Seeta Aur Geeta* blossomed steadily into a deep and profound relationship during the making of *Sholay* – the biggest film of their careers and perhaps their lives.

6

The Colours of Spring

'There has never been a more defining film on the Indian screen. Indian film history can be divided into *Sholay* BC and *Sholay* AD.' Shekhar Kapur's words have perhaps served as the most befitting description of what *Sholay* (1975) meant for Indian cinema. Taking off from the hugely popular American genre, the spaghetti Western, this was one film that doffed its hat to several cinema greats – from Akira Kurosawa to Sergio Leone. But it was the finer nuances, from the framing to the engaging screenplay, from its characters to the poignant sense of unhurriedness, and the underlying tone of tragedy that made this solely a director's film. With *Sholay*, Ramesh Sippy outdid himself. Whether any other film has come close to the craftsmanship or popularity of this monumental effort will always be a matter of debate.

The story of *Sholay* can be summarized in four simple sentences. The village of Ramgarh is plagued by Gabbar Singh (Amjad Khan) and his goons – a band of ruthless dacoits. A retired police inspector, Thakur Baldev Singh (Sanjeev Kumar), settled in the same region, vows to put an end to the menace. The Thakur also has a deep personal grudge against Gabbar, having lost his family and his arms to the dreaded bandit. He hires two fugitives on the loose – Jai (Amitabh Bachchan) and Veeru (Dharmendra) – to nab Gabbar. What follows is a revenge drama of epic proportions.

After owning author-backed roles in films like *Andaz* and *Seeta Aur Geeta*, Hema was initially reluctant to play the role of Basanti, who would have all of five-and-a-half scenes. 'This isn't your film. This is Thakur and Gabbar's film. But your role will be very interesting,' Ramesh assured her. Having worked with him closely and knowing all too well what this director was capable of creating, Hema needed no further convincing. She recollects, 'Well, at the time we never knew we were doing something that would become this big. At first I looked at the script and was a little surprised that they wanted me to be a tangewali. I mean, you've heard of tangewalas but never of a tangewali, right? In fact, the entire set had to give me time after each day's shoot to get acquainted with how to ride a tonga!'

True to this actor–director association, *Sholay* tested every nerve, every limit in Hema – not just her acting prowess but, equally, her indomitable spirit. Apart from playing a motormouth and having to rattle off several pages of dialogue every time she came on screen, being a gutsy tangewali meant braving risky chase sequences and even dancing on glass. Hema did it all, in a film that would truly be her grandest effort on celluloid.

'It was a great experience,' she confesses. 'I was habituated to Ramesh-ji by then. He would give me three pages of dialogues that I had to deliver breathlessly. It wasn't easy. I still remember the action sequence that Ramesh-ji shot with me. It was very risky. Riding a horse-driven cart is very difficult, but somehow I managed. *Sholay* will remain a special film for me.'

The making of *Sholay* was as epic as the film itself, with enough anecdotes to fill up an entire book! Salim–Javed drew some scenes from real-life incidents too. For example, the scene where Jai goes to Basanti's Mausi with Veeru's marriage proposal was borrowed straight out of the writers' lives! It is believed that Javed was in love with Honey Irani and wanted to marry her, but neither her mother nor Salim was keen on the alliance. Javed coaxed Salim to convince Honey's mother. That's when a reluctant Salim went over with the proposal, seemingly singing Javed's praises, but in reality undercutting every one of them. Like almost every other scene in *Sholay*, this too is one for the ages.

Interestingly, many of the dangerous scenes belonged to Hema. One of the most difficult scenes was the chase where she had to ride her tonga at ferocious speed while trying to escape the dacoits out to grab her. Most of the shots for that sequence were taken from a camera vehicle that towed the tonga. For some shots, the camera was placed inside, next to Hema, but the horses were removed to minimize danger. For the long shots and the scene where the tonga overturns, a double – Reshma – was used. In fact, during that last shot, Reshma lost her footing and fell in front of the cart. The wheel went over her and she lost consciousness.

Another remarkable feat on Hema's part was shooting for the pre-climax number, '*Jab tak hain jaan*'. Basanti is forced to dance before the leering band of dacoits outside Gabbar's den on jagged rocks. A gun is cocked at Veeru's head, while his arms and legs are bound. '*Jab tak tere pair chalenge uski saans chalegi … tere pair ruke toh yeh bandook chalegi*' (As long as your feet keep moving, he'll keep breathing … if your feet stop this gun will go off) – Gabbar spits out his threat. Being a consummate dancer, the steps were easy for Hema, but the stage wasn't. To make the struggle look real, Ramesh wanted to shoot the song in summer under the scorching sun, on location, near Bangalore.

'Why not shoot this in January?' Hema asked him.

'Because I want that expression of torture due to the extreme heat on your face,' replied the director.

The song was shot in May. But Bangalore, known for its unpredictable weather, only added to their troubles. The days were blisteringly warm while the nights brought rain. By morning the rocks were damp and slushy. Shooting could start only by midday, once the production unit hastened the drying process with fans and blowers. By the time the crew was ready for the day's shoot, the rocks were scalding. Characteristically, despite the situation, Hema refused to dance with pads on her feet. It made her uncomfortable, she said. For the long shots, though, Ramesh insisted on them. 'I don't want to torture you unnecessarily,' was his reason. After each shot, Hema's spot boy would rush to splash water on her feet to provide temporary relief. But that wasn't all. Halfway through the song, as the script went, a couple of dacoits throw glass bottles on the rocks. Basanti has to dance on broken glass. Although plastic was predominantly used for this portion, for the actual bottle-throwing shot, they used glass bottles, and Hema's feet, already blistered, ended up with a few splinters. Anyone else would have probably thrown a fit at what would seem like the last straw. But not Hema. She carried on till the last shot was canned, delivering with a flourish right till the end.

Ramesh Sippy looks back at the *Sholay* days and Hema. 'Hema-ji has a tremendous memory. She would deliver those 340 words of dialogue at one go. She would not get the proper accent in one take, but we made up for that during the dubbing. I think for Hema-ji, playing a tangewali was a revolutionary act in Hindi cinema. In fact, the dialogue where Basanti tells Veeru, "*Agar Dhanno ghodi ho kar tanga khinch sakti hai toh Basanti ladki ho kar tanga kyon nahin chala sakti?*" (If Dhanno being a mare can pull a tonga, why can't Basanti being a girl drive one?) is one of the strongest feminist lines that I have used in my films. She was not just the comic relief in the film, but she was representing women power in it. There is an action sequence that has been wonderfully portrayed by Hema-ji. I can't think of anyone else but Hema Malini as Basanti.'

Ask anyone from the *Sholay* team and they will tell you that shooting for this film was, without doubt, one of the most exciting chapters of their lives ... one of those phases that seem like an unbelievable dream in retrospect. As for the couple that was slowly falling in love, the backdrop couldn't have been more paradisiacal.

That Dharmendra was by now plain besotted with Hema was known to all in the crew. In love and unafraid to wear his heart on his sleeve, tales of how he wooed her have now become legendary. It is said that Dharam would tip the light boys to slip up during the romantic scenes, so they would have to do retakes! He had worked out a code with them. If he pulled his ear, they would either mess up the trolley movement or drop a reflector; if he touched his nose, the shot was okayed! The tip could go up to a hundred rupees for each take. On a 'good' day, the light boys went back richer by at least a couple of thousand rupees!

Dharam roped in Ramesh Sippy as well, pleading with him to play cupid. 'Please say nice things about me to her. I want to marry her,' he would tell Ramesh beseechingly. Ramesh also had Hema's unflinching trust. He was the only one on the sets she used to confide in. Over time, she began confessing her growing feelings towards Dharam. Soon, the two became inseparable. As Hema admitted years later, while talking about those days, 'It was such a beautiful atmosphere that everyone was in love ... even the old cameraman!'

When asked about these tales, Hema says, '*Pata nahin kitna sach hai yeh sab baton mein* (I doubt if all these stories are true). I remember reading in various interviews and articles that Dharam-ji used to bribe spot dadas so that they would deliberately create some mischief and he would get a chance to do those romantic scenes over and over again. I think I should ask Dharam-ji directly, if at all he did anything like it!'

When *Sholay* was released it was initially declared a disastrous flop. Trade pundits fell over each other, sniggering at the film's dismal failure. Newspapers reported how the audience simply did not react to the scenes, that it was all 'thanda', no fire just smoke. Ramesh Sippy too, after considering a last-minute salvation by reshooting the climax, finally gave up on the idea and eventually the film. Until the unthinkable happened. Crowds slowly began increasing in number. A few more weeks and theatres were now running housefull. What had at first seemed like tepid pubic response was actually the result of a crowd too stunned to react – such had been the impact of the film.

Sholay went on to run for five consecutive years in theatres. Apart from audio cassettes of its songs, this was perhaps the only film in the history of Indian cinema that had its dialogues recorded and released separately in cassettes for its fans. No other film has left as deep or as lasting an imprint in the consciousness of cinemagoers. More than forty years after its release, *Sholay* continues to be a grand enigma, with no one quite able to pinpoint what exactly made the film what it became, or why it had such recall value.

Sholay's record run at the Minerva Theatre was broken by Yash Chopra's *Dilwale Dulhania Le Jayenge*, that ran for almost two decades at Maratha Mandir. A senior trade analyst, however, points out, '*Sholay* ran on merit for five years to a packed house. *DDLJ* ran mostly on emotional grounds, because Yash-ji and Adi Chopra shared a very good bond with the theatre owner, and even though the seats would remain empty, they would still not bring the film down.'

When Hema talks about *Sholay*, her eyes light up. 'I didn't even realize that Basanti would become an iconic name. Every year, the media calls me for an interview on 15 August for *Sholay*. We celebrate *Sholay*'s anniversary in India as much as we celebrate Diwali and New Year. That shows the popularity of the film. Even today when I make public appearances, people expect me to rattle off lines like '*Chal Dhanno, aaj teri Basanti ke ijjat ka sawal hai*'. The songs from the films are so popular that they are remixed at every pub and social do.'

Karan Johar had once shared a story. 'I was in love with Hema-ji's dance [in the song] "*Jab tak hai jaan*", and as a kid I once tried to dance on broken pieces of glasses, when my mother (Hiroo Johar) came and slapped me.'

Hema seems mildly shocked when she hears about Karan's attempt. 'Really?' she asks with a surprised look. 'I think the film created a euphoria. I still get fan mails for *Sholay* from various parts of the world. Earlier they used to write letters, now they tag me on Twitter and Facebook.'

While *Sholay* earned Hema unprecedented accolades as an actor, she faced problems during her live classical dance shows post the film. People would always want her to dance to the Holi and '*Jab tak hai jaan*' songs onstage. 'I think it's the organizers who would give false hope or promote the show as Bollywood star Hema Malini's dance show. I think they wanted to sell their tickets at high prices, and thus resorted to these cheap routes. But once I would start my classical recitals on stage people would enjoy them too and the situation would be under control,' says Hema.

It was certainly a disappointment for her fans when Hema didn't receive any nominations for *Sholay* at the Filmfare Awards that year. Others from the movie like Sanjeev Kumar, Amjad Khan, Salim–Javed, G.P. Sippy (producer), Ramesh Sippy, R.D. Burman (music), Asrani (who played the role of the jailer) and M.S. Shinde (editor) were nominated, but finally only M.S. Shinde went on to bag the award for Best Editor. 'I was nominated (as Best Actress) for *Khushboo* and *Sanyasi*, along with Jaya Bhaduri in *Mili* and Suchitra Sen in *Aandhi*. But Laxmi won the award for *Julie*,' Hema adds with a smile. 'From that year I decided that I will focus on my work and not pay much heed to awards.'

With the roaring success of *Sholay*, Hema Malini was at her zenith.

If she had been one of the popular actresses thus far, with this film, she decimated all competition to claim her position at the top. She was the highest-paid actress in Hindi cinema by now and went on to hold the numero uno spot for the next decade.

The commercial circuit was hers, but arthouse cinema continued to elude Hema. Even as her popularity soared, critics dismissed her acting skills, relegating her to being nothing more than a 'glamour doll, incapable of a soulful performance'. In one of the editorials of a Bengali film magazine, *Anandolok*, director Rituparno Ghosh quoted a film veteran talking about Hema. Ghosh wrote, 'Hema Malini had such a beautiful face that even when she cried she looked beautiful on screen!'

Those who know Hema closely would tell you that one of her most astounding qualities is her self-assuredness – an unwavering self-belief that gains invincible strength in the face of any challenge. Through all the criticism she faced, all she did was wait.

In the same year as *Sholay*, Hema had a second release – a social drama called *Dulhan*. Directed by C.V. Rajendran, the film revolved around the tragic life of a young married woman. Hema played the central character – one who loses her doctor husband in a boat accident, mistakes his lookalike for him and later, upon realization of her mistake, returns to her village as a widow who finally succumbs to a cardiac arrest. 'I remember the film for Lata-ji's song "*Aayegi zaroor chithi*", as well as some high-voltage drama scenes. It was a completely different space, and I enjoyed working with Dadamoni (Ashok Kumar) and Jeetu-ji (Jeetendra),' she says.

The film had a disastrous run at the box office. But significantly, Hema's performance – understated and poignant – was nothing short of stellar. It made critics take note. If *Dulhan* helped usher in a hitherto unexplored side to the actor, with her next few films, Hema Malini would silence her critics once and for all.

7

Tryst with a Poet ... and Poetic Cinema

It seemed an unlikely combination: a film-maker with a rare sensibility and an eye for deep, nuanced stories, and an actor who was the czarina of the box office. And yet each served as the other's inspiration through some sensitive collaborations.

Gulzar first met Hema Malini on the sets of *Andaz* (1971), for which the former wrote the screenplay, the two striking a chord almost instantly. Years later, while receiving the Filmfare Lifetime Achievement Award from her, the director professed, 'What I admire most about Hema Malini is that she has led her life with conviction. She's a feminist, a truly liberated woman. And she has done it without slogans.'

For Hema, no film-maker has earned the respect and dedication she so instinctively reserves for Gulzar saab – a deference that was amply rewarded by his faith in the actor, which led to some of the finest performances of her career.

Their first film together was *Khushboo* (1975). Based on Saratchandra Chattopadhyay's short story 'Pandit Moshai', the movie was set in the hinterlands, an unusual storyline devoid of loud characters or any extravagance. This was Gulzar giving us a film that championed its women. *Khushboo* explored several social prejudices, subtly undermining each, but at heart, it was the story of Kusum – a woman who repeatedly falls victim to circumstances but refuses to succumb to them. As a young girl, Kusum is betrothed to Brindavan (Jeetendra). But as it happens, they don't end up getting married. Years later, when Brindavan returns to the village as a doctor, they chance upon each other. He is already married and the father of a young boy; she, having loved no other man, is devastated, but resolves to take it in her stride, going as far as developing an extreme fondness for his son. As the film progresses, we see ample instances of a woman betrayed but not cowed down. She is hurt and yet nothing comes before her pride. Even in the face of opportunities to get back with the man she loves, she decides not to – the offer seems out of pity and Kusum knows that that is no reason for a union. In a social milieu where one expects a woman to cower and concede, Kusum stands tall – a woman dignified, self-assured and strong.

If Gulzar made a powerful statement through *Khushboo*, it was Hema who ensured that it got delivered to perfection. In a role that saw her without a touch of makeup, dressed in plain cotton saris, she enacted her character with staggering honesty. Her eyes did a lot of the talking in the film – a window into how deeply the actor herself resonated with the innate strength and beliefs of a fearless, independent woman.

What makes Hema's effort in *Khushboo* even more significant is the fact that while shooting for this film she was also shooting for *Sholay*. For an actor, there couldn't have been a greater test of virtuosity. Hema recalls, 'I am grateful to him (Gulzar) for giving me the best films in my career. He was the only director who had immense faith in me and allowed me to experiment with different characters. *Khushboo* was a different experience. I had never played a Bengali woman earlier. It was difficult for me to work practically without makeup and wigs. He emphasized on natural acting and facial expressions. It was a challenge for me because I was simultaneously acting in Ramesh Sippy's *Sholay*, which demanded a lot of blabbering. Later, we worked together in many films, but *Khushboo* remains special to me.'

After the success of *Khushboo*, Gulzar brought Hema and Jeetendra back together on screen for *Kinara* (1977) – this time, to her delight, in the role of a retired Kathak dancer. Hema delivered once again. After her character loses her paramour (played by Dharmendra) in a car accident, her only wish is to get his novel published. Later, when she meets Jeetendra, she gradually learns it was his reckless driving that had taken her husband's life. As the story unfolds, Hema's character too tragically loses her eyesight. The plot gets more complicated thereon, with many turns.

Talking about the film, Hema says, 'It was like a dream come true. I always wanted to play a dancer's role. I remember meeting Gulzar saab for the first time on the sets of *Andaz*. I think he had written the dialogue for the film. Ramesh-ji would ask him to sit with me on my dialogues. After we would be through with our lines, he would chat with me. During those times, I had told him that no matter what happens, I would never stop performing on stage. That films would remain an integral part of my career, but dance was my life. So, the fact that *Kinara* was based on a Kathak and not Bharatanatyam dancer was a treat for me. When Gulzar-ji narrated the script, I got so excited. The choreography was done by Kathak exponent Pandit Birju Maharaj-ji. The character was great, with lots of shades. Another important issue in this film was that I was playing a physically challenged character for the first time. Gulzar-ji wanted me to wear contact lenses during the dance numbers to restrict the movement of my eyeballs. The lenses would help me convey the stillness he wanted in my eyes. But I avoided using lenses and assured him I would deliver what he wanted from me. And I did.'

The title track of *Kinara*, 'Naam gum jayega', rendered by Lata Mangeshkar and Bhupinder Singh, remains one of the most popular tracks from Hema's films. The song was such a hit that much later, when director Sudipto Chattopadhyay went on to make a tele-series loosely based on Bengal's legendary actress Suchitra Sen, he named it *Naam Gum Jayega*. The series was aired on Doordarshan and Hema Malini played the role of Suchitra Sen.

Kinara fetched Hema Malini a Filmfare nomination, but the award went to Shabana Azmi for *Swami*; incidentally, a film produced by Hema's mother. 'I was hoping to win for *Kinara*. It was so close to my heart – I had never played the role of a physically challenged woman before this. Apart from that, I had such beautiful Kathak numbers in the film, which was again rare for me as a performer. I have such wonderful memories related to that film. Dharam-ji agreed to do a cameo in it once I told him the story,' she adds.

Not many know that Hema had also been trained in Kathak

earlier, under Shambhu Sen. 'He was a very talented teacher, who would pester Amma to allow him to teach me Kathak. I was not interested in Kathak at all, but my mother almost forced me to meet him. But after I met him and started practising, I enjoyed it. In fact, I did one full-length Kathak performance at Shanmukhananda Hall. But that was my first and last Kathak performance on stage. Somehow, I always felt I was born to be a Bharatanatyam dancer, and no other form of dance has ever excited me,' she confesses.

After the success of their first two ventures, Gulzar wanted to make the third, one that would really count. It was to be his dream project – the story of Devdas – and he had wanted his most trusted protégées to be on board. While Hema Malini and Sharmila Tagore would take up the roles of Paro and Chandramukhi respectively, Dharmendra would be cast as Saratchandra's immortally flawed protagonist. To be produced by Kailash Chopra, by May 1979, the first song for the film had been recorded. Bhupinder Singh lent his voice to a score that carried the magic of R.D. Burman, with Gulzar's lyrics. By July, shooting had begun. But unfortunately for Indian cinema and all of us, the film was shelved before it could make any further headway.

Gulzar was once asked, many years later, if Dharmendra – known mainly for his brawn – had perhaps been the wrong choice for a character like *Devdas*. The director had defended his decision. 'I was very close to the book … the charm of Saratchandra's Devdas is the adolescence of the Devdas, who never grew out of it. While the two women Paro and Chandramukhi were mature … Dharmendra was certainly a better adolescent romantic lover, which he still retains…'

Talking about the aborted film, Hema recollects, 'It was a great experience. The script was brilliant. I was playing a Brahmin girl, Parvati or Paro, who was in love with Deva or Devdas.' She still remembers those Bengali 'tant' saris and the typical style of draping them. 'They (the costumes) weren't as gorgeous as in Sanjay Leela Bhansali's film (*Devdas*, 2002). Aishwarya Rai (who played Paro) looks like a princess in that movie. My costumes were similar to those in *Khushboo* – realistic and aesthetic at the same time,' she says.

The real reason for the film being shelved was shared twenty-five years later, when the producer finally broke his silence. 'It was my dream project,' Kailash Chopra confessed. 'I approached Gulzar because he was a brilliant film-maker. Initially I wanted to take Amitabh Bachchan as Devdas. Amitabh had already agreed. But then Gulzar told me that he had already committed to Dharmendra for the role. I thought that the director was the best person to take those decisions. But from the first day, I could see that Dharmendra was not happy with his role. He used to grumble, *"Ye kya dhoti aur side parting hairstyle kar diya aap ne?'* Even Sharmila was not satisfied. Hema didn't have any problems. After five days of shooting, I realized that the stars were reluctant. So I called Gulzar and said, "I want to shelve this film!" By then I had already invested ten lakhs. But I didn't want to do a film where the artistes themselves were uncomfortable.'

The great never waste time in lament. Gulzar, it is believed, had a spectacular vision for *Devdas*; the director had even planned an alternative ending. But it didn't take him long to accept the inevitable. Weeks after *Devdas* was abandoned, Gulzar moved on to what would be his first attempt at devotional cinema. And not surprisingly, Hema was signed on once again.

For Hema, *Meera* (1979) was probably the one film she was born to do. Being an ardent devotee of Lord Krishna herself, ever since she was a little girl, for her to be able to enact Meera's story seemed nothing short of divine intervention. What only added to the fortuity was the fact that she had her most trusted director behind it.

When Gulzar conceived the idea of Meera, he had no hesitation on who he would cast for the titular role. 'She (Hema) is the living Meerabai,' the director had once said. 'I can see the bhakti and shraddha in her face. Other than Hema, I can't think of anybody as Meerabai.'

As always, Gulzar had put in a lot of thought and study behind how he would tell this story. His portrayal of the sixteenth-century poetess, popularly upheld as a saint, was a brave departure from every other cinematic depiction till then. The director was keen on removing the mystique that shrouded her, so that she could develop before the audience's eyes into who she truly was – a profoundly independent woman, one who consistently discarded social expectations, stood up for her beliefs and laid them down clearly.

Meera's story always fascinated me. As a young girl, when she asks her mother who her husband would be, the mother points towards an idol of Lord Krishna. The little girl treats her word as gospel. She falls helplessly in love with the Lord and nothing – not time nor marriage – can lessen her devotion. Eventually, Meera is married off to a Rajput royal. But for her, nothing changes. In an age and time when the concept of a defiant wife was unthinkable, she is matter of fact when she tells her husband the reality of her situation. The film throws up several incidents where she is derided – for her failing to bear a child, or for her refusal to cook meat sent by the head priest from a ritual sacrifice, as per the royal tradition – but she is unmoved. Social norms and practices stand no chance before her divine commitment. And that is where the essence of Meera lies, in the strength of her conviction.

Talking about the scene where she refuses to cook meat, Hema recalls, 'That was a very critical scene; we were conscious of not offending those who believe in that ritual, but at the same time we wanted to convey our message through the dialogues. These scenes were never shown in any other versions of Meera. She was not just a poet who composed dohas and died peacefully, she was a rebel and fought for justice,' she explains.

The story of Meera had been adapted into film six times before Gulzar's version. Going against the popular grain, this version naturally didn't please its audience. But it is a fact that no other director, over the decades, has had as deep or as intuitive an understanding of the poetess–saint.

Hema reminisces about the shooting. 'I was already familiar with her life and was always taken up by it. I remember Gulzar saab would tell me the scene and insist on no makeup, not even powder. My face was kept completely clean. Once on the sets, I'd get into the skin of the character. It wasn't difficult. In fact, it was a beautiful experience … particularly because I was shooting for *Meera* in the mornings and for *Razia Sultan* (1983) in the evenings. That (Razia Sultan) required getting into these elaborate costumes. I remember how good I felt doing the role of Meera – romancing the Lord. It was lovely … I owe all the credit to Gulzar-ji because he used to explain every shot to me in such great detail. He was a perfectionist. Somehow I can never think of delivering a mediocre performance when he is around.'

The making of this film had its own share of setbacks. When Lata Mangeshkar agreed to inaugurate the production by sounding the clapperboard, everyone assumed she would naturally be the main playback singer for the film. But when she announced that she couldn't take up this film because she had already cut a record of Meera's bhajans, it came as a huge blow to all. When one thinks of Meerabai and her legendary voice, who else comes to mind as being capable enough?

In an interview, Premji, the film's producer, recollects, 'Lata-ji, in a way, is Meera in the public's eye. We very much wanted her to sing in the film, but she refused the offer on the mahurat day itself. And then the music director duo Laxmikant–Pyarelal refused to score music because they were not willing to work without her. So finally we signed on Pandit Ravi Shankar and singer Vani Jairam.'

The decision didn't go down very well with Hema. She tried her best to convince Lata, calling her up several times to make her change her mind, but to no avail. But signing on Pandit Ravi Shankar and Vani was a call they didn't have to regret. 'I still remember, Hema-ji came over once or twice just to see my recording,' Vani recalls. 'I guess she was worried about my voice because she was already familiar with Lata-ji's voice. But after the recording she complimented me and I guess she did justice to my voice on screen.'

Despite all the despair and heartbreak, the soundtrack, once completed, was a sensational success. In fact, it is still considered one of the most sought-after collections of Meera's bhajans.

The second big roadblock Gulzar found himself facing was finding a suitable actor to cast as Meera's husband. His first choice was Sanjeev Kumar, but everyone knew that wasn't an option. What made the process harder was the fact that the director wanted to cast a big name, even though the role would be minuscule when compared to that of the protagonist's. He narrowed down on Amitabh Bachchan.

'Hema was a superstar and I wanted an equally weighty name opposite her,' Gulzar recollects. 'But Amitabh refused to do a cameo in this film. So I signed Vinod Khanna opposite Hema. I think he did a fantastic job.'

There has been speculation around why Vinod Khanna agreed to do the film. It is believed that he wasn't very keen on doing it either, but couldn't refuse Gulzar since the director had given him a break as a male lead in *Achanak* (1973). But the actor never admitted to this story. Talking about the film, Vinod Khanna once said, 'I am proud to be a part of *Meera*. I wish Gulzar had signed me as Meera! It's one of the best characters that I have ever seen in my life. Hema is just brilliant.'

When everything finally seemed to be on track, the production almost fell apart once again. It is believed that right in the middle of production, Premji ran out of funds. Having the top-rated commercial actress on his roster didn't help matters either. Being in the kind of soup that he was, the producer decided to go with the most sensible option – to be honest about the situation. After a heart-to-heart with Hema, it was decided that she would be paid on a daily basis instead of hefty instalments. The actor gracefully accepted. That this film was no ordinary commercial affair for her was by then a well-established fact; with this decision, she removed any traces of doubt. Premji would hand over an envelope every day at the end of the shoot to Hema. What the producer doesn't know, perhaps, is that those envelopes still lie with her – sealed and unopened till date.

Hema recalls, 'After the film got over, I realized that he was paying me one or two thousand rupees per day. I didn't care much about the remuneration because Gulzar saab had mentioned that we all do films for a living, but sometimes we also take up a film for the sake of art. *Meera* was my contribution to Indian cinema.'

Meera remains one of the most talked-about films in Hema's career. 'Gulzar saab had mentioned that *Meera* would end up being a film I could watch with every generation. I have watched *Meera* with my daughters Esha and Ahaana, and hopefully I will be watching it with my grandson Darein and Esha's kid too,' Hema says.

When *Meera* released, it was greatly appreciated by critics and film connoisseurs. For Hema, the reaction hardly mattered. It had been her most satisfying and significant work yet, and she was grateful for the chance.

8

Colleagues Extraordinaire

Apart from Gulzar, if there is any other name that Hema has always held in reverence, it is Dilip Kumar. It had been a long-cherished dream for her to work with the thespian and the year 1979 finally seemed to hold the promise of fulfilling it. B.R. Chopra was planning a film, *Chanakya Chandragupt* – a massive two-and-a-half crore-rupee project – with Dilip Kumar as the protagonist and including Hema, Dharmendra, Parveen Babi and Vijayendra in the cast. But for reasons still unknown, the film was never completed. Hema had to wait another two years before providence stepped in once again.

Manoj Kumar's 1981 production *Kranti*, going back in time to the year 1825, when the earliest seeds of revolution were sown, remains one of Hindi cinema's most popular patriotic films. It is the story of Bharat (Manoj Kumar, of course) and a freedom fighter he idolizes, Sanga (Dilip Kumar), and how they plan an underground movement to fight the British Raj on two fronts: the imperialists as well as the treacherous Indian princes. Woven intrinsically into the plot is the story of Meenakshi (Hema Malini), a beautiful princess of a mighty state who joins the freedom struggle while also falling in love with a prince who betrays his own state.

'Working with Dilip saab was a great honour,' Hema recollects. 'I respect him for his experience and his dedication. Unfortunately, after *Kranti* we never worked together again. I still remember that he agreed to give the clap for my directorial debut *Dil Aashna Hai*

(1992). He spoke highly about me and loves me a lot. I am also close to Saira Banu-ji – she is a wonderful lady.'

Not one to go out of her way to build associations, Hema always shared a great regard for senior actors. From Dilip Kumar to Dev Anand to Manoj Kumar, her rapport with each of them was special, a kind of respect and appreciation that was always heartily reciprocated.

Much before *Kranti*, Hema had worked with Manoj Kumar in *Sanyasi* (1974). The story of a self-proclaimed brahmachari who eventually falls in love with a woman and gives in to his heart, the film was a success, earning itself three nominations at the Filmfare Awards in 1975. *Sanyasi's* success was quickly followed by *Dus Numbri* – another hit for the on-screen pair. Though the films that released after that didn't quite climb the charts, Manoj Kumar and Hema continued to share a congenial association off screen and have always been vocal about it.

Manoj Kumar once said, 'Hema is a beautiful lady. One of the best human beings I have come across. She is polite and humble in nature. Though she was the number one actress, she never carried that aura around with her. She gave respect to all her seniors and adored her juniors also. Though she maintained her dignity and privacy, she would never behave [in an] arrogant and egotistical [manner] on the sets. She was probably the most hassle-free actress that I have worked with. Hema has not only grown beautiful with time, but has carved her niche as a woman of substance in the truest form. I am proud of Hema, rather we all are proud of Hema.'

Surprisingly, in *Kranti*, Hema was seen sporting a choli for a rain dance that was shot on a ship deck. Known to be extremely cautious when it came to wearing 'bold' costumes, many an eyebrow had been raised when she did this song. 'He (Manoj) would never let it look vulgar,' Hema says. 'Manoj was an extremely sensitive and talented actor and film-maker. Whenever he approached me for a role as a director he knew his screenplay thoroughly. I could trust him. That is why I didn't have any inhibitions when it came to things like costumes.'

It may come as a surprise to most but of all her co-stars, Hema had a great fondness for Vinod Khanna. Their first film together was *Patthar Aur Payal* (1974), in which he played a negative role, after which they went on to do eight films together. Hema said, 'If I can do anything for Vinod and Gulzar, I feel happy.'

Their second film, *Haath ki Safai* (1974), proved to be a difficult project for Hema. Not only did she have a rough time with director Prakash Mehra, she also didn't quite get along with Randhir Kapoor, who was cast in the film. Talking about those days, Hema says, 'I am not going to work with Mr Prakash Mehra again. He'd call me night after night to shoot at Powai and other far-off places, and deliberately not take a single shot of mine. Even when the scenes only required Randhir Kapoor and Vinod, he would never let me leave the sets. I couldn't understand his attitude. Why take an actress like me, pay so much, and not use me at all? One night, realizing that I was not required I walked out of his sets, the one and only time I've ever done such a thing. And sure enough, he made a big noise about it. I have always shared a cordial relationship with my co-workers. That was the first and last time anything like that happened.'

About Randhir Kapoor she says, 'I have never refused to work with Randhir. After *Haath Ki Safai*, I never received any offer opposite Randhir. It's not that we didn't get along personally though I admit that I don't talk much when I am with him, but that's because when Randhir starts talking he doesn't stop, and nobody else gets a chance!'

Hema quickly adds how Taimur Khan Pataudi (Kareena Kapoor Khan and Saif Ali Khan's son) looks just like Randhir. 'I recently saw Daboo's (Randhir Kapoor) grandson Taimur. He looks exactly like his grandfather, chubby, fair and handsome!'

Incidentally, Hema did work with Prakash Mehra (*Mohabbat Ke Dushman*, 1988) and with Randhir Kapoor (*Chacha Bhatija*, 1977) again. But the making of *Haath ki Safai* had left a bitter taste.

In the middle of all the chaos during the shooting schedule of *Haath ki Safai*, Hema had found a confidante in Vinod Khanna, and that marked the beginning of a genuine and warm friendship. Decades after, Hema signed Vinod Khanna for her home production *Marg*, but the film was never released officially.

Marg explored a bold subject, on the politics at play in an ashram. Hema played a god-woman while Vinod Khanna essayed a reformed criminal in search of salvation. Mahesh Bhatt, who directed the film, recalls, 'The subject of spirituality has tormented me for a long time. When Hema approached me to make this film, I was very excited. I always wanted to work with Hema, and Vinod was a friend. The subject was so intriguing.'

The film, however, didn't find a distributor and was finally canned. Hema tells me, 'It was unfortunate because the film was produced by my mother. She had always wanted to make a film on the subject.'

Years later, Hema again approached Vinod for *Dil Aashna Hai* but he couldn't accommodate the dates. On her part, however, she played a cameo in Vinod's home production, *Himalay Putra* (1997), which had been designed to launch his son Akshaye Khanna. Outside of films, Hema also accompanied Vinod many times during his political campaigns. Incidentally, Hema's latest release, *Ek Thi Rani Aisi Bhi* (2017) directed by Gulbahar Singh, stars Vinod Khanna as the male lead. Based on the life of Rajmata Vijaya Raje Scindia, the film was stalled for almost ten years before it got released. 'Vinod was already suffering from cancer and could barely work. But he still gave time to Gulbahar to finish his scenes. In fact, the death scene picturized on him was his last day of shooting. He has been a great friend, and I cherish the fact that we worked together till the last scene of his life,' a visibly emotional Hema shares about the dear friend she lost recently. Vinod Khanna succumbed to cancer in April 2017.

With more than a dozen films behind them, Shatrughan Sinha was another co-star with whom Hema shared a sincere and honest camaraderie. After Dharmendra and Jeetendra, Hema perhaps did the maximum number of films with him. He once said, 'Hema Malini is a powerhouse of talent. She can do everything under the sky, gracefully, without making a hue and cry. I have seen her grow from an incipient flower to a charming daisy. I remember seeing her for the first time at Filmcity studio, she was shooting with Dharam for *Tum Haseen Main Jawan, aur unko dekh kar mein dharashayee ho gaya* (I was clean bowled when I saw her). I would tease her by saying that men would either call out "Hey Ma" when in trouble or "Hema". She has been more like a family friend since we started working together. Poonam and Hema are friends, Esha and Ahaana are very close to my kids, Luv and Kush.' Incidentally, the two actors have been neighbours for years and their children spent a lot of their playtime together while growing up.

It has to be to Hema Malini's credit that even someone like Raaj Kumar – known for his volatile temperament – was quite in awe of her! Talking about working together in *Lal Patthar*, the actor had declared, 'I can't think of anybody else but Hema Malini in *Lal Patthar*. Hema is the most versatile actress in Indian cinema. I have worked with her in many films, and each time I have seen a better Hema. She is beautiful from outside, because she is far more beautiful from inside. I don't know who named her "dream girl", but I am sure that person was a farsighted one.'

According to some sources, the producer of *Lal Patthar*, F.C. Mehra, had initially wanted Vyjayanthimala for Hema's role. Apparently, Raaj Kumar insisted on giving Hema – a relative newcomer – the chance instead. Mehra agreed but it wasn't an easy decision for Hema to take. Several people around had dissuaded her from taking up the film. Finally, it was Raaj Kumar once again who helped swing the balance. 'I remember Raaj Kumar was such a big star then. He requested me to watch the original Bengali film *Lal Pathar*. After watching the film, I was sure about the role and decided to go ahead with the film,' she says.

'Congratulatory flowers and cards filled my drawing room after the film's release,' Hema remembers. 'People loved my scene with the stuffed tigress. It was my first period drama, and that too I was playing a jealous Bengali thakurain!'

It was rumoured that Raaj Kumar had fallen in love with Hema during the making of the film and even contemplated marriage, a claim he refuted in an interview to *Stardust* in 1983. 'Marriage? Oh no! Marriage was never on the cards at that time. It came to my mind much later. I was not very keen on getting married. In *Lal Patthar* we were just co-stars. We worked in great harmony. Hema was new and liked to be told certain things. It was one of the best performances of her career. Besides, such things happen to all artistes at some time or another, there is nothing very sensational about it. If I had contemplated marriage, there was no question of it not happening!' he had characteristically stated.

As a top-billed actress carrying a reputation of being a thorough no-nonsense professional, directors seldom had any trouble while casting for a Hema film. In 1973, an interesting episode unfolded, which gives a glimpse of her professional approach.

C.V. Sridhar wanted to make a film for which he had Hema, Jeetendra and Amitabh Bachchan in mind. Going by their history, the industry was certain he would stand no chance when he approached her. But as has often been the case with Hema Malini, she surprised everyone. Not only did Hema agree to sign up for *Gehri Chaal* (1973), not a word was spoken about Sridhar's insult that had, in fact, left a deep and lasting scar on her mind.

'It was very unfair on his part to make such derogatory statements about me,' Hema finally breaks her silence on a subject she has studiously avoided all these years. 'I didn't want to become an actress. He had spotted me and wanted to cast me with Jayalalithaa in the Tamil film *Vennira Aadai*. I looked hideous in that film, but my opinion was never asked for. He had decided to change my name to Sujata because he thought Hema Malini was a very old-world name and wouldn't work in the film industry. My mother was naïve then. Though she was very fond of my name, she still agreed to change it. Once again, I was not consulted. We had gone to Madurai for the shoot, and Jayalalithaa was also there with her mother and brother.' Jayalalithaa, it seems, barely spoke to Hema during those days. 'I have never spoken about her (Jayalalithaa) in the past, because I wanted to forget the entire chapter. Now that I think about it, I remember her as a very fair and pretty girl. She was of my age, probably a few months older. I was told that she was very good at studies and she was also well groomed. She did come across as overconfident and had an attitude on the sets. But when we were not shooting, she was a completely different person. She would mingle freely with Amma and me.'

A young Hema Malini with her parents and brothers Kannan (L) and Jagannath (R)

Hema as a child

Practising Bharatanatyam in Chennai

A playful Hema with her appa, Vengarai Srisailesha Rangaramanuja (V.S.R.) Chakravarti

Jaya Chakravarthy helping Hema get ready for her dance recital

With Dharmendra at the premiere of
Asmaan Mahal, where she met him
for the first time

With her maternal grandfather,
Parthasarathy Thathachari

With her family at Kannan and Prabha's wedding

At a house-warming ceremony in Chennai with her amma and appa

L to R: Kannan, Prabha, Jaya Chakravarthy, V.S.R. Chakravarti, Hema's Das mama aka Narasimhan and his wife Bhanu

Hema and Dharmendra at their wedding

At their traditional Tamilian wedding at Jagannath's house Sea Palace in Juhu

Hema and Dharmendra on honeymoon in Switzerland. Dharmendra is wearing a jacket gifted by Hema

With Dharmendra, Esha and Ahaana at their Goregaon house

A photo of baby Esha clicked by Dharmendra

With baby Esha, wearing identical kaftans. Hema gifted her kaftan to Esha during the latter's pregnancy

With her brother Kannan's family in Chennai

A family portrait: L to R (standing): Shanta's son Mohan, Dharmendra, Ashish, Prabha Raghavan (Pappu), Smita and Hema; (sitting): Kannan, Hema's aunts Saroja and Shanta, Jaya and Jagannath; (on floor): Esha, Ahaana and Jagannath's son Arjav

At Esha's mehendi
ceremony

A loving father:
Dharmendra with
Ahaana and Esha

Ahaana with
Dharmendra and
Sunny Deol

With Jagannath and his wife Smita

With Kannan and his wife Prabha

Bottom: Their mother's daughters: Ahaana (L) and Esha

Hema with Sunny Deol, Dharmendra and her cousin Prabha Raghavan (Pappu)

Hema and a young Esha with Guru Ma Indira Devi

At Esha's engagement (L-R): Dharmendra, Hema, Esha, Bharat Takhtani, Sunny Deol, Vijay and Pooja Takhtani

Hema and Dharmendra at Ahaana's wedding reception in Delhi with Ahaana's in-laws Vipin Vohraa and Pushpa Vohraa (R) and Pooja Takhtani (L)

With Vyjayanthimala at the Synergy show in Chennai

Abhay Deol at Esha and Bharat's wedding

Madhoo with Vyjayanthimala at Esha's reception

Esha and Bharat

Bottom: Ahaana and
Vaibhav with their son
Darien

The doting grandparents with Darien

Hema and baby Darien

An eternal love story

After shooting for almost a week or so, Sridhar decided to drop Hema, signed A.B. Shanthi, renamed her Nirmala, and launched her. Nirmala acted in 200-odd films, including some Malayalam movies, as Usha Kumari. 'It was Jayalalithaa's Tamil debut, and we were both supposed to be launched in the same film. But somehow destiny had other plans for me.' Hema smiles.

Gehri Chaal was completed in record time, and although not a box-office draw, it opened avenues for something much larger and grander: a treat called the Hema–Amitabh on-screen pair.

In *Gehri Chaal*, Amitabh and Hema were cast as brother and sister. At a time when the Dharam–Hema romance was in full steam, trade pundits completely missed the potential of this brand-new pairing. It took director Arabind Sen to finally see their on-screen chemistry and within the next year, he had cast them opposite each other in his film *Kasauti* (1974). An interesting story that centred around a strong-headed woman who decides to fight her demons with the help of a simple and good-natured taxi driver, *Kasauti* was proof of how this pair was nothing short of magic. From *Sholay* to *Satte Pe Satta* (1982) – no two actors could play off each other the way Hema and Amitabh did. Their comic timing worked like a finely tuned orchestra – seamless and impeccable. In fact, their lines from *Satte Pe Satta*, a film that can still bring the house down, are rattled off by fans even today.

Speaking about Amitabh Bachchan, Hema says, 'I did a number of films with Amitabh. He was a wonderful co-star – totally different from the others. I remember him as two different, contrasting personalities. At times, he was very aloof and quiet. He would say very little, speak to the point. At other times, he would be a lot of fun – jovial, making you laugh. His professionalism was, is, will be legendary. He was always prepared when he came on the sets. He was very easy to work with. In fact, I had a cordial relationship with all my heroes – some like Jeetendra or Shatrughan Sinha are very funny. Amitabh, on the other hand, was more serious, more professional. But at times you would get a glimpse of his boyishness when he was in a light-hearted mood, particularly on Manmohan Desai's sets. It was as if he was more at home with him. He was in a great mood when we were shooting for *Naseeb* (1981) and *Desh Premee* (1982). With Amitabh, I did some good films but he had become so popular that all the attention was focused on him and there wasn't a balance between our roles. As an actor, he had the gift of converting his minuses into pluses. When he came into films, everyone said he was very tall. All kinds of comments were passed about him because he was very different from the normal heroes. He has this tremendous capacity to transform his personality. Everybody should learn from him. That is so very important ... that you can develop yourself into anything you want.'

Amitabh Bachchan has always been vocal about his admiration for Hema Malini. 'I met Hema-ji much before the shooting of *Gehri Chaal*. Where ... when ... and how ... I really don't remember. But it was great working with a thoroughly professional star like Hema. She was reserved and yet not arrogant. There is a very thin barrier between arrogance and anchorite. Hema strictly maintained the barrier. People ask me that though we were at the number one position at that point in time, why didn't we work together in comparatively more films? Well, I guess this depends on the distributors and producers. I would have loved to work with Hema in any second film, but my choice is not the final verdict in this business. Hema is a brilliant dancer too. The reason how she keeps herself fit. She is a very good daughter, wife and mother. After seeing her ballet *Draupadi*, I was astonished. She looks like a goddess on stage. She is a good friend of Jaya's. Even Abhishek and Esha share a healthy relationship. Dharam-ji is like my elder brother. So, for me, Hema and her daughters are just like extended family. She is, in the truest term, a woman of substance. She deserved more, but whatever she has achieved in this lifetime, it's a rare treat for any human.'

As mentioned earlier, Hema worked with Dev Anand in many films, of which most were blockbusters. Hema says, 'My mother was a huge fan of Dev saab, so I grew up hearing his name and watching his films. How was I to know that one day I'd go on to do many films with him? I started my career with one legendary actor, Raj Kapoor, then I quickly did *Johny Mera Naam* with Dev saab. You can imagine how nervous I was. I was so young and he was a huge star. But he never made me feel like a newcomer. Both Dev and his brother Vijay Anand took such good care of me. The film was a runaway hit, my first blockbuster. We were signed for several films together. I had the privilege of being directed by all the three brothers, Chetan, Dev and Vijay Anand. Dev saab was a perfectionist.'

From legends like Ashok Kumar, Pran, Raj Kapoor and Balraj Sahni to sensations like Rajinikanth, Kamal Haasan and Mithun Chakraborty, Hema has under her belt perhaps one of the longest lists of professional associations. She says, 'I think I have worked with almost every star and superstar there has been! They have taught me something or the other in life. I am eternally grateful to the Lord for bestowing me with such opportunities. I can keep talking about all my colleagues, but I think we should reserve that for another book!'

9

An Eternal Love Story

It's true what they say about love – it catches you when you're unprepared. And before you know it, there is no looking back. Your heart and mind are at loggerheads; you convince yourself you're still in command, but something much stronger, much deeper, has taken over you.

Till I met Hema and spent many an evening learning about the kind of person she is, I couldn't quite fathom how someone so meek and docile in front of her parents could fall in love, defy her family and marry an already married man. The thought seemed incredulous. But after talking to her about what must have been the most difficult phase of her life, I realized that the answer was simple. For someone who was used to listening to her heart, when love announced its sudden arrival, she could head in only one direction. As one of the most beauteous faces of the silver screen, Hema had a perpetual stream of admirers. But she kept her distance from all of them ... till she met the 'one'. For him, she was willing to give up the world and everything she had ever held dear till then.

A close friend of Hema's once told me that falling in love and marrying Dharmendra was possibly the only time Hema had rebelled against her parents. Till then, not only were her mother's words as good as gospel for her, she was also her most trusted confidante. Even something like the Sanjeev Kumar affair – where hardly anyone till date knows what really happened – was known to Jaya. In an interview to *Stardust* in June 1974, Hema had said, 'It's become a habit with me to tell everything to my mom. I can't remember having lied to her at any time. When I got involved with Sanjeev Kumar I needn't have told her about it. But I didn't hide anything from her. She had nothing to do with the break-up. There were other reasons involved – reasons which are too personal and complicated to be disclosed.'

This was also the time when the Hema–Dharmendra on-screen pair was gaining popularity and being cast in films, one after the other. Jaya had, in fact, been relieved by this. A married co-star – she had no reasons to worry for her daughter, she told herself.

Truth was, Hema was intensely in love with Dharmendra by then, as was he with her. When Jaya got a whiff of the situation, not surprisingly, she raised hell, but this time she held no sway. For the first time in her life, Hema kept the relationship a secret from her parents and did everything she could to keep meeting him. Once, to the horror and utter disbelief of her family, she disappeared for an entire day. When she came back, they were too relieved to rebuke her, but Jaya increased her watch over them. The couple had little choice but to restrict their meetings to film sets, which was often enough, since they were doing so many movies together by then. It was about now that Jaya felt that getting Hema married seemed the only way out of the situation. She didn't need to look too far. At the time, Hema was working with Jeetendra on two films – *Dulhan* (1974) and *Khushboo* (1975) – and it was obvious that the two got along famously. Jeetendra also had a soft corner for Hema and had been pursuing her for a while. When Hema consistently showed disinterest, he finally made peace and the two settled on becoming good friends.

Over the years, Hema and Jeetendra grew to become each other's confidantes. Hema, in fact, was one of the few who had known about his affair with Mumtaz. But although theirs was a platonic friendship, Dharmendra was never happy about it. It is believed that he had always been suspicious of Jeetendra, and being the possessive lover he was, he once went as far as to storm on to the sets of a Hema–Jeetendra production and drag Hema into the makeup room in a rage, while the latter stood dumbfounded.

Meanwhile, Jaya kept working on her plans. Every day was spent convincing her daughter to marry Jeetendra. She managed to coax Hema to meet his parents, and once Hema did, things started spiralling. Jeetendra's family was ecstatic – they could hardly wait for the alliance. A close friend of Jeetendra's remembers him saying, 'I don't want to marry Hema. I am not in love with her. She is not in love with me. But my family wants it, so I might as well. And she is such a good girl.'

For all practical purposes, it was to be a marriage of convenience. It had to be quick – before either party changed its mind – and it had to be a clandestine affair, so that no 'untoward trouble' could take place. Hema, Jeetendra and their families had flown to Madras and the wedding was supposed to happen there. But an evening daily got a whiff of the sensational news and their next issue carried the 'big story'. It left much of the industry in a state of disbelief but more importantly, it gave Dharmendra a jolt he was clearly unprepared for. Recovering his wits quickly, he rushed to Shobha Sippy's house – then Jeetendra's airhostess girlfriend – and the two took the next flight to Madras to take matters into their hands.

When they reached Hema's house in Madras, the scene, ironically, was no less dramatic than a blockbuster. Hema's father couldn't contain his rage and almost physically pushed Dharmendra out of the house. 'Why don't you get out of my daughter's life? You are a married man, you can't marry my daughter,' he repeatedly yelled. But a pleading, helplessly sentimental and slightly inebriated Dharam could not be budged. Finally, they agreed to let him talk to Hema alone in a room, while everybody else – Hema's parents, Jeetendra's parents and the registrar of the marriage bureau – waited outside on tenterhooks.

Inside the room, the two were going through an emotional turmoil of catastrophic proportions. Dharmendra, distraught and on the verge of falling to pieces, kept begging Hema not to make such a 'big mistake'. Outside, it was Shobha's turn to give vent to her rage. When a nonchalant Jeetendra announced to Shobha his decision to marry Hema, apparently all hell broke loose.

When Hema finally came out of the room – puffy-eyed and visibly shaken – her voice quivered as she asked everyone if they could wait for a few days. Jeetendra and his parents, livid by now, declared that

that was not an option. The marriage had to happen now or never. As everyone waited desperately for an answer, Hema quietly shook her head. The insult was far too much for Jeetendra and he stormed out of the house with his parents.

This incident occurred in 1974. It took Hema another two years before she finally spoke to *Stardust* about this tumultuous event.

'I did not propose to Jeetendra. His parents made the proposal to me. I was confused. It was the most unexpected thing that has ever happened to me. They came over in the morning. By evening Shobha and all landed there – and the matter ended there. But as far as the press was concerned that's where the story began!'

The tabloids now went crazy speculating and concocting all kinds of stories around the three actors. But even while all three maintained a stoic silence before the press, the episode took its psychological toll on each of the dramatis personae. It must be said of Jeetendra that even though he was portrayed as the villain in most of the stories and, to an extent, was given the short end of the stick, he never struck back. He got married to Shobha right after. Moreover, he continued accepting films with Hema and the two worked together as though nothing had happened.

But Dharmendra was not happy with that arrangement. He made Hema promise she wouldn't work with Jeetendra again. Sympathetic towards the man she loved, Hema initially agreed, but despite the pacification, his insecurity didn't abate. As his demands on her grew, so did his fears, and soon he took to drinking. Paranoid calls from Dharmendra in the middle of the night to check her whereabouts became all too frequent. For Hema, the possessiveness was suffocating. To defy him, she went back to signing films with Jeetendra, *Jyoti* (1981) being the first. Once again, Jeetendra was made the pawn in the equation. Getting the message, Dharmendra decided to mend his ways and agreed to every condition Hema laid down – marriage, naturally, heading the list. But it would still have to wait.

After this, every Hema–Jeetendra film under production had to now sign on Dharmendra as well. He also made it a point to ensure that no romantic scenes between Hema and Jeetendra featured in any of the scripts. Interestingly, while Jeetendra's wife was fuming at the ridiculousness of the situation, Jeetendra remained unaffected. In a smart move, he gradually started signing up with younger co-stars like Jaya Prada and Poonam Dhillon, ensuring a final exit from this long-playing mess.

Who would have known that for Hema and Dharmendra, the moment of truth would finally arrive with a film called *Hum Tere Ashique Hain* (1979)? Based on the classic *My Fair Lady* (1974), this Prem Sagar venture featured Hema and Jeetendra once again, and upon release did reasonably well, making it to the top twenty films of the year. In it was a scene where Jeetendra plants a kiss on Hema's cheek; in yet another scene, she had apparently cried without the need for glycerine, which, of course, could be taken to mean that she was living her emotions. It is said that one of those instances, if not both, finally drove Dharmendra to take a decision. On 2 May 1980, Hema and Dharmendra got married.

It was one of the biggest stories coming out of the Hindi film industry, but is to Hema and Dharam's credit that no one dared to ask them directly about their marital status.

Describing their relationship, Hema says, 'I just knew that he made me happy. And all I wanted was happiness. I never wanted to make any other person unhappy. I didn't know what to expect of him or of the future. People asked me, "What do you expect?" My family asked me too. All they got in answer were blinks. I didn't think. I didn't plan. He did not woo me with any style. He was simple, sincere, and that's what I liked about him. I don't think that he's ever complimented me, to this day. That way he is exactly like my mother. He doesn't ever praise me. That is why I am surprised when I hear the constant flattering lines heroes say to heroines in our films. Nobody said such lines to me. I am told that he praises me to people behind my back, but not to my face. He would always say, "You are okay!" Just like my mother. Who knows, it was probably these familiar traits, "Do this ... don't do that" that got me hooked to him.'

She continues, 'It was no ordinary relationship. Fingers were pointed. Accusations were flung at us. Nobody said anything in front of me, but I was not a fool. I knew that they discussed me behind my back. It wasn't easy. During that phase, when we first made our relationship public, I thought that I should shift to Bangalore. I love that city and felt I would be happy there. But since there were many incomplete films, I continued working in Bombay, without making any announcements. And as time went by, people stopped discussing us and our marriage.

'Finally, the dust settled. We Indians have a bad habit of discussing other people's lives and passing judgements. I don't know why we do that. Everyone should be left to lead his or her own life. Even today some journalists, in the course of a serious interview, ask me embarrassing questions about my co-stars like Jeetendra or Sanjeev Kumar or my marriage. But I remain unruffled. There are phases, there are changes. Everything is not meant to be discussed with the press.

'There were so many prospective grooms my father brought before me, but things didn't work out. Why? Why did I only feel for him (Dharmendra)? It is destiny. It happened. Also, something like this cannot be one-sided. He has to feel equally, support me, be on my side. I had no intention of hurting anyone. Time and again, I have been referred to as the "first lady of second marriages". I don't like it. It's not fair. Maybe I was the first one of my generation, yes, but I cannot be held responsible for others. It all comes down to circumstances. I can go on and on discussing this but considering I have not talked about it all these years, why do so now? My life is my own, and I should be allowed to live the way I want to. I know there are sections of people who discuss me with pity. They make me out to be someone who is weeping and mourning at home, pining for my man who is not around. I am not a police officer who needs to keep tabs on him. And I don't need to show people a roll-call register as to how many days he visits me and how many days he doesn't. He knows his duty as a father and I've never had to remind him of it. Dharam-ji still treats me like he did in the initial days. He still feels that I have to be carefully explained what's right and what's wrong. At the same time, he has immense faith in my capabilities. He looks tough but he is a soft man at heart...'

That people spoke behind their backs is a gross understatement. Magazines, tabloids, newspapers – nothing spared the couple. This was much before live television had made its entry, but the coverage and sensationalism that the print media whipped up did equal damage. What surprises me is how the entire film fraternity remained completely neutral on the issue. Hardly anyone stood up for or against the marriage. I've always upheld my point of view and no matter what the world says, I've wholeheartedly stood by Hema and Dharmendra. Love needs to be fair and this couple has lived up to that. The ultimate measure of a man lies in the stand he takes in the face of a challenge. And in choosing to stand by both the women in his life – not ready to abandon either, no matter how heavy a price he has to pay – I believe Dharmendra proved much more than any other man in the industry till then.

Dharmendra has always refused to talk about the subject. He had once said in an interview to *Stardust* in 1985, 'Look, I've never been open about all these things to the press nor will I open up now. These things were very personal matters and even now they are more personal. Anyway, I am uncomfortable discussing that "chapter", so let's avoid it. I am really touchy about these things.'

While Hema and Dharam thought that the storm had died down, it hadn't. In fact, one of the biggest controversies surrounding their marriage was its illegitimacy under the Hindu Marriage Act, since Dharmendra was already married. It was reported that the two had converted to Islam and changed their names to Dilawar and Ayesha Bi, and a nikaah was performed to solemnize their marriage in 1979. Only once this was done were they permitted to get married once again, according to the Iyengar tradition. This came to light only as recently as 2004, when Dharmendra stood as a BJP candidate for the Lok Sabha elections. The Congress pointed out that in his declaration of assets, he had mentioned only his first wife Prakash Kaur's properties and not Hema's. Twenty-four years since they had tied the knot, they were still under the scanner, their marriage was still easy fodder for sensationalism.

Hema calmly declared at a press conference during this controversy in 2004, 'When some people go out to do something great, there are others who always try to pull them back. But I hope he (Dharmendra) sails through it.' When she was asked why Dharmendra had not mentioned her as his second wife in the affidavit, she said, 'This is extremely personal between us. And we will sort it out between ourselves. Nobody else should bother about this.' The matter didn't rest there. Soon after, the Congress went as far as to demand a cancellation of Hema Malini's nomination as a member of the Rajya Sabha, alleging that she had furnished wrong information about her name and religion. 'There is no truth in these allegations. I have nothing more to say about this,' Hema said, defending her position. 'This is the time of competition. It is natural that each party would try to project itself as the best. It has been nearly three years since I started taking part in electioneering, and I don't think anything has changed this time.'

Around the same time, Dharmendra gave an interview to *Outlook* magazine, where he categorically denied that he had changed his religion: 'This allegation is totally incorrect. I am not the kind of man who will change his religion to suit his interests.' When asked about the Congress charges, he asserted, 'If there is any truth in this charge, let someone prove it with evidence. If this a lie, let the public decide.' The actor too dismissed the whole controversy as an attempt to disrupt his highly successful campaign. He criticized the Congress for 'stooping low' to defame him. Incidentally, after all this, Dharmendra won from the Bikaner constituency by a margin of 57,175 votes. Hema, on her part, continues to be an immensely successful BJP Lok Sabha member.

It seems the people, after all, had had the last say.

10

'Hunterwali' Hema

Over the years, the Hindi film industry has seen its fair share of popular on-screen couples, but none have come close to the kind of saleability Hema and Dharmendra garnered in their heyday. Decades after the two stopped working together, their popularity remains hard to beat. Of the twenty-eight films they did together, sixteen were hits. If you are into number crunching, the earnings translate into a whopping Rs 7,36,04,88,423. For all that has been said and written about the legendary Raj Kapoor–Nargis pairing, their success rate is estimated at nine out of fifteen films and the monetary benefit stands at nearly half of that of Hema and Dharmendra's.

After marriage, Hema's on-screen avatar went through a metamorphosis. Deliberate or not, the transition seemed seamless. Hema was one of the earliest actors to bag such a high number of women-centric films – twenty, to be precise. Film scripts and dialogues were written keeping her specifically in mind, a considerable feat in an industry obsessed with its male stars. When top stars like Dev Anand and Rajesh Khanna hit a rough patch in the 1970s, it was their films opposite Hema Malini, *Amir Garib* (1974) in the case of Dev Anand and *Prem Nagar* (1974) with Rajesh Khanna, that boosted their careers.

If the 1970s saw her in glamorous and demure roles, with the onset of the 1980s, the audience witnessed the firebrand in her. From owning her dacoit characters to relishing those 'hunterwali' roles, Hema was unstoppable. She needed no male star to support her – she was an army in herself.

Ever since she faced the cameras, much had been said about Hema's drop-dead good looks. From her amber eyes to her captivating smile, paeans have been dedicated to her beauty. But what I have always found most fascinating about Hema is her laughter – uninhibited and free-flowing, like a waterfall. It's interesting, though, how incongruous it seems to be with the kind of person she is. But when I think about it, it seems more an affirmation than an incongruity – an affirmation of the fact that beneath her quiet demeanour lies a spirit that's always been in command ... the captain of her ship, riding the ebb and tide with élan. Hema's choice of films from the 1980s onwards seems to be a brilliant manifestation of that.

The new era began with Pramod Chakraborty's *Jyoti*. This was also the director who had come up with the maximum number of Hema– Dharam hits. With this one, though, he was out to prove a different story. *Jyoti* was to be a remake of the Guru Dutt classic, *Bahurani* (1963). Based on the Bengali novel *Swayamsiddha*, it tells the tale of Gauri (Hema). When a rich zamindar Raja Saheb (Ashok Kumar) chooses Gauri to be the bride of his spoilt son from his second marriage, Niranjan, his second wife (Shashikala) is left fuming. She has been working hard to ensure that her son inherits Raja Saheb's fortunes, going as far as reducing his first son and legal heir, Govind (Jeetendra), to an opium addict. On the day of the wedding, she insists that Gauri marry Govind instead – the poor nobody-of-a-girl seems more suited to the illiterate and helpless Govind. That's what finally happens. Despite the turn of fate, Gauri remains undeterred. From that day, she undertakes a mission to nurse her husband back to good health and to fight the atrocities life throws at her.

'Hema had that personality. She could carry off such a role with élan,' Pramod Chakraborty said in an interview with me. 'I deviated from the original novel and showed a bullfight scene with Hema, just to make it more interesting. Needless to say, she was brilliant. Hema had the largest fan following after Amitabh Bachchan in India – they clapped in the scenes where Hema used to fight back. She was considered on par with her heroes. After *Jyoti*, I made her do a few action sequences in my film *Nastik* (1983) opposite Amitabh. I was planning to make a full-length action film with Hema, but it didn't materialize.'

Both *Jyoti* and *Nastik* were hits. It was clear that Hema was making a foray into a genre yet unexplored by her or any other female actor of her times, but that didn't stop the stereotypical film offers from coming in. She acted in conventional roles like in *Justice Choudhury* (1983) and *Qaidi* (1984). Typical of the films of the 1980s made by south Indian banners, these got her a lot of flak, particularly *Qaidi*, which had her matching awkward steps with Jeetendra in an embarrassing dance number. For her fans who had cheered her on through her brave and unconventional choices, this was a letdown. To be fair to Hema, though, she had been reluctant to take up either film but had gone along anyway, a decision she lived to regret, as she admits. Those were perhaps the last few films which had her pandering to stories that were mere crowd-pleasers. After that, she chose every film with utmost consideration.

In 1985, with the Shyam Ralhan film *Ramkali*, Hema spearheaded a trend to beat all others. With her turn as the rifle-toting dacoit, spewing venom and spreading fear, the transformation from 'dream girl' was sensational. She wasn't the first female actor to take up such a role. Rameshwari and Rita Bhaduri had attempted this before, but no one could match the command and comfort with which Hema slipped into the character. She seemed born for it.

'Viewers have always loved me in action roles with a vendetta theme and a lot of bloodshed!' Hema says with glee. '*Ramkali* was full of action; plus heroine-oriented dacoit films leave the viewers feeling that women aren't as weak as they are normally shown to be. My film *Durga* (1985), which was directed by Shibu Mitra, was a hit because I kill all the villains in that film. I just love the idea of a heroine taking on wrongdoers instead of the hero – it's something different.'

Riding high on this trend, came *Sitapur ki Geeta* (1987). Again a Shibu Mitra directorial, this one also starred Rajesh Khanna and Pran – big names for a film that rode solely on its female protagonist. Geeta (Hema) is a village girl whose husband is ruthlessly killed by the zamindar and his goons. They rape her too. The rest of the film is about Geeta planning and extracting her pound of flesh. A revenge drama to its core, with Hema living up to her dacoit queen avatar, the crowds lapped this up as well. 'People think that dacoits are basically Robin Hoods at heart, which makes changing the storyline very difficult,' Hema confesses. 'Even the costume and basic appearance remained the same (as in other such movies). The hair-band, tika, bandoleer, etc., were the same. In any case, this concept was selling.'

The trend took off and many after Hema jumped on to the bandwagon. From Rekha to Sridevi to Dimple, many an actor attempted the role of the dreaded dacoit over the years, but none could pull it off with as much flair, except perhaps Seema Biswas as Phoolan Devi years later, albeit in an entirely different genre of film. Hema remains the master of the genre even today.

Pretty early on in her career, it had been evident that action sequences were second nature to Hema. From riding motorbikes to tongas, playing bandits to cops, doing swordfights to lashing out with a whip, directors had a gala time experimenting with this leading lady, for whom no stunt was off-limits. Director B. Subhas remembers how smoothly Hema carried off the sword-fighting scenes in his film *Aandhi-Toofan* (1985). 'Hema-ji was an experienced actor. We didn't have to work much on her. She was very particular about her shots and used to rehearse a lot. The sword-fighting sequence with Danny (Denzongpa) in the film is awesome. She moves like a butterfly from one place to another. Holding the heavy sword was not a matter of much effort for Hema-ji. In fact, Danny, who is brilliant at action sequences, was surprised by Hema-ji's flexibility.'

Amitabh Bachchan, who worked with Hema in *Naseeb* and *Andha Kanoon* (1983), recollects her action sequences in those films. 'Hema, being a dancer, was very comfortable with her body movements. Action sequences in films are well composed, like the dances. So, it wasn't a tough job for Hema to execute. Moreover, she looked extremely smart and intelligent as a police inspector. In fact, she was doing action sequences since my first film *Gehri Chaal* with her.' He adds, characteristically, on a lighter note, 'Rather, I used to be always relaxed in films with Hema. She used to share the burden of action sequences with me! Hema is probably the only actress who did action sequences in my films.'

Despite Hema pulling off these roles with aplomb, the fact remains that most of the films she did in this phase did nothing to enhance her reputation as an actor. For someone who has often placed a premium on her performances, even within the constraints of mainstream cinema, it begs the question: what made her take on clangers like these?

The answer lies in the financial soup she found herself in in the 1980s. Not having paid her taxes on time, she was expected to cough up close to a crore, no ordinary sum even for someone like her. Dharmendra offered to help, but she would have none of it. It was her mistake and she would do whatever was needed to make amends.

'My father would keep reminding Amma that we need to pay the taxes, but my mother, being naïve, felt it was unfair to expect us to pay so much tax since her daughter was working so hard to earn that money. They would often have arguments about it. Unfortunately, only after my father's demise did we realize that we had got into a financial soup over the years. We had to clear a lot of pending taxes.' She recollects how Sunil Gupta, a chartered accountant, helped her out in several ways. 'He not only sorted out my financial issues, but also got back the extra money we had paid the government as tax,' she adds.

To pay off her debts, Hema signed on a number of films, most of which would fall under what is called 'B-grade cinema'. None of the big banners had anything to offer her as she was a mother of two. Those from the world of parallel cinema weren't sure if she would take up projects that had small budgets. When film-makers like S.K. Kapur, B. Subhash and Shyam Ralhan offered her lead roles and a huge pay, Hema lapped up the films; she had little choice but to do so.

'It was the worst phase of my life, and it lasted for almost ten years,' she recalls. 'I had to clear my debts and barring these films I had nothing. Dance shows would keep me going, but the majority of the money came from movies.'

Those were difficult times for everyone. Esha remembers, 'After Ahaana was born, I realized that Mom had started shooting a lot. She would barely be at home. Later on, when we watched a few films like *Durga, Anjaam* (1987), *Sitapur Ki Geeta* and *Jamai Raja,* I remember asking her why she was doing these movies. That is when she told me about the debt.'

Although these films opened up fresh avenues for her as an action star and helped her tide over financial difficulties, they afforded her little by way of opportunities to showcase her potential as actor. She was still waiting for a film that would give her a character that would demand every ounce of her talent – from exposing vulnerabilities to demonstrating the czarina within – a well-rounded role.

When Kamal Amrohi signed Hema Malini for his magnum opus, *Razia Sultan* (1983) – based on the story of the only female queen of the Delhi Sultanate – it left the industry puzzled. Hema was still, no doubt, a name to be reckoned with, but there were several other promising talents he could have considered. Also, during its production, Hema Malini had opted for marriage and, as the industry wisdom went, must have lost some of that earlier charm. But the director was certain. 'I can't think of anyone else other than Hema as Razia Sultan,' he had said, echoing Gulzar's words when he had signed her on for *Meera*.

The thought of casting Hema for this film had apparently occurred to Kamal Amrohi much after the decision to make it. At first, he had considered giving the role to a newcomer. It is believed the director had changed his mind after he chanced upon a description of the historical Razia Sultan by a foreign traveller. '*Agar Razia ke ruksar ke kareeb ek genhu ke bal ko rakhte toh ek hi palak mein jal kar raakh ho jata* (If you held dried wheat close to Razia's cheeks, it would turn to ashes in a second!).'

'Who else other than Hema Malini would have done justice to this compliment?' Kamal Amrohi's son, Tajdar Amrohi, recalls.

Kamal Amrohi was always known as a director with a penchant for spectacular productions. Many considered his obsession with grandeur excessive, sometimes unreasonable. But reason has seldom produced brilliance. Produced under the Rajdhani Films banner with a mammoth budget, *Razia Sultan* was one of the costliest films to have been made in the Hindi film industry. (Sanjay Leela Bhansali's Rs 50-crore extravaganza, *Devdas* [2002] finally broke its record.)

The film began shooting in 1978 and took close to five years to complete, which was not surprising given that Kamal Amrohi's *Pakeezah* had taken over fifteen years to make. *Razia Sultan* would also star Dharmendra as Jamaluddin Yaqut, Pradeep Kumar as Iltutmish, Ajit as Balban, Parveen Babi as Khakun and Vijayendra Ghatge as Malik Ikhtiar-ud-din Altunia. Who better to score the music for a historical than Khayyam? Lavish sets were constructed at Kamalistan Studio and hundreds of horses and camels procured. Clothes and jewellery were especially designed to bring alive a lost era. Bhanu Athaiya, who later won an Oscar for costume design for the film *Gandhi* (1982), did the costumes. The stage was set for yet another fantastic production.

Tajdar Amrohi, the only 'authorized' person to talk about the film, has some interesting stories to share. 'My father had called Hema-ji at Ashoka Studio at Juhu Galli, Andheri. She was amazed after my father narrated the story to her. Without thinking twice, she accepted the role.' He also remembers his father telling Hema, 'Come to my set as a first-timer, as if you are making your debut. And I shall think just the opposite, that Hema knows everything, so I will have to be attentive. If we both surrender to each other, it will be a masterpiece.'

Going by production standards it was indeed a masterpiece. Art director N.B. Kulkarni (who won the Filmfare award in 1983 for this film) had created massive sets to replicate the Durbar-e-Aam, the Durbar-e-Khaas and the Moti Mahal. 'Nearly ten lakh pearls were used to make that Moti Mahal,' Tajdar adds. The costumes designed by Bhanu Athaiya too were exquisite. 'We had to hire some horses from Rajasthan and some other localities to recreate an army. The soldiers were all given outfits to wear and after the day's work, they just ran away with the clothes! Incidentally, we had hired a temporary tailor who would stitch innumerable army costumes every day.'

During the long and elaborate shooting schedule, while the rest of the cast and crew treated themselves to a grand feast of chicken and mutton, Hema's food would be brought separately from her house. Tajdar remembers a funny incident from the shooting days. 'There was a sequence where Razia's chambermaids would read out proposal letters to her which had come from various parts of the country. The actors were reading those letters in chaste Urdu and Hema-ji was supposed to reject the suitors. Suddenly she called for a "cut" and in her typical Tamil accent told my father, "*Yeh kya hai, Kamal saab, ek bhi word samajh mein nahin aata hai…* (What is this, Kamal sir, I can't understand a single word…)" and we all broke into laughter. She would always try to understand each and every dialogue, so that she could give the best expression.

'My father used to say, "*Hema mein woh sab hunar hai jo ek sultan mein hone chahiye. Hema-ji jab chal kar aati hai toh lagta hai ki bijli karak rahi hai.* (Hema has all the qualities of a sultan. Her gait alone seems to have the power to evoke thunder and lightning.)" She has that royal characteristic in her blood. Frankly speaking, my father had to hardly work on Hema-ji because her stance, her walk and her facial expressions were as good as (the real) Razia's. In fact, she never grumbled or complained about anything. She was the number one heroine but she used to come half an hour early to the set and would wait until the shots of the other actors were over. It happened once or twice that she was waiting in her make-up room and my father was taking some other shot. She would never make a fuss about it. Not only that, Hema-ji, being an early riser, would call Bhanu at her place for costume rehearsals. She had even squeezed out time from other films and during lunch breaks to sit and work on the jewellery and costume combinations. I remember the sandstorm sequence where twenty blower fans were on and Hema-ji was feeling uncomfortable, but not once did she ask my father to change the shot. Every day after pack-up, she would come to my father and ask, "*Theek tha na?* Are you happy, Kamal saab?" *Aaj ki tariq mein itni dedicated actress milna mushkil hi nahin, balki namumkin hai*! (In today's day and age, finding such a dedicated actress is not just difficult, it's impossible!)'

What adds weight to Tajdar's observation is the fact that Hema was pregnant during the making of this film. Hardly anyone on the sets was aware of this. Hema being Hema, she carried on with the shooting – riding horses and enacting swordfights – with complete nonchalance. She recollects, 'I didn't want to let anyone know that I was pregnant. The only person who knew was, of course, Dharam-ji. I wanted to keep it a secret from the rest of the world. It was our child and I didn't want everyone criticizing and asking questions. I hadn't even told my mother or Shanta aunty at home. Luckily, I didn't have any problems, like morning sickness or fatigue, during the early months. So, I quietly went on with my work without telling anyone. But however much I tried, this (with a pat on her now flat stomach) began showing. And my mother got suspicious and asked me about it. I still didn't tell my producers and continued shooting well up to the sixth month. I had to do a lot of horse-riding scenes. It was a nightmare doing them in my condition. After I dismounted, I would feel as if my insides were being torn apart. In fact, I almost collapsed one day. So *Razia Sultan* will remain a special film in my career and in my life as well.'

The publicity for this film had been as extensive as it was elaborate. In fact, the first two weeks witnessed a huge turnout at the theatres. The film's music, too, had become immensely popular. Lata Mangeshkar herself once admitted, 'I have sung the maximum numbers of songs for Hema. But my favourite still remains "*Aye dil-e-naadan*" from *Razia Sultan*. Hema was simply awesome (in that).'

It is true that Hema gave her all to this film. But once released, it failed miserably at the box office. Several reasons were cited for its dismal performance but since it was an all-in-all Hema film, much of the flak was directed towards her alone. Soon producers started hesitating in taking up films that starred Hema and Dharmendra, while Hema's box-office ratings began to plummet. To be fair to her, she had done more than her best. One of the more plausible explanations for the box-office response to *Razia Sultan* was given by journalist Mahmood Farooqui when he said: '*Pakeezah* (1972) was the last commercially successful film in Bollywood which was based on a subject that had chaste Urdu dialogues and a Muslim backdrop. It was released in the 1970s, a period when things rapidly began to change both within the film industry and the country at large.'

By the time *Razia Sultan* released, the Hindi film industry had already turned a page. At a time when Amitabh Bachchan was creating a sensation with his brand of 'angry young man' films, something like *Razia Sultan* appeared odd and untimely. The use of chaste Urdu left many viewers of the era flummoxed as they could not make sense of what was being said. The fact that Kamal Amrohi took so long to finish the film only added to the problem. Written off soon after its release as a film with big ambitions, a bigger budget but no soul, *Razia Sultan* eventually sank without a trace.

However, it remains an important film in the context of Hindi cinema. For one, it was perhaps one of the earliest movies to explore the subject of bisexuality. Razia's relationship with Khakun (Parveen Babi), the daughter of her wazir (Sohrab Modi), is treated with mystery and intrigue. 'Razia (the historical figure) refused to be called "Sultana"; she was always Razia Sultan,' Tajdar points out. 'She had apparently said, "I am not an empress, I am an emperor. I am not a queen, I am the king." She also refused to wear the purdah, saying, "My citizens are like my children, why should a mother hide her face from her own kids?" She was born courageous. She was as strong as a man.' Historians like Stanley Lane Poole have written: 'She did her best to prove herself a man, wore manly dress, and showed her face fearlessly as she rode her elephant.'

In the film, Kamal Amrohi treats Razia's possible bisexual orientation with subtlety. There is a scene where Razia and Khakun embrace each other in a boat at night, though hidden behind an ostrich plume. Parveen caresses Hema and sings a lullaby to her. That scene is said to be the first in the history of Indian cinema to suggest sexual love between two women.

Interestingly, the film press never asked her about this aspect of the film. Neither was Parveen Babi. Their co-actor Vijayendra Ghatge, who played Malik Ikhtiar-ud-din Altunia, shares his view on this particular scene, 'Well, there was a scene between Hema-ji and Parveen Babi, which had a hint of bisexuality. After the film was released, the press and public did talk about this scene and I still remember that years later when the film was shown on Doordarshan, this particular scene, followed by a solo song sequence by Parveen Babi, was cropped. I really don't know whether Razia was a lesbian or not. I guess Kamal saab would have been the right person to answer this question. But I would also like to say that both Hema-ji and Parveen did a fantastic job. It was aesthetically done. In a way, Hema-ji deserves kudos for having the guts to do that scene.'

Vijayendra continues, 'I still remember that we had a fight master, Naseer, and another foreign fight master. While we used to rehearse for our shots, they used to fight with each other! Hema-ji is an excellent action artiste. I remember the swordfight sequence between us. We had to rehearse that for two days. It was shot in scorching sunlight and we had to use reflectors on our eyes. That's when I saw her dedication. *Ek bar bhi unhone koi nakhra nahin kiya.* (She never made any fuss.) She was thoroughly committed. That is the reason she remained the queen of Bollywood for more than a decade!'

Hema was pushed to her limits for *Razia Sultan*, and that is reason enough for it to be considered amongst her most significant works.

An interesting episode unfolded a few years after the film's release. Richard Attenborough, it is believed, was contemplating a movie to match up to, or perhaps surpass, the standards he had set with *Gandhi*. After much deliberation, he decided to make a biopic on Rani Lakshmi Bai, the invincible queen of Jhansi. The selection for the lead actress was finally narrowed down to two names – Shabana Azmi and Hema Malini. Both actors, naturally, were extremely keen on bagging the film but Shabana, it is said, had an upper hand since she had already worked in several international collaborations. Apart from her wide network, she also had a loyal set of friends who had worked in *Gandhi* and backed her wholeheartedly. Word was out that Hema wouldn't stand a chance before her. At this point, Hema made a request to the great director. She asked him to watch a particular film of hers and only then arrive at a final decision.

Immediately after Attenborough watched *Razia Sultan*, he wasted no time in announcing Hema Malini as the lead in his next film. Fascinated by the poise and presence Hema displayed in the film, he was certain that no one else could play a queen with as much flourish. Shabana's friends tried hard to change his mind, but the director was adamant. Unfortunately, the film ran into financial trouble right after the final stages of pre-production and had to be shelved.

Razia Sultan had been a long and challenging schedule. Once it was over, Hema decided to work on a home production. Keen on a woman-oriented subject, but with a difference, she zeroed in on Irving Wallace's *The Second Lady*. She decided to title the film *Sharara*.

Directed by Rajendra Singh Babu (with whom she had worked in *Meri Awaaz Suno* in 1982) and starring Hema in a double role opposite Raaj Kumar and Shatrughan Sinha, *Sharara* (1984) gave her a chance to learn the ropes of film production. She recalls, 'My mother had produced films earlier but I was never involved in production matters. *Sharara* was my first production. I was very satisfied with the final product. I had participated in every segment of the film, from artiste selection to story to production to direction. It was quite thrilling. But I still had a lot to learn when it came to financial affairs. Thankfully, I didn't have to suffer difficulties, but I didn't make any money either.'

All this while, Hema also kept herself busy with a couple of challenging roles, in films like *Ek Nai Paheli* and *Ek Naya Itihas* (1984). She was still pregnant, but despite keeping up with the gruelling schedules, Hema faced a lot of criticism from producers who accused her of dishonouring her contracts. In her defence, she says, 'I am a very conscientious artiste. I have never allowed my personal problems to interfere with my work. I did not ditch my producers. I was definitely not the first Indian actress who became pregnant during a shoot of a film. But yes, I was the first actress who did not take advantage of my physical disability, to cause any inconvenience to my producers. I did not let them feel the change in me. I performed all my scenes the way I would have if I were not pregnant. I even shot a fight sequence without a double in *Meri Awaaz Suno* in this condition. And yet, instead of appreciating my cooperation, I was criticized. I did not cancel shootings or hold up films. I was blamed for not giving dates to Kamal Amrohi to complete *Razia Sultan*. I must clarify that I had completed all my shooting, except the patchwork for the film. In fact, the only thing that was left was the dubbing, which Kamal saab wanted to do in London.'

11

'Amma' Malini

'When you are a mother, you are never really alone in your thoughts,' Sophia Loren has once been quoted as saying. 'A mother always has to think twice, once for herself and once for her child.'

For Hema, the desire to experience motherhood superseded every other. And when her ardent prayers bore fruit, she didn't need anything else. Life, for her, became as perfect as it could ever be.

Esha Deol was born on 2 November 1981. Both Hema and Dharmendra had been sure their first-born would be a boy, though. In fact, all the shopping was done with that in mind – the room painted and brimming with all things blue.

'Those were my happiest days,' Hema reminisces. 'Feeling the child growing within me was a wonderful sensation. Both Dharam-ji and I had dreamt of getting the best of everything for the baby, so much so that we even considered having the delivery abroad. But then things didn't work out. So instead I took off to Bangalore in my seventh month. From there I decided to go to Ooty to rest. But I did a very foolish thing. Before going on the long drive from Bangalore to Ooty, I had a very heavy meal. Those hours on the road were killing. By the time we reached, I was in a terrible state. I had the most acute cramps in my stomach and was rolling in agony. I felt as though I would deliver any minute. And yet I wasn't quite sure whether they were genuine labour pains. Oh, it took them ages to locate a doctor in that place and I, of course, wanted the best. Luckily nothing happened and I miraculously survived those pains. It's only later that it dawned on me what a stupid thing I'd done, taking off to Ooty like

94

that. Of course, by then everyone knew I was pregnant. I really had a tough time hiding it from the world. I remember during those early days, at the shootings too, I just couldn't stop eating. I would keep asking for all kinds of sweets and I'm sure, although they didn't say it, everyone must have guessed my secret. But I realized only later what problems I'd caused, for I wasn't really sure about the date of delivery. My calculations were two weeks off the mark. It was only when they did a sonography in the later stages that we realized that I was due almost twenty days before the date I'd believed to be the D-day.

'On the night of 1 November, Dharam-ji was going for a film preview,' she continues. 'I pestered him to take me along. He refused, because he didn't think I was in a condition to see a film. He was right. As soon as he left, I had to be rushed to the hospital. They didn't take me in my usual van to avoid recognition. We went in another car. My doctor was already with me, apart from the others. Generally, I can cope with any situation. But this one time I couldn't. I was suddenly very scared. I lay quiet, my head in my doctor's lap. Dharam-ji was called back from the preview. I wasn't getting the pains so they had to induce labour. My one distinct memory during my most agonizing pains was a shrill cry – the cry that brought with it so much solace and made me a mother! In a matter of minutes, my entire family was by my side, but nobody told me that I had given birth to a girl because they felt it might upset me. But when I saw her, I forgot everything else. The first thing I noticed about her was her hair. Unlike me, she wasn't bald at birth. She means more to me than any son!'

Pammi Gautam, journalist and close friend of Hema's, recalls those initial days of sleeplessness and giddy euphoria. 'I was there to share what was, as Hema put it, the most happy and rewarding moment of her life. I still remember Hema's ecstatic face, radiating pride and happiness. For the first time, I saw Hema drop her defences. She laughed more easily and could talk of little else but her newborn. Holding a couple-of-weeks-old Esha in her arms, she was beaming. "Everyone thinks that she looks like Dharam-ji, and even though I think so too, it's too early to say anything yet!" she had gushed.'

Hema had always shared a deep friendship with both her sisters-in-law. It is through Prabha Chakravarti, Kannan's wife, that I learned how crazy Hema had always been about children. Prabha tells me, 'When my daughter Suchitra was born, I was at my parents' house in T Nagar (Chennai). Hema was shooting for *Prem Nagar* with Rajesh Khanna at that time. She used to be mad about babies. She would come over at 11.30 at night, wake up the whole house, wake up the baby and spend at least half an hour with her – whenever she was in Madras. When Suchitra was the only child in the family, Hema used to shop for boxes and boxes of stuff for her. Hema and I have always been close – we had hit it off from day one!

'When she was carrying Esha, she worked till she was six months' pregnant,' Prabha continues. 'At every stage, she would call to give us updates on what happened each day. When Esha was born, I remember Kannan describing her as a very cute and big baby with curly hair! Hema was so mentally prepared that she had learnt cooking just for her daughter. Hardly anyone knows that she is a wonderful cook. She learnt cooking for her children's sake. Whenever they travelled abroad, they would take up a flat and she would cook for her children. Sometimes when she would get stuck with a recipe, she would call me from there and would follow instructions on the phone and complete the dish.'

When I ask Hema why she decided on the name 'Esha', it is as if she had been hoping I'd ask her that question. 'Esha is a Sanskrit word, derived from the Upanishads. It means "the divine beloved". Her birth has made me realize how incomplete my existence was before her. There is in me an overwhelming emotion, alien to me. I feel different. There is a sense of belonging. At last, here is someone who is all mine and whom I don't have to share. A daughter is a mother's gender partner, her closest ally in the family confederacy, an extension of herself. And mothers are their daughters' role model, their biological and emotional road map, the arbiter of all their relationships,' she finishes, with a blissful look on her face.

Despite the doting mother that Hema was, it seemed that she had taken a conscious decision to never overindulge her children. She herself had had an extremely strict upbringing. Going by the usual human psychology, the tendency should have been to go overboard and spoil her children – ensure they received all the pampering she perhaps didn't. But that wasn't the case. Soon after Esha's birth, Hema went back to work, even though it broke her heart. She had restricted her schedule to one shift a day, but missed her daughter immensely through it. Those days she had said, 'Dharam-ji is a strict father. He's dead against the child being brought to the studios. Even before she was born he'd made it very clear that he wasn't going to let her anywhere near the studios. When I return home in the evenings, sometimes I find her restless and crying, till I take her in my arms. Otherwise she is a well-behaved baby. You know she's a Scorpio. I am told Scorpio girls are very difficult to handle!'

Anyone who has seen Hema and Esha together will tell you about the kind of relationship they share. Each time I do, I come back with a feeling of warmth. This mother–daughter duo is unique. The two are a team in every sense of the term … cohorts and in tandem, communicating a kind of harmony that is rare to find. I have often caught them share a glance and break into laughter or finish each other's sentences … always intuitively aware of and deeply sensitive to the other's state of mind.

How does such a close relationship develop? The answer perhaps lies in being brazenly honest with each other – honesty that is encouraged from one's earliest years. The honesty one finds in friendships more than familial relationships. And that is perhaps the secret here as well – this is no didactic hierarchical relationship, but a friendship amongst equals.

Months after Esha was born, Hema had written a letter to her. Naturally, it would be many years before any of it would make sense to the little girl, but the thought behind this letter reveals a lot about how Hema wanted to nurture this relationship.

> My Dearest Darling Bittoo,
>   I am writing this letter to you because I love you dearly. I know you are too little to understand what I want to say, but I'll write it anyway … Bittoo dear, everyone calls you Esha, but you shall always be Bittoo for Mama and Papa only! Do you know the meaning of your lovely name 'Esha'? It means the Divine's beloved, and I want you to grow up into an extremely lovable person and live up to your name. I can see that you are going to grow up into

a beautiful little lady, but what is more important to me is that you should be a beautiful person, like your papa. I want you to be big-hearted, kind, selfless and loving, like he is. I know you love him and rush to him as soon as you see him, but that is only because he plays with you, buys you everything you like and pampers you a lot. But if you only knew what a self-made man he is, you would love and adore him and be all the more proud of him. I'm sure you'll realize this as you grow older.

In this letter, dearest Bittoo, I want to thank you for the beautiful, lovely, divine feeling you gave me when you happened to me. No doubt, I did get a lot of love and affection from my mama and papa and from your papa too, but the joy you have given me is something which no one in this world could have blessed me with. It is a feeling which I cannot express in words. When you were born, there was a lot of expectation because you were born to me. The press, fans, well-wishers, everyone was curious to know more about you. But I didn't want to share you with anybody. I strongly felt that you were mine and only mine! You were someone who was too personal and dear, to me and my family, to be shared with millions of people!

Bittoo, at present you are at home all the time, with your toys in the nursery and with your own family. But the moment you step out into the world, people will give you extra importance because you are a daughter of well-known personalities. Darling, I want you to keep your head on your shoulders and not get carried away with this undue importance – because your parents have struggled for it. Success didn't come to us on a golden platter, you know. I want you to learn how to value it.

Esha, do you know I was a totally different person before you were born? My world was restricted only to work and dance. That was my life till I met your father and experienced some of the most beautiful, precious moments. But even in those times my parents were strict with me and didn't hesitate to give me a slap when I was in the wrong! However, I am really glad they brought me up that way, because I am what I am today, only because of them!

So also, I want you to grow up into an obedient child. Even if I scold you or correct you at times, I want you to take it in the right spirit and know that I am doing it for your own good. Though I'm writing all this, deep inside me, I know I will never have the heart to shout at you! You are too adorable, intelligent and lovable for that! Anyway, I think Papa will set you right!

I still remember the first time I set my eyes on you. You looked like a little doll! I wanted to hold you in my arms and play with you forever! Ever since then, I have enjoyed every bit of your growing up. The first word you uttered was more rewarding than a thousand compliments I've received in my career. The first time you called me 'Mummy' was more thrilling than anything in this world. The first time I saw you toddle, it was the most beautiful sight I'd ever seen, even though you fell down after taking a couple of steps! I'll never forget the first time you held my little finger and walked with me – because that was something I had always visualized and wanted you to do ever since you were born…

One more important thing I want you to know is that I have fought all odds and married your father in spite of all the controversies, knowing very well that my career, which was at its peak then, would be affected. But I made my choice. And once I got married to the man I loved, I wanted to bring you into this world. Because I wanted to be happy. A different kind of happiness, the kind all women want to experience. Now, my world has changed because of you. I am a much more fulfilled, complete, happier person because of you. Today, the moment I come home from work and set my eyes on my little puppet, I forget all my tiredness and worries and am as fresh as a flower again!

Now, of course, you will ask me why I go out at all? Why don't I stay at home with you, day and night? Why do I have to work? For the time being, I have to work for various reasons. But maybe by the time you grow up and are able to reason things out and can ask me these questions yourself, I won't be working … I shall be all yours and only yours…

Four years after Esha, Hema and Dharmendra had their second daughter, Ahaana. When I ask her if they were disappointed for not having a son yet again, Hema tells me, 'Yes, we were expecting a boy. I suppose every mother wants a son and a daughter. I had Esha, so it was natural to expect a boy child. But I now think that Ahaana is far, far better than any son I'd hoped to have. I have no regrets.'

It was about now, as a mother of two, that Hema contemplated giving up films. She wanted to devote all her time to motherhood. However, it didn't take her long to realize that she wasn't meant for that. Listening to her talk about how much of her sense of self came from her passion for work, I remember being reminded once again of how forward-thinking she really is. There was no single identity Hema Malini could think of tying herself down to – there were several realms she drew from and several lives she led synchronously.

She confesses, 'At one stage I tried getting out of films. That was after I had got married and had children. But I couldn't. This industry is like a whirlpool, it dragged me back. It's only work that keeps me going. It gives me the strength and confidence to go on.'

After ruling the scene in Hindi cinema for more than ten years as its most popular leading lady, did becoming a mother change things for her, I ask. 'Oh yes!' she says emphatically. 'I didn't like it, initially. To be honest, after Esha was born, I would accompany Dharam-ji for his shoots. I would see Rekha, Jaya Prada, Sridevi, Anita Raaj and many other actresses playing the female lead. It used to hurt me, because till a few months ago, I enjoyed that position opposite Dharam-ji! Not that these heroines misbehaved with me or anything of that sort. In fact, after pack-up, they would all visit me and Esha and spend time with us. They would talk about new films and other actors. I barely had any films in hand then, so I would listen to their stories. After a point, I felt that I was being a pile-on at the shoots. Not only was I not adding any value, I thought that my presence at times would be intimidating for the other heroines, especially when they had to do scenes with Dharam-ji. So, I decided to stay away. I asked myself then what I really wanted. I had wanted to marry a man whom I loved and have a baby. Now that God had bestowed both upon me, I realized that I should respect his blessings and give my hundred per cent to my family. That's when I decided to spend most of my time with Esha and Ahaana. I wanted to enjoy these moments and not regret anything later.'

12

In and Out of the Box

King Raghunath of the Vishnupur kingdom in Bengal staggers into the room. Chandraprabha, his wife, is awake. A constant feeling of anxiety throbbing away at the pit of her stomach has rendered sleep almost unattainable. Even so, his entry into the room leaves her startled.

Like every other day, Raghunath reeks of alcohol and juhi – a nauseating combination that has become all too familiar. Chandraprabha's disgust is perhaps more evident today as she watches her husband fumble in an attempt to explain himself. He seems to be in the mood to talk. She wonders if the other times are better, when all he manages are a few clumsy steps to the edge of the bed. 'Chandraprabha,' he mumbles, 'you know that I go to Lalbai's place just to listen to music … not because she is beautiful.' He pauses. 'Of course, she is beautiful … but …' He trails off as he sinks into a heavy, dreamless sleep.

In the well-known Famous Studio of south Mumbai's Mahalaxmi area, the shoot is on for a television serial for Doordarshan, *Terah Panne*. Even though it is November, the heat is unforgiving. With those last lines, the camera zooms in on Hema's face … the look of anguish, of a wife betrayed, is so real that you find yourself trapped along with her in that moment of helpless rage. It is only when Vikas Desai, the director, yells 'Cut!' from a distance, that the spell is broken.

The world of television is different from that of films. On the surface, it seems like a step down; perhaps even an easier medium to

101

work with. At one time television was, in fact, considered a last-ditch option for out-of-work film stars and desperate theatre actors. But none of those arguments are valid. Working on tighter schedules and budgets, with a turnaround time much lower than in films, a well-executed television production is often more gruelling.

For any actor, working in television is a far greater challenge. For Hema Malini, however, the ones given above weren't the only challenges she faced when she decided to give the small screen a shot. Having given birth to two daughters, she had taken a conscious decision to make a clean break from acting. Two years later, once the kids were a little older, she decided to get back to acting, but with a difference. The passion to be part of the storytelling process was still what intrinsically drove her, but this time she would change the medium. From the world of cinema to that of the small screen – Hema decided to take a leap of faith.

The industry, of course, slammed her for taking a 'suicidal' call. Many predicted the end of her run with films. 'She must be running out of film offers … why else would a star of her calibre move to television?' many speculated. But Hema took the plunge. And today we can only thank her and some of the others who followed, for decimating that unwarranted sense of hierarchy as well as many of these misconceptions associated with television.

'Gulzar and Vikas came to me and told me that they wanted me to act in this serial about the great women of India. The subject was so interesting that I immediately agreed to do it,' Hema says about her decision. 'It's much more interesting than films. In a film, you shoot for forty days for the same film and the same role, but in this, every four days I changed from one character to another. There was a change of sets, the atmosphere changed. It was a real challenge for me.'

Terah Panne was a string of stories on the lives of thirteen historical women figures. From Rani Roopmati to Pannabai to Nati Binodini – this was a fascinating anthology that was received with cheer and acclaim. Not only were these stories compelling in themselves, but fans now had the chance to watch their favourite leading lady from the comfort of their homes. For Hema, the connect with her audiences had never felt this close or real. 'I was in Ooty when I heard women discussing this serial,' she remembers. 'Every evening they wanted to rush home early to watch television. I don't think films can ever have that effect. Imagine, throughout India from Kanyakumari to Kashmir, everyone is watching you on screen!'

Being immensely satisfied with her debut in television didn't mean she was closing the gates on films. Having experimented with every possible genre the industry had to offer, by now Hema had every right to be fastidious. Close on the heels of her television serial came a film offer worth reckoning. Sukhwant Dhadda's *Ek Chadar Maili Si* (1986), based on the prolific Punjabi writer Rajendra Singh Bedi's short story, seemed fascinating from the word go. A social drama based in the heart of rural Punjab, the film sought to explore the custom of widow remarriage within the same family – a sensitive subject that few dared to discuss. The film, Hema realized, would need able handling.

When a poor village woman and a mother of two tragically loses her husband, the entire village insists that she get married to her younger brother-in-law. Horrified at the thought, she resists, but fails to stand her ground before the might of the panchayat. As a prevailing custom, the marriage is almost forced upon them.

Ek Chadar Maili Si made a powerful statement, as much for Hema's understated performance as for creating the character of Rano – a progressive, thinking woman. The role seemed tailor-made for Hema. (No wonder Dharmendra considers it his favourite Hema film.)

It is almost ironic that Dharmendra had been offered the same film many years ago. He was to take on the role of the brother-in-law, while Geeta Bali was to play the role of Rano. But while shooting for this film, the vivacious actress, who was thirty-five at the time, died of smallpox. The film had to be shelved and no other producer was willing to make another version. Finally, a newcomer, Sukhwant Dhadda, chose to ignore these superstitious beliefs and take up the subject. Hema too had been hesitant to accept the offer at first.

'It was great to work with Rishi Kapoor as the male lead,' Hema

says about her co-actor in the film. This was in fact the first time the
two had been paired together. 'He is an extremely talented actor, and
he played the role perfectly. My role demanded the body language of
a Punjabi lady. I drew inspiration from the many women I had met
while I used to travel with Dharam-ji in the villages of Punjab. The
film was critically well received.'

In his recently published biography, *Khullam Khulla*, Rishi
Kapoor admits that he had lost out on working with Hema Malini in
more films because he looked so young. Producers apparently used to
have a hard time finding him suitably aged heroines. Those like Hema
Malini and Rekha were considered senior, though in real life they
hardly were. 'Working with Hema-ji was a delight. The film remains
close to my heart because it was completely different from what I was
playing in other films. Probably my first venture into offbeat cinema,'
he mentions.

With films like *Marg* (1988) and *Awaargi* (1990) after *Sharara*, Hema
by now had already had a taste of film production. For both *Marg* and
Awaargi, she had signed on Mahesh Bhatt as director, and while the
first didn't manage an official release, the latter failed miserably at the
box office. Today, Hema admits that those were her early days in the
producer's role and she knew little about what was needed. In fact,
she was completely dependent on her uncle, P. Raghunathan, and her
brother, Jagannath.

'My uncle and my brother were supporting me. My first home
production *Sharara* went over budget. It cost us Rs 1 crore 50 lakh.
We shot at five outdoor locations. My brother yelled at me because
it was a very expensive idea. But that's my problem, I cannot think
of anything on a small scale. The director Rajendra Singh Babu was
good; he had made many successful Kannada films, but this time
he wasn't clear about what he was shooting. If a director is weak in
planning, it's a very big setback for a producer.'

The other films, *Marg* and *Awaargi*, took a long time to finish.
One of the main issues with *Awaargi* was Govinda, who was playing
one of the leads. '*Awaargi* was supposed to be a start-to-finish project.

It should have been ready within a year. But we couldn't get the combined dates of Anil (Kapoor), Meenakshi (Sheshadri) and Govinda. Specially Govinda's. It's torturous the way he used to drive himself, doing five to six films a day! Around the same time as this I was supposed to act in a film called *Ghaav* with him. Instead of reporting at 10 a.m., he would report at 10 p.m.! I had my kids at home and I explained to my director that if this continues I would have to excuse myself from the film. *Awaargi* was also held up because of his erratic behaviour,' she says.

There were reports that, frustrated with Govinda's behaviour, Hema had to finally take help from her husband. Apparently, it took one call from Dharmendra to set things straight!

Incidentally, *Ghaav* also had Shashi Kapoor as part of its initial cast, but the project was delayed to such an extent that when it was resumed by its director, Lawrence D' Souza, Shashi had given up acting. *Ghaav* was supposed to be Lawrence's debut film. The first schedule had been shot in 1986 while the rest was put on hold till Hema and Govinda had put their differences behind them. In the interim, the director took up another project called *Saajan* (1991), a resounding hit featuring Sanjay Dutt, Madhuri Dixit and Salman Khan. Finally, when he got back to *Ghaav*, he decided to rename it *Maahir*. The film finally saw the light of day in 1996 but failed to make a mark at the box office. Three years later, Hema and Govinda went on to work together in an action drama, *Paap Ka Ant* (directed by Vijay Reddy), that was well received by its audience.

While her tryst with films continued, Hema was already planning her next move in television. This time she was adamant on sticking to a subject after her heart. It would have to be a dance-drama.

Going by the great rapport she had shared with Vikas Desai through the making of *Terah Panne*, Hema approached him with the concept of *Nritya Yatra* – the tale of a dancer who has to give up on her passion because of her husband, but finally, unable to resist, goes back to it.

It was said that the then information and broadcasting minister

Ajit Kumar Panja had insisted on Hema producing this serial. 'Yes, I had discussed this idea with a close friend, who incidentally happened to mention it to Ajit Kumar Panja. He said that it was a good idea if I could perform the classical dances myself. It would be a good opportunity for the public. But he also said that I would have to submit the script and go through the regular channels,' she clarifies.

Unfortunately, after shooting for a few episodes, *Nritya Yatra* had to be shelved. It is believed that Hema and Vikas had very different visions for the production and they thought it best to leave it at that.

'I guess Vikas didn't understand my thought process,' Hema says. 'There was a vision gap between us. He thought from his point of view and I thought from my perspective. So, I dropped the idea.'

Nritya Yatra may have been shelved, but the idea of creating a visual story around classical dance continued to haunt Hema. In her mind, the concept was a living, throbbing reality; all she needed was a director who matched her sensibility. After rounds of meetings with several directors, her family urged her to direct the serial herself. Reluctant at first, it was finally Gulzar's push that gave Hema the courage to launch HM Creations – her very own home production. In 1990, *Noopur* – a serial centring around the life of a classical dancer – was telecast on Doordarshan.

'I never thought that I would be a director one day,' she tells me. 'I never plan my tomorrow, so I was unaware. But when my mother and even Dharam-ji pushed and inspired me to direct my own serial, I started giving it serious thought. After all, I have been working for so long in this industry. I think I might have gathered some knowledge about the medium. I always wanted to make a feature film based on the life and times of a classical dancer, but I guess times have changed and people aren't really interested in classical dance anymore. It would have been risky to make a film on that subject. So, I thought of making a serial. I had worked hard on the script and Gulzar-ji helped me with the dialogues. Camera wasn't a problem because I was always watching the monitor. Each episode of *Noopur* had one classical dance item. From Bharatanatyam to Mohiniattam, from Kuchipudi to the Durga dance ballet, I included everything in it.'

Being actor, producer and director would not have been easy

for Hema. But whenever she looks back at what was her first such attempt, she is deservedly proud of herself.

'It was a brilliant experience and great fun. The only problem was acting and directing simultaneously,' she recollects. 'I am glad that I took up *Noopur* despite my initial reluctance. A lot of people tried to dissuade me, but I am happy that I plunged into it headlong. The subject had been with me for too long. I agree that the serial wasn't technically perfect. I made several mistakes. We all do in our first venture. All these years, I have done what the directors asked me to … stood where he asked me to … spoken the lines he gave me. Now, at last, I was doing what I wanted … speaking the lines I wanted to say … performing the movements I found beautiful! Sometimes it works, sometimes it doesn't. One doesn't have to be perfect. It's a wasted life if there are no surprises.'

Noted actor and film director Anant Narayan Mahadevan spoke to me at length about working with Hema Malini on television serials like *Noopur* and, later, *Women of India*.

'Those days I used to be working with the Bombay Publicity Service, which was headed by V.P. Sathe. While there I got a call from Hema-ji's office. Initially I thought it was a prank call, although I was already a popular face in television after my serial *Ghar Jamai* (1997–98). I still found it hard to believe that Hema-ji would call me for her serial. Finally, I went to meet her and it was the first time I actually saw Hema Malini. She was working on *Noopur* and wanted me to play her cousin brother. I remember getting off to a great start with her on that first day itself because she felt I looked a lot like her own brother! Coincidentally, my nickname was also Kannan! So, I guess she always had a soft corner for me. I still remember that I was shooting for Sanjay Khan's *Tipu Sultan* in Jaipur in those days and Hema-ji required dates in Madras. But she was extremely cooperative and adjusted her dates to accommodate me.'

He continues, 'There is a scene in the serial where I go completely bald. Actually, I had to shave off my hair for *Tipu Sultan*, and later when I entered Hema-ji's set I still remember how she had screamed! "Aieeyo, what has happened to you?" she said. I then suggested we use a wig, but she actually changed the script to keep it real. *Noopur* was

a very difficult project. To convert classical dance into an interesting
television series is not an easy task, although it had its discerning
audience. I remember, in the last episode, I realized that my character
was missing. So, I actually went up to Hema-ji and requested her to
put me in some scene. She asked me, "How can I put you here?" I
told her, "Give me a chance." I sat down and wrote a scene and she
liked it. That's how I was there in the last episode. I didn't expect any
director to be liberal enough to accept suggestions from character
artistes. That serial also fetched me the Best Supporting Actor Award
at the Uptron Television Award Ceremony. Hema-ji may not have
been a very good technical person, but she is a brilliant storyteller.
Like Gulzar, Hrishikesh Mukherjee and Basu Chatterjee, Hema-ji
too tried to narrate simple stories on screen. She didn't believe in
technical jugglery.'

It's a relationship that Anant Mahadevan obviously cherishes,
though almost all their future collaborations failed to take off. 'Hema-
ji had always wanted to make an upgraded version of *Lal Patthar*. She
wanted me to write and probably direct the film. We had even got down
to writing, but somehow things didn't materialize. Later, I directed the
pilot for Hema-ji's production *Hulchul*. It was a brilliant story, based
on a child who travels all the way from his house in Chennai to Kerala
in search of pearls. We had submitted the episodes but the channels
played dirty with us and the serial never saw the light of day. Then I had
worked with her in her serial *Women of India – Urvashi*. I played the
role of Narad Muni in that serial with Madhoo. Later, when Hema-ji
became the chairperson of National Film Development Corporation,
she sanctioned one of my projects. Titled *Mausam Ki Tarah*, the film
was based on a true incident in Kolkata, during the Naxal movement.
NFDC wanted Ajay Devgn to play the main protagonist and he was
willing to do the film. But the budget was just Rs 80 lakh and we
couldn't afford him. So, that too was shelved. I have also met Dharam-
ji at Hema-ji's place. As a matter of fact, Hema-ji wanted to produce a
film for him, which would have been his comeback film. I had already
narrated the subject to Hema-ji, which was based on a professor's life.
But somehow Hema-ji got involved in NFDC and her dance ballets,
so the film remained a dream.'

Noopur, however, did reasonably well. More importantly, it gave Hema enough confidence to now move to the big screen as a director. Soon she announced her decision to direct her first-ever feature film, *Dil Aashna Hai* (1992), one that would go down in history for totally unexpected reasons.

13

The Debut of King Khan

Hema Malini is the first mainstream female actor in Hindi cinema to have ventured into directing a full-length feature film. It had been a long-cherished dream.

Based on a popular Shirley Conran novel, *Lace* (1982), *Dil Aashna Hai* was a fairly bold story to begin with. Any other first-time director would perhaps hesitate to bet on something as audacious as this, but Hema, after reading the book, had been convinced that this was the right subject for her.

The film is about a popular cabaret dancer, brought up in a brothel, on a mission to track down her biological mother. The mother could be one of three women – college friends who had each fallen in love during their younger years, one of them giving birth to a baby girl. Which of the three is the mother is a secret only the friends have access to and they had vowed to keep this information to themselves. With all the suspense and lots of drama, the story had the necessary ingredients to make for a perfect potboiler. In fact, this wasn't the first time the novel had been adapted for the screens. In 1984, director William Hale had used the same story for an immensely popular television series.

Hema talks about the making of the film: 'As a woman, I had strong feelings for the subject. But I knew it was a very difficult task to transform an English novel into a Hindi film. So, I approached Imtiaz Hussain to write the story and screenplay. Though I wanted to write the story myself, I hesitated. I thought that a professional person would do justice to it. I didn't want to disturb the soul of the subject, but at the same time wanted to put it in an Indian context. I knew it was a difficult job, but I have never done easy jobs in my life.'

Launched on a grand scale, Hema specially invited Dilip Kumar and Saira Banu for the film's mahurat. The thespian made a rare public appearance. Hema cast Dimple Kapadia, Sonu Walia and Amrita Singh as the three college friends. Divya Bharti (already a name in Tamil films) played the role of the young cabaret dancer, while a relatively new actor, Shah Rukh Khan, was cast as her love interest. The young man already had a considerable fan following among the younger generation after two hugely successful television series, *Fauji* (1989) and *Circus* (1989–90).

Actor Anant Mahadevan narrates how Hema had signed Shah Rukh on. 'I clearly remember that Hema-ji was desperately hunting for a fresh face for *Dil Aashna Hai*. At that point in time, we were shooting together for Khalid's (Mohammed) unreleased film *Nargis*. During the break, Hema-ji asked me about Shah Rukh. Frankly speaking, I was doubtful about Shah Rukh then. But Hema-ji insisted that her daughters liked him very much and they wanted her to cast him as the hero. So, I gave her Vivek Vaswani's number and Hema-ji got in touch with Shah Rukh. Not many know that the first film Shah Rukh signed was *Dil Aashna Hai*, though his first release was *Deewana* (1992).'

Talking about her film directorial debut, Hema recalls, 'After two decades in the film industry, I wanted to do something different. I was getting film offers like *Jamai Raja* (1990). I was very disappointed with the presentation of my character in that film. While directing *Noopur*, I decided that I will make a masala film, with fights, romance, good music, a typical Hindi film. I had full confidence in myself so I launched *Dil Aashna Hai*, which in Urdu means 'my heart knows'. I didn't act in that film because it was difficult for a woman to direct and act at the same time, plus I had to look after the production too. It is easy for a man to do both because he only has to apply a little make-up, comb his hair, look into the mirror and shoot. But for me, everything has to be perfect – the dress, make-up, hair, etc. To direct and at the same time to look presentable on screen gives me additional tension. In *Noopur*, I had to look after the dances, keep going back to my guru-ji for consultations, then dance before the cameras, direct the shots and do so many other things. I lost 5 kg after *Noopur!*'

Dil Aashna Hai received a tepid response at the box office. In fact, it lacked in several departments and, as it happens, Hema wasn't spared the criticism. It would be a lie to say that she was unaffected. No film-maker would be. The film didn't even manage to recover its production investment. But what is truly commendable is the spirit with which Hema faced every criticism that came her way. She had believed in the subject and saw it through to its very end – how many of us can say as much about ourselves? Today, when Hema talks about her first film, she has a characteristically unique way of looking back at the experience.

'I was happy with my life,' she says. 'I have heard people say that I am a liberated woman. But what does liberation mean? It does not mean that one should throw off everything (clothes) and run on the streets. Being liberated means to be strong, firm, to do what you feel is right, to have a career, to never stand back and complain. I do think that no woman should sit idle, she should do whatever she can.'

For all the criticism that *Dil Aashna Hai* received, there's no taking away from the fact that it gave Hindi cinema its next superstar. Shah Rukh Khan remains indebted to Hema: 'I am grateful to Hema-ji who introduced me to this world of 70mm gamut,' he says. 'I see Hema-ji as an epitome of responsibility. I think the one and only real numero uno actress in Bollywood was Hema Malini. Whoever we had after her was only because we were trying to find a replacement for Hema Malini.'

Hema confesses that she never anticipated that Shah Rukh would come this far. 'I never thought that Shah Rukh will become such a big star,' she tells me. 'But Indira Ma (her guru-ji) had told me that he would become a phenomenon. When she saw his photograph for the first time she told me that Shah Rukh is a star and he will change the industry. Since then, I knew that something big was going to happen with my movie. The day he signed my film, the same week he had signed four other films, including *Deewana, King Uncle* (1993) and *Kabhi Haan Kabhi Naa* (1994). Every second day I would come to know that Shah Rukh had signed a new film. That's when I knew that Indira Ma was right. She could foresee what none of us could.'

When Hema finally decided to cast him, she asked her cousin and personal assistant, Prabha Raghavan (Pappu), to call Shah Rukh to her Mumbai office. But when Prabha called up the young actor, he was sure it was one of his friends pulling a prank. Finally, Prabha left the office telephone number with him and asked him to call back so he could clarify all his doubts. It was only after he made the call that he finally believed her. The next morning, as he stood outside Hema Malini's bungalow, waiting to be escorted inside, he was in a daze.

Hema remembers how nervous Shah Rukh had been during that first meeting. Apparently, every question of hers was met with a breathless, incoherent reply! The first audition left her dissatisfied. Shah Rukh's hair had been all over his forehead, making it impossible for her to see the expressions in his eyes. Hema suggested they try again – this time with his hair gelled back and his colourful jacket replaced with a plain tee. The results were satisfactory but just to be doubly sure, Hema called Dharmendra over to come and meet the young actor. Dharam, it is believed, took a liking to the young man instantly.

In a recent interview, Shah Rukh recalled those initial days and his meeting with Hema Malini. 'I was an odd-looking boy, I spoke too fast and I was not from a film background, but they gave me an opportunity. Hema-ji is not here, but tell me who gets an opportunity in his life to sit across the Dream Girl and she says, "I like your nose, it's very aristocratic and you got into my film because of that." *Vo naak jisko main chhupata phirta tha, vo naak Hema Malini ko pasand hai!* (The nose that I went about hiding, that's the nose Hema Malini likes!)'

In an interview to NDTV, Shah Rukh spoke about what it was like working with Hema, the director. 'It was 26 June 1991 and I was shooting a romantic scene with Divya Bharti. There was a dialogue where I had to tell Divya that I would stand by her decision, as her boyfriend. I still remember the lines, "*Laila, chahe kuch bhi ho jaye, main tumhare saath kadam se kadam mila kar chalunga...*" We were shooting this in a bungalow near Yari Road. It was a moonlit night, romantic sequence. I think Hema-ji was not happy with the way I was doing the scene, so she enacted the scene for me and showed me what exactly she was expecting from me as an actor. There I was, standing behind the pillar, looking at Hema-ji's face on a moonlit night. I couldn't believe that the 'Dream Girl Hema Malini' was actually enacting my scenes and showing me how it should be done. After she was done, I told her, "Hema-ji, what you did was nice. But I can't do it like you. You are beautiful. So, whatever you do on screen looks beautiful. I am not. Can I please do it my way?" She was gracious enough to give me that space as an actor and deliver my lines. I don't know if she was happy with that particular scene or not, but she okayed the shot and we moved on to the next scene.'

Hema also found an unexpected friend in the young star. She shares, 'He (Shah Rukh) was already married when he started his career as a movie star. I remember meeting Gauri during the shoot of the movie and at the music launch. They complemented each other. Dharam-ji was also extremely fond of Shah Rukh. I remember an incident which I have never shared with anyone till today. During the shooting of *Dil Aashna Hai*, Esha was having her exams. One day she called me up and wanted me to come home. She said something like she wouldn't study if I didn't get back and be with her. I was naturally very disturbed. I felt torn between my roles as a mother and a director, and I didn't know who I could talk to at that point. That is when I found a friend in Shah Rukh. Realizing I was disturbed, he came to me and asked, '*Kya hua, Hema-ji*? (What happened, Hema-ji?)' When I told him everything, he said, '*Aap cameraman and chief assistant director ko scene samjha dijiye, main isko kar dunga. Aap ghar jaiye!* (Explain the scene to the cameraman and chief assistant director and I'll manage it. You go home!)' He was so young, but his assurance had that maturity. I could see in his eyes that he was sincere and would not let me down. That day, he did those scenes without me. And later, when I saw the rushes, I was happy to see that he knew exactly what I had wanted from him!'

Hema wasn't just the first director Shah Rukh had worked with – she was also the first woman director. Over the years, rumour mills might have had a lot to say about the differences that had cropped up between them, but Shah Rukh has never lost an opportunity to express his deepest regards for her. He recalls a particular instance, 'I was too young, and I remember that *Stardust* magazine had published my interview with a headline that quoted me as saying: "Hema Malini doesn't know direction!" I realized that I was misquoted. But that was the least of my worries, because I had to still face her on the sets of *Dil Aashna Hai. Main chhup chhup ke set ke andar hi ja raha tha*, when she immediately noticed me and called me. I sat beside her, petrified of the consequences. But to my surprise, in her inimitable style, very sweetly she said, "Look, magazines only write about famous people. So, either I am famous or you are famous. These days I hardly work in films, so it has to be you. And when you become famous, magazines will write all sorts of rubbish about you. So, that's fine!" That was a big learning for me, from a living legend like Hema-ji.'

In 2011, almost two decades after *Dil Aashna Hain*, Hema's second film directorial venture, *Tell Me O Kkhuda*, was set to release. It featured her daughter Esha and newbie Arjan Bajwa. Incidentally, Shah Rukh's home production *Ra.One* was also scheduled to release on the same date. The media had a field day reporting on how Shah Rukh had been unhappy about the clash and he and Hema had stopped talking to one another. Before the release of both films, Shah Rukh decided to show up at the music release of *Tell Me O Kkhuda*. If that wasn't enough to stop the frenzied stories, his words at the event put an end to all speculation.

'Hema-ji, I have not been able to thank you enough for what you have done for me. I remember that my first cheque as an actor was signed by "Hema Malini" and I knew that I had arrived. Whatever my family, my wife, my kids and I am enjoying today, in terms of success, stardom, blessings from fans, is all because of you. I am what I am today because of you. I am sorry, Hema-ji, that I have not been able to say that often, and people made stories out of ignorance. Deep down, I know what you mean in my life. I know what I learnt from you in my first film. I know what your contribution has been in this industry. I wish you success in whatever you do in life. Inshallah, your film will be a hit and my duas will always be with you.'

After *Dil Aashna Hai*, young Divya Bharti had also been on a roll, delivering consecutive hits early on in her Hindi film career. Her sudden and untimely death a few years later left the industry in shock. It remains unclear whether she was the victim of an accident or something more sinister. Hema remembers, 'She was a very bubbly girl, but used to go through severe mood swings. At times, she would be very chirpy and extremely warm, and suddenly she would sulk and behave strangely. I used to like her a lot as a person. I couldn't believe that she died so early.'

Long-time associates Mithun Chakraborty and Jeetendra were also part of Hema's first Bollywood venture.

'Hema-ji has always been an idol for any actor,' says Mithun. 'The day she approached me with this film, I said yes without thinking twice. I had never worked with a woman director till then. Not that I didn't want to, but it never happened. Hema-ji was the first. I share a very cordial relationship with her. Even when Hema-ji had turned producer, she had asked me to play a cameo in *Sharara* with Tina Munim. I had done that role as well. There are two people in this industry I can never say no to – Hema-ji and Amitabh Bachchan-ji. My wife Pinky (Yogita Bali) is also a great admirer of hers. I had a very small role in the film, but I thoroughly enjoyed working in it. I had worked with Hema-ji in a couple of films (earlier) and I already knew her temperament. Years later we again worked together in G.V. Iyer's *Swami Vivekananda* (1998). I was playing the role of Ramkrishna and Hema-ji was Goddess Kali. She looked divine as Ma Dakshineshwari Kali. In fact, I had turned vegetarian during the shooting of this film, and it was she who had inspired me. I have seen how dedicated an actor she is even for a guest appearance. I was given the National Award for that film, but I feel my best scenes in the film were all with Hema-ji.'

As an actor who has shared the screen with her in innumerable films, Jeetendra was elated when Hema decided to take to direction. 'I think Hema is the best. In a career span of thirty years, I had never worked with a woman director. In fact, after working with her, I didn't feel any difference because of the gender. She is as competent as her male counterparts. I have always shared a wonderful camaraderie with her and I would love to work with her in any project. She is a beautiful person and a magnanimous personality.'

I ask Hema how she felt sitting on that director's chair. Her memories from those days are still fresh. 'I was very clear and sure of what I wanted from my artistes. I used to do my homework before going to the sets, but once I was there I used to constantly improvise, and all my homework would go to waste! I am a spontaneous person. That's why I used to sit on the sets, absorb the atmosphere, discuss the angles, etc. As a director, I felt I should be on the sets, see the lighting, think of different angles. But I used to get so confused with so many angles that I finally left it to my cameraman Peter Pereira!

'For *Dil Aashna Hai*, I wanted to sign Vinod Khanna. But he couldn't do the film because he couldn't accommodate those dates. Actually, I had originally approached Amitabh Bachchan to do this role, but at that time he told me that he wasn't signing any films. For the younger roles, I did speak to Aamir Khan and Vivek Mushran, but they had already committed their dates to other producers. I signed Divya Bharti because I liked the bubbly attitude and the naughtiness in her eyes, which suited the character in my film. I wanted Dharam-ji to play an important role in my film, but he was not willing to act under my direction. People said all kinds of things after the film's mahurat because Dharam-ji couldn't attend the party. But there was no truth to that. He couldn't attend it because he was in America. Every day I used to update him about the film's developments. He was a great support. My daughters too were particularly excited about this film.' (Later, Dharmendra made it a point to attend the audio release of the film and the premiere show.)

'On the mahurat day, when I said "Action" for the first time, I was so excited that after the artistes had said their dialogues I forgot to say "Cut"! I had already rushed on to the stage! It was Subhash Ghai who saved the situation and said, "Arre, cut"!' she recalls, laughing.

14

Taking a Different Direction

Two years before her maiden directorial film was released, Hema landed herself a film that would shape much of her journey as a filmmaker. Arunaraje's *Rihaee* (1990) not only gave Hema her first dyed-in-the-wool parallel film role, it also had her working with a female director for the first time.

'Apart from a brilliant script and good cast, I was interested in working with Arunaraje. I wanted to learn how a woman director manages her work. So, it was a learning experience for me,' she says.

The storyline was a sensitive one and the subject would have left most people scandalized, if not downright offended. In a village where most of the menfolk have migrated to cities, the women are alone and lonely. While the men often visit brothels, the women have no such option. Takku Bai (Hema) is one such, married to a carpenter (Vinod Khanna) who is barely ever home. When a stranger from Dubai (Naseeruddin Shah) pays the village a visit, she finds herself inexplicably drawn to him. The attraction is mutual and, over time, they fall in love. When Takku Bai conceives his child, her husband is consumed with rage. He refuses to accept the illegitimate baby while Takku refuses to abort. What follows is the story of a woman standing up for herself and her choices before a rigid and patriarchal village panchayat.

Hema being cast in Takku Bai's role came as a surprise to most. When I spoke to Arunaraje, she told me how Hema had, in fact, not been her first choice. She had always wanted Smita Patil for this movie, an actor better suited and more experienced in the arthouse genre. Smita had also wanted to assist Aruna directorially on this film.

'The news of Smita's death came like a thunderbolt. I was shattered,' Aruna recalls. 'I thought of not making this film at all. Though my project was sanctioned by the National Film Development Corporation (NFDC), I was reluctant about doing it with any other actress. But my friends insisted that I complete it, at least as a tribute to my best friend Smita. I was puzzled as to whom I should cast. It was a strong character – a lady who doesn't speak much, but still stands by her beliefs. I thought of Hema Malini for the role. I saw a certain integrity in Hema-ji. She is not pretentious about her life. She never made bold feminist statements but still lived a life that she believed in. My character Takku Bai in *Rihaee* was somewhat similar. Hema-ji and I are both Librans; my birthday is just a day after hers. So, we gelled well. She was very excited about the script and she too respected Smita. So, she wanted to do the film.'

Having watched the film, I ask Aruna how she convinced Hema to perform some of the explicit lovemaking scenes. I was surprised to learn that Hema didn't have any reservations while shooting them. 'Well, Hema-ji didn't have any qualms with those scenes,' Aruna tells me. 'She is a director's actor. When I narrated the lovemaking scenes with Naseer, she asked me how to do them. So, I literally lay on the chatai and showed her the movements. After that she was absolutely comfortable. Apart from that, I guess she trusted me as a woman. In fact, Naseer was tense. When I asked him to kiss Hema-ji's neck, Naseer immediately raised his hand and said, "*Na baba na, Dharam-ji aa kar bahut peetenge!* (No, no, Dharam-ji will come and beat me!)" And we all burst into laughter. I guess these explicit scenes weren't a problem with Hema. She had some other issues. During the first schedule, she used to always ask me, "Why aren't you taking my close-up shots?" Actually, she was just another villager in my film, along with other co-actors like Reema Lagoo, Ila Arun and Neena Gupta. In a couple of scenes Hema-ji is just part of an audience. She was not habituated to that. But later when I explained this to her, she understood and there was no such problem again and she was extremely cooperative.'.

The actor might have adapted quickly to the demands of her new role, but for her fans she was still 'Hema Malini'. When word got around of her shooting for a film in an outdoor location, the crowds came in throngs. Suddenly the production unit was faced with a deluge they certainly weren't anticipating. Aruna recollects, 'We were shooting for twenty-eight days at a village called Vadnagar, which was a ninety-minute drive from Ahmedabad. Hema-ji was put up at a bungalow with her make-up man and hairdresser. Every day during the shooting, people used to come in trucks and tempos to see Hema Malini. Nearly 50,000 people gathered just to get a glimpse of her. They had two reasons to come – one, to visit the Hatkeshwar Temple and two, while returning, to get a glimpse of the screen goddess. Finally, the police had to lathi-charge and they in turn threw stones at us. I got hurt along with my actor Mohan Agashe. I realized that she was still a very popular star even then.'

The entire team was fairly anxious before the film's release. The response could swing either way. Aruna recalls, 'During the press conference of *Rihaee*, one journalist asked me whether I was asking for rights for women to sleep with anyone of their choice. That's utterly ridiculous. Can one really stop anyone from behaving according to his or her wish? Another reporter had questioned, "How can you say such a thing, our women are not like that, etc." Who exactly did this person refer to as "our women"? Were they from his community or was he referring to prostitutes? And why do we think in this manner? Can't we look at it as a natural urge, something that exists in our society? It is a need for both the sexes. I was even warned before the release of the film that people might demonstrate against it, stage morchas, dharnas, etc. But nothing of that sort happened. It is only the media that reacted in a strange manner, while the film received an overwhelming response from men and women. Hema-ji was very happy with the response. In fact, I went to a theatre in Connaught Place in New Delhi, where men clapped on each dialogue of Hema-ji's. It went for the National Awards, but the jury members felt that it was a film against men, and that women should not speak out like that in our society. So, it didn't win a single award.'

As a matter of fact, Hema was nominated in the Best Actress category for *Rihaee* at the Filmfare Awards but lost out to Madhuri Dixit for *Dil*. After receiving the award, Madhuri confessed, 'I still can't believe that I have won this award. I guess Hema-ji was brilliant in *Rihaee*.'

Aruna's concluding words say it all: 'I have seen actors and actresses in India lobbying for awards. But Hema-ji has never bothered to pitch for an award. I guess Hema-ji was never given her due as an actress. She is the most underrated actress in India and directors simply failed to extract the best out of her.'

Perhaps inspired by Arunaraje, when Hema announced her next directorial venture, it was a radical departure from the kind of subjects she had dealt with so far. The telefilm for Zee, called *Mohini*, was a take on Malayattoor Ramakrishnan's novel *Yakshi* (1967) that explored the concept of witchcraft. However, it did not deal with the occult or anything mystical – it was more a subversion of male psychology. In the film, a professor meets with an accident and his face gets disfigured. People begin to avoid him. As matters get worse, the woman he loves, unable to come to terms with the dramatic change of events, walks out on him. Left to himself, by now a recluse, the professor takes to reading up obsessively on occultism. Over time he meets, falls in love and gets married to a beautiful woman. However, he feels that she is not an ordinary woman but a witch with supernatural powers, out to destroy him. His fear soon reaches manic proportions till it drives him to a point of utter despair.

Hema launched a relative newcomer, Rituparna Sengupta, in this telefilm. When asked about her, Rituparna remembers fondly, 'My name was suggested by Mithun-da. I was very excited. Obviously, I couldn't believe that Hema-ji wanted to cast me in her film. I had grown up seeing her films and admired her for her achievements. She looked at me and said, "*Arre, kitni dubli ho...* (How thin you are!)" and then every day she used to give me health drinks! I played a cameo in *Mohini*. After the shooting was over, Hema-ji said, "If I would have got your dates earlier, I would have extended your role. You will make it big." I admire her. I am grateful to Hema-ji for making me a part of her project.'

Rituparna went on to become a big star in the Bengali film industry and even won the National Award for her performance in Rituparno Ghosh's *Dahan* (1997). Recently, when she met Hema at the airport, they recollected memories from the *Mohini* days. 'I want to produce a film for Hema-ji. I have a wonderful subject, and I want to make that film with her,' Rituparna says.

In *Mohini*, Hema's skills as a director were on ample display. From scripting to camerawork, she had come a long way from the *Noopur* days. Talking about this film, Hema recalls with typical confidence, 'I wanted to make a film on this subject. I don't believe in the concept of making women-centric films because one is a woman. Films are either good or bad. I want to make good films and *Mohini* was a bold subject.'

Mohini was also significant for another more personal reason. It was on this production that Hema worked with her cousin Madhoo, the actress who had shot to fame with her debut in Mani Ratnam's *Roja* (1992).

Not many know about Hema's relationship with Madhoo. Madhoo happens to be Jaya Chakravarthy's brother P. Raghunathan's daughter, but Hema and she have been known to share a slightly bittersweet association. According to Madhoo, the equation between them got tumultuous once she entered the film industry.

Madhoo, who has so far been tight-lipped about the situation, finally opens up.

'Hema and I share a huge age gap, as my father is last but one amongst eleven siblings. Amba (Jaya Chakravarthy) was the eldest. My mother had expired at an early age and she had handed over the responsibility of bringing me up to Amba. Ever since I can remember, I have been aware that Hema Malini is a superstar first and only then my cousin. To be frank, as a child, I used to hate it. In school, my friends used to call me *Hema Malini ki behen* (Hema Malini's sister), which used to annoy me. I didn't have an identity of my own as a child. I was scared to make friends because most of them tried to be friendly with me only because they wanted to meet Hemu (that's what I always called her). I clearly remember that at one point I didn't want to be associated with her.

'Of the eleven siblings, only Amba, Shanta aunty and my father used to stay in Mumbai. We stayed in Juhu, which was very close to Hemu's bungalow. The rest of my uncles and aunts stayed in Chennai and Delhi. Because we were in Mumbai, we often gathered at Hemu's place and played with the other cousins, Prabha Raghavan and Mohan Raghavan (Shanta aunty's children). We were all in the same age group. Every day after school I used to go to Amba's place for lunch. I still remember, after *Sholay* released, we used to play "Sholay" in Hemu's garden. I would be Dharam-ji, Prabha would play Hemu's role and Mohan would always be Gabbar! We would scream out those lines from the film! Gradually and unwittingly I started getting drawn and then addicted to the world of films and glamour.

'Hemu always used to be extremely busy. We hardly ever got to spend time with her, even though she wanted to. As a child, I always thought very highly of Hemu's life. I used to tell myself that it was the perfect life – one where people were running after you, your photographs were being published every day in newspapers, fans were sending innumerable mails ... what more could a girl want?

'My first trip abroad was with Hemu. It was for a song sequence in *Dream Girl*. I was playing an ordinary role of a kid and got the opportunity because of her. Hemu must have told the producer, "I have a little one at home, can I take her too?" It was a simple part where I just had to run from one corner to another, but we had great fun. I remember those rides in Disneyland which Hemu took us for. She was like our guardian there. We had tremendous respect for her.

'However, I still remember an incident on that trip that left me a little hurt. One day, Hemu complained to my aunt about how I had dirtied her bathroom. She said to my aunt, "Papu (as I was called at home) should not do such things in future." She was disappointed with me and I was upset that I had offended her. That is one thing I did not want to do. I haven't mentioned this to anyone, but maybe when Hemu reads this book, she will know that I knew she had complained about me!

'My initiation into swimming was also because of her and guess who my trainer was? None other than Dharam-ji! I still remember how Dharam-ji was swimming and I was standing with Hemu and watching him when he looked at me and said, "*Chal pani mein aaja!*

(Come into the water!)" I was so scared. Then Hemu took me to the pool and Dharam-ji taught me how to paddle. Dharam-ji is a fantastic swimmer. Even now when I meet him, he smiles and says, "*Maine hi tujhe swimming sikhayi ... bhulna nahi.* (I'm the one who taught you how to swim ... don't forget!)" He is such a wonderful person. I am really happy that Hemu has got a gem as her life partner.

'As cousins, we were never close. We never had extensive chats. Sometimes she would play with us and before leaving for outdoor shoots, would kiss us, but that was it. So, there was not much I knew about her as a person. Even when I was in college, she used to be so busy that she must have not noticed how much I had grown up. I ended up developing an opinion of her based on what I had heard and read – which, at that point of time, wasn't the greatest. Now I know that it's not fair to judge anyone. One should learn to accept the person for the way he or she is.

'After I joined the film industry, Hemu and I somehow drifted apart. I remember I used to have preconceived notions about her, but I am not sure what exactly happened back then. Over time I became a successful star and got my share of recognition. Subsequently, I started visiting her house and talking to her and that is when I realized what a wonderful person she is. Everything that people had said about her was rubbish. We began to share our views and ideas about films. After seeing my film *Roja*, she wrote me a letter saying, 'You are such a wonderful actor; I hope you have more such roses (Roja) along the way...' I still have that letter. Gradually, I began to understand why people had negative views about Hemu. She was a big star and had to maintain a stern demeanour, otherwise people would start walking all over her. Hemu didn't approach me directly for *Mohini*; she asked my father. In fact, I did television for only one reason: I wanted to work with her.

'This brings me to another controversy that had cropped up when I joined the film industry. The press and the media started hounding me with a question I had no answer for: they wanted to know why Hema Malini had not taken the initiative to launch her own cousin. For a long time, I refused to answer a question of that kind, but then finally I couldn't contain myself and one fine day I just exploded. I couldn't handle the pressure. I behaved in a juvenile manner. Later, I realized what a fool I had made of myself. The truth was that Hemu had been casting for her film *Dil Aashna Hai* and she had signed Divya Bharti for the lead role. At that point of time I had also asked myself the same question – why not me? I did feel bad. Later, she clarified that the role was not suitable for me. Now when I sit back and think I thank my stars for it, because if she had launched me, I might not have received any credit for myself as an actor.

'On the first day of the shoot of *Mohini* at Essel World, in a restaurant scene, I was sitting with my co-actor Sudesh Berry. Just before the shot I wanted to ask my director something but I had a problem. How do I address Hemu? Since childhood Amba had taught us to address her as Hemu and not didi. But here she was my director, so should I address her as Hema Malini or Hema-ji or Hemu? Being the brat that I was, I shouted out from my chair, "First, please tell me what I should call you … Hema, Hema-ji or Madam?" She looked at me calmly and said, "I am Hemu for you … always. Call me Hemu!" And that was what finally broke the ice for us! I realized that she was my sister and one who still loved me in spite of everything. Thereafter, there was no looking back.'

After *Mohini*, Hema went on to direct Madhoo in serials like *Women of India – Urvashi* and *Tell Me O Kkhuda*.

'As a director, Hemu knew exactly what she wanted. Her conviction in her subject was rock solid. I liked her work so much that we worked together again in *Urvashi*. In my personal life, too, Hemu went on to play an important role. I didn't realize it then but I ended up modelling my life after her. If you had asked me this question a few years ago, I would have hated admitting it, but now I know that I have merely followed Hemu's footsteps. I trained in classical dance with Guru Kalyanasundaram of the Raja Rajeshwari dance school. I joined the film industry. She was the first one to know about my marriage plans. I wanted to have two daughters like her. And now that I want to work again, I find myself going back to her with my decision. I still feel that her life is perfect and I will be lucky if I could emulate her in more ways than one.

'At my wedding, Hemu did everything that a mother is supposed to do. Amba was around but she was weak, so Hemu took over. Earlier I may have idolized her only as an actress, but later I realized that there are so many things about her worth admiring.

'Even now she wants to and tries her best to spend time with my daughters. The other day she called me and said, "I would love to see Keya and Ameya." That want is genuine! In fact, when I conceived my first baby, my doctor came and asked me to select a date and time for the delivery of the baby. I selected the number sixteen as the birthday of my elder child, because it matches Hemu's birthdate. I wish my daughter's life unfolds like hers. I want my daughter to be as lucky and famous as Hema Malini!'

Continuing her sojourn in television, soon after *Mohini*, Hema signed her first mega serial as an actor, *Yug*, for director Sunil Agnihotri. It had Hema play the role of Nirmala, a freedom fighter. The serial got off to a grand start and was received warmly by its audiences, but continued only for ninety episodes. It seems the producer, Sattee Shourie, and Hema had some differences over certain financial issues, driving her to walk out of the project. The serial had to be taken off air abruptly.

Barring an exception or two, Hema had had a fruitful and deeply satisfying association with television by now. She had also come to enjoy and understand the medium well. In no time, she announced her next – another pet project that had been waiting to take wings. The story of Amrapali, the beautiful dancer in the court of Magadha who later embraced Buddhism, had been made into a film way back in 1966, by Lekh Tandon. Vyjayanthimala was cast as the central character. Hema had several reasons to love this film. For the televised version, she decided to take up the role herself and direct the tele-series too.

'It's a dream role for me,' she had gushed at the time. 'As a dancer, this character fascinated me. And Vyjayanthi-ji's fluid, energetic classical dances in *Amrapali* are still considered magical in Terpsichorean terms. I have seen her film and loved it. In television, you get a chance to narrate the subject in detail. I have worked a lot on research, costumes and sets. These are short series based on famous women personalities from India. I am glad that I am playing the character of Amrapali, finally!'

Amrapali was an enormous success. In fact, the DVDs of the series were available till as recently as a few years back. Actor Pankaj Dheer, who played the role of King Bimbisara, recalls: 'It was a great experience working with her. The research was authentic and the music in the film was great. I wouldn't call Hema-ji a technically brilliant director, as she has to go a long way as far as the technicalities of film-making are concerned. She is not a trained director, but she is passionate. She puts her heart and soul into a project.'

Sometime in the early 1990s, a young enthusiastic Bengali director waited patiently outside a dubbing centre in Mumbai. He had a detailed bound television script in hand and was waiting for Hema Malini to come out of the studio so he could beseech her to listen to his story. Hema apparently had already expressed disinterest, but Sudipto Chattopadhyay wasn't ready to give up. He recalls, 'It was raining and Hema-ji was waiting for her car to arrive after the dubbing. I somehow managed to narrate the synopsis of my serial and then, all of a sudden, she was interested! After that things went smoothly.'

That's all it took to convince Hema Malini! She made her way to the film studios in Kolkata's Tollygunge for the first time, for a young and relatively new director, only because he had convinced her with a good script. The Hindi serial, *Naam Gum Jayega*, was loosely based on the life of Bengal's greatest actress, the legendary Suchitra Sen. 'It was a very nice experience. The role was different and I had never worked in Kolkata, though I had heard a lot about this city from my brother (Kannan),' Hema remembers.

Hema continued her tryst with stories of powerful Indian women on television, with the production of *Jhansi Ki Rani*. Soon after completing Sudipto's serial, Hema had in fact been cast as the fiery Rani Laxmibai in director Kawal Sharma's mega serial by the same name for Zee TV. But this time, Hema was keen on producing the series herself. The dream to work with Richard Attenborough had remained unfulfilled; perhaps she saw this as an opportunity to make amends.

Although the project was delayed for a considerable period, when it finally took off, there was no stopping it. Starring Varsha Usgaonkar as the feisty queen and directed by Ravi Chopra, this fifty-six-part series was a huge success. Talking about it, Hema says, 'This subject had always fascinated me. I read Vrindavan Lal Verma's Hindi novel *Jhansi Ki Rani* and thought of adapting it into a serial. We researched the 1857 Sepoy Mutiny extensively. I didn't play the role of Rani Laxmibai because of the age factor. She was very young and died young too. Moreover, as a producer I have added tension. I didn't want to direct this particular series in *Women of India* because a subject like Jhansi Ki Rani demanded action and grandeur, which Ravi would handle with élan.'

Three years after *Jhansi Ki Rani*, Hema was approached by Puneet Issar for his serial *Jai Mata Ki*. In 1999, she played all the avatars of Goddess Mahamaya. 'We wanted Hema-ji for our serial for obvious reasons. Can you think of a face other than Hema-ji's that can radiate bhakti and shakti simultaneously?' the director asks. 'Another factor that played an important role in signing her was her classical dance. People did ask me about her age, but does Hema-ji look her age? I don't think so. I clearly remember the first day of the shoot. It was at Film City. Hema-ji reported at 9.30 a.m. sharp and went inside the make-up room. She took exactly two hours to complete her make-up and costume. She is such a professional that she would always ask for her dialogues in advance and would come to the set with those dialogues learnt by heart.

'Hema-ji had been very impressed to see me with my bound script for all twenty-six episodes. In fact, she was extremely cooperative. The first day, we announced pack-up at around 7.30 p.m. The second day it went on to 8.30 p.m. and on the third day it extended till 10.30 p.m. That day, I remember Dharam-ji calling and asking her, "*Arre bhai kahan ho aap?* (Where are you, my dear?)" Despite being a superstar, she never threw any tantrums. We made her run, walk and do action sequences on rocky terrain, but she never grumbled. She was tremendous in the action sequences. My serial topped the TRPs only because of Hema-ji. No one else would have been able to do justice to these characters. Unfortunately, we had to end the series abruptly because Doordarshan had crashed and they demanded more money, which was economically not feasible. Later, we did a rerun on Star Plus and again it topped the TRPs.'

In the world of television, Hema had become a force to reckon with. Even though she had explored acting in mega serials like *Yug* and *Jai Mata Ki*, apart from being behind the scenes as producer and director for so many others, she wasn't yet finished with all the options the medium provided. In 2000, she took on an altogether new role – as anchor for a popular show called *Rangoli* on Doordarshan – one that served as a retrospective of old Hindi film songs. The show once again was a resounding success. Ravi Malik, then general manager of television marketing at NFDC, recalls, 'Hema Malini is a very disciplined and competent person. When I did this Hindi film-song-based programme for Doordarshan, Hema Malini was our host for 162 weeks. We had quality songs and avoided cheap gimmicks, yet made it very popular. She made it look sophisticated and rich. In fact, we used to get letters in which fans requested her to talk more and show lesser songs. That's a rare thing, where viewers want to see the anchor more than the main show.'

Soon there was a demand for a televised version of the health-and-beauty magazine *Meri Saheli*, of which Hema was editor. Producers wasted no time in launching a 150-episode show called *Aap ki Saheli* in which Hema would advise viewers and give them health and beauty tips. As on 70mm, on the small screen too, she had grown to become a much loved and revered name.

Hema is possibly the only mainstream Hindi film actor to venture into producing regional content for television. After the success of *Jai Mata Ki*, she went on to produce two Marathi serials – *Songati* and *Umbartha* – both revolving around stories of ordinary women in difficult life situations. For someone who had never worked in a regional film in all these years, this came as a surprise to most.

She reveals, 'Whenever I used to travel to the interiors of

Maharashtra to conduct dance performances during the Ganesh festival, my fans often asked me to make a Marathi serial. I was excited by the idea.'

Forever ready to portray mythological characters, Hema had even performed a one-hour dance show called *Mahisasurmardini Durga* for Kolkata Doordarshan Kendra years ago. The ballet had been choreographed by Bharatanatyam exponents Thankamani Kutty and Govindan Kutty and had been made in both Bengali and Hindi.

She followed this up in 2001 with yet another dance drama, *Robi O Radha*, in which she played the role of Radha. Based on Rabindranath Tagore's *Bhanusingher Padabali*, the audiovisual show was directed by Bandana Mukhopadhyay, while Kavita Krishnamoorthy rendered Hema's tracks and Pandit Jasraj composed the music. 'It was my humble tribute to Rabindranath Tagore and the rich culture of Bengal and Bengali music,' she says. 'I always wanted to be a part of Bengali dance drama. In fact, Tagore's is the most powerful character that I have ever come across.' Going by her penchant to take up new challenges, one wonders if Tagore's dance dramas are on the horizon for her.

15

Dancing Diva

In the middle of a conversation, Hema suddenly turns to her cousin Prabha who, over the years, has also come to play the role of trusted lieutenant for her. With evident irritation in her voice she tells her to ask the production controller from the previous night's dance performance why her sari had come in late for the 'vastraharan' sequence.

We are sitting in Hema's suite at Kolkata's Taj Bengal hotel and catching up over cups of adrak chai. Hema is in Kolkata for her dance ballet *Draupadi* – possibly the finest in her repertoire. 'You know what happened last night?' she tells me with exasperation. 'I had to move away from the light so that I could take the sari. It was handed to me from backstage. It was so difficult. I hate it when things are so disorganized. *Toh phir itna rehearsal ka kya faida*? (Then what's the point of rehearsing so hard?)'

The first time I saw Hema Malini on stage was during her dance ballet *Mahalaxmi*. I remember being spellbound by how uncannily she was in character – the goddess of power and strength. From Adishakti to Pallavi to Ashta Laxmi, she exemplified all the avatars, walking in and out of each with impeccable fluidity. Most importantly, she made it look easy, as though nothing came more naturally to her. She was fifty-four, and an unstoppable force of energy and radiance. Since then, I haven't missed a single chance of watching Hema Malini on stage. The image of a 3,000-strong crowd at the Science City Auditorium giving her a standing ovation isn't one that fades away easily.

Hema's story would be incomplete without bringing up her relationship with dance and how much it has shaped her very existence. I call it a relationship because it has been nothing less for her. Her most steadfast companion, her call to the spiritual realm, her raison d'être – it has been a deep-seated and long-enduring affiliation. What keeps this relationship thriving is also the fact that Hema is possibly one of the most vociferous champions of classical dance and dance ballets in the country today. Desperate to keep the tradition alive and, more importantly, relevant, Hema's ballets are a constant experiment in reinvention.

In *Draupadi*, for instance, the dance performances were interspersed with visuals that had been shot earlier, making the recital a unique amalgamation of two separate media vehicles. It had been the costliest ballet from her stable, with sixty-odd performers on stage at the same time – a grand, extravagant affair. In one of my interviews with her for *The Asian Age*, Hema had spoken at length about *Draupadi*, how she had built its script from Pratibha Ray's award-winning novel *Yajnaseni*, and what had gone into its arduous preparation.

> Draupadi is my ninth production. I have always been fascinated with this character, but have not found the right way to interpret her on stage, until I came across Pratibha Ray's novel, on which I based my script. I used to call my choreographer Bhushan Lakhandri and give him ideas, as to what I felt could be highlighted. It took me a year for the pre-production of my ballet. I wanted to make it look grand and that's how it has finally shaped. It's good to see that the audience appreciates my efforts. My ballets are neither too old-fashioned nor too modern, but at the same time, lyrically beautiful. I try to narrate a simple story interspersed with dialogues and shlokas that make for an interesting viewing. I have often been asked why I always work on mythological subjects. Well, these subjects make for better stage presentation. Apart from that I can't use the form of Bharatanatyam or Odissi in a contemporary subject; it will simply look out of place.

Having premiered in Mumbai, Delhi, Kolkata and Chennai, *Draupadi* was showcased in several countries as well. Not to forget the smaller towns, where folk theatre and dance recitals have always been a huge draw. Hema's *Draupadi* has been said to have drawn up a five-lakh-strong crowd in the hinterlands on a few occasions. The three-hour-long performance is a universal rage.

It had always been on the anvil, but it took years of meticulous planning and passionate hard work before Hema could finally announce her very own dance academy. Natyavihar Kalakendra opened its gates to the world in 1986 with the dance drama *Meera*, choreographed and co-performed by Bhushan Lakhandri. Born in Darjeeling, Bhushan is a trained classical dancer and went on to become the institute's first choreographer. He recalls, 'I was playing the role of Vishnu in Ramanand Sagar's serial *Ramayana*. Meanwhile, Hema-ji got in touch with me. She wanted to do a dance ballet. I had already played the role of Ram in dance ballets in Delhi. So, playing Krishna in *Meera* was a cakewalk for me. But performing with a mega star like Hema Malini was the only factor that created butterflies inside my stomach. I was very excited. *Meera* was accepted by the viewers and thereafter Natyavihar Kalakendra never looked back.'

Meera was special for another reason, as Bhushan tells me. 'We used to rehearse in the backyard of Hema-ji's bungalow. Esha was a little kid. Hema-ji never treated her like a star kid. So, she used to play and at times sit and watch our ballet. One day, she went up to Hema-ji and whispered, "Mummy, can I play young Meera in your ballet?" Hema-ji was surprised. She never wanted to thrust anything on her kids. But she always wanted her daughters to be trained classical dancers. Hema-ji agreed and Esha was launched as baby Meera in her ballet.'

Most of us were introduced to Natyavihar Kalakendra only in 1986 with *Meera*, but its foundations, in fact, had been laid as early as the 1970s. Born in an environment where dance and the classical arts were entrenched into everyday lives, Hema had opened the academy, albeit on a small scale, in her residential premises itself in Chennai. The purpose was to get the young interested and involved in classical dance forms. Her own stature as an accomplished dancer helped rope in like-minded professionals as trainers, and within no time the academy grew into a purposeful centre for learning. It took almost a decade to open a wing in Mumbai, and with that came the realization that it was perhaps time to adapt and reinvent.

'It was at this time that we realized the need to offer more than solo recitals of Bharatanatyam, Kuchipudi and Mohiniattam. We then began to work on dance dramas,' Hema says, recalling the birth of what would end up being her most successful stage experiment.

Meera, Durga, Ramayana, Mahalaxmi, Geet Govind, Radha Krishna, Yashoda Krishna, Rukmini Parinay, Savitri, Draupadi – Natyavihar Kalakendra went on to produce some of the most stellar dance dramas this country has witnessed. Each ran to packed houses. Hema explains the phenomenal success: 'Dance drama as a concept is really not very well understood by many in India. It is an art form that is a coming together of dance, music and drama. Often, what one sees is that many performers choose to concentrate on the "dance" aspect of the dance drama. The theatrical aspect gets relegated to the background and thus it becomes an extension of a dance presentation. That has to change. It is not enough if one understands only the basics of dance drama. What is equally or perhaps more important is the way it is presented. Presentation would imply everything from stagecraft to lighting, costumes and make-up. The artistes must first understand and then work to coordinate all these aspects with their performance, for any dance drama to make complete sense.'

With decades of industry experience behind her, not just as the czarina of the screens but as a director with a deft and keen eye behind the lens, there couldn't have been a better-suited exponent of the craft. Not to forget the backbreaking effort and scrupulous planning Hema invariably puts into each production. Most of the songs in her ballets are usually rendered by Kavita Krishnamoorthy (who had, incidentally, been launched by Hema's mother), while the music used to be composed by Ravindra Jain. Hema's ballets might all be based on mythology, but they stand out brilliantly in terms of interpretation, execution and treatment. As always, many naysayers have pointed out that what really draws crowds to these performances is her name and not what she brings to the stage, but Hema clarifies that that cannot be the only reason.

'Actually, that factor (her name) is quite important. But once they see the performance, they forget the star and become one with the character that I perform. First, the medium of dance and music that I have chosen for most of our productions so far has been classical. My shows are costly and thousands of people gather to see my ballets. They will get bored with the same "varnam" and "jatiswaram". Instead of showcasing my classical talent I thought of narrating a story instead ... one that would be entertaining. So now I get invites from countries like Dubai, Muscat, Kuwait, America and England. Recently I performed *Mahalaxmi* in Pakistan as well, for Imran Khan's cancer hospital.'

The story of *Meera*, based in the northern belt of India, for instance, is delivered exclusively through the delicate subtleties of Kathak that originated in north India. On the other hand, *Nritya Mallika* (a name suggested by Jaya Chakravarthy) – an amalgamation of life stories – is vibrantly diverse in treatment. One of the stories in it, called 'Triveni', draws from the legend of three of our mighty rivers – the Ganga, the Yamuna and the Saraswati. The story of each river is represented through three distinct styles – Bharatanatyam, Odissi and Kathak.

One of Hema's most successful shows is *Geet Govind* – a representation of the immortal epic poem penned by the great twelfth-century poet, Jayadeva. The piece is of astounding lyrical beauty and is, at heart, a complex exploration of the relationship between Radha and Krishna. It takes us through myriad levels of human dynamics and comprehension, and by choosing to focus on the famous Kanta Padavali section of the poem, Hema made a brave choice. Madhurya Rasa, or the mood of erotic love, is what laces most of this segment; and it takes a genius to translate its truest, deepest meaning for the stage.

Geet Govind was choreographed by Professor Deepak Mazumdar, with Hema in charge of costumes and direction. Showcasing verdant forests, humming bees and languid, moonlit nights, the quality and scale of production were impeccable. It had reviewers gushing over how 'Hema had brought Vrindavan to the metropolitan cities'.

But beating the records of all the others, and by far her most spectacularly popular presentation, is *Durga*. Launched more than a decade ago, Hema still draws full houses for it. There is a certain enigma attached to this particular ballet, with several stories adding to its charm and mysticism. It is said that after watching Hema in this production, Ramanand Sagar was adamant that he would cast her in his serial, *Jai Durga*, in 1998. His son Prem Sagar had declared, 'When you see her ballet *Durga* you realize she is into the role not only physically but even spiritually.' The jewellery she uses for her ballet is kept strictly off limits. 'They vibrate a certain energy,' he had said.

After a particularly successful show in Kolkata, I remember a relaxed and immensely satisfied Hema Malini talking about her favourite production: 'People love to see me as Mother Goddess. I have tried to break the general myth of Durga wearing a red sari; in my ballet, I wear a blue sari. Actually, I play various avatars of Mata. My ballet is mainly based on Durga Saptasati, divided into three segments: Sati, Parvati and Durga. I have worked a lot on the costumes and song recording. Ever since I started performing *Durga*, I have started fasting on Fridays. It has helped me a lot. No, it has nothing to do with the myth; I am not so rigidly tradition-bound.'

Contrary to popular perception, the success and popularity of her dance ballets didn't come easy. During the early years of her tours, Hema took time to get accustomed to the frenetic demands of a dynamic, live performance. Talking about those early years, Bhushan tells me how uncomfortable she was with the quick-change costume system. Invariably, she would ask him to stretch his piece so that she could get more time for a change. 'I always tried to keep her onstage for the maximum amount of time,' he says. 'She is the star, and people are paying tickets for her. Gradually, she understood the importance and organized herself. Now she gets ready even before the other co-dancers. Her costumes, hair, jewellery – everything is always organized. It's a rumour that she keeps her Durga costumes separate as it vibrates shakti. Hema-ji believes in God and so, whenever or wherever she travels, she carries her Krishna and Ma Indira's photographs.'

Bhushan has been with Hema since their very first production of *Meera* in 1986, and though now retired from the stage, he continues to be the chief choreographer in Hema's troupe. 'It's my home,' he says nostalgically. 'We have both worked hard to make Natyavihar Kalakendra a name to reckon with in the dance arena. I still remember two funny incidents that happened with me. Once, during the ballet of *Meera*, Hema-ji asked me to stop the show because she wanted to have a Coke and rest for a while. She forgot that she was not shooting but performing live! Another incident happened during *Durga*. It was our first show. We were all tense. Just before the curtains rose, Hema-ji turned around and started asking me, "*Accha, Bhushan, iske baad kya step hai?* (What's the next step after this one?)" I was really puzzled because I had no time to explain the steps. I told Hema-ji, "*Jo aapko achha lagta hai aap wohi kijiye.* (Perform whichever step you would like to.)" She is such a perfectionist that she would keep thinking about her steps. Even when she was doing her make-up, she would play a small tape recorder and would practise her mudras. I am sorry to say that I haven't seen that much of dedication in any other actor in Bollywood.'

Interestingly, one of Hema's toughest performances, in terms of logistics and costume change, was a piece suggested to her by Ma Indira. Keen on performing for her guru-ji, Hema had planned a private screening of the ballet *Ramayana* for her in Pune. She describes what happened. 'After the show, Ma Indira blessed me and insisted that I should play the role of Ma Durga as well. That stayed with me, and I discussed this with Bhushan. He immediately looked up mythological books and figured that during the war between Ram and Ravan, the former had worshipped Ma Durga to seek her blessings to kill Ravan, who was protected by Lord Shiva. This is popularly known as the akal bodhan (untimely worship). For that particular scene, I had to rush back to my make-up room, change my costume from Sita to Goddess Durga and immediately change back to Sita. That was a huge task for me.'

Not many are aware that Hema's ballets, over the years, have been planned around several charitable causes. Her performances abroad have often been steered towards channelizing funds for health programmes in India. In 2003 alone, Hema toured ten cities in the US with her dance drama *Radha Krishna*. Organized by the American Association of Physicians of Indian Origin (AAPI), the proceeds from the shows went towards setting up thirteen health clinics in India.

Even when the popularity of her ballets soared, Hema didn't stop her classical dance rehearsals. No matter how well appreciated or far-reaching her dance ballets have been, nothing comes close to the pride of place Hema has always reserved for the classical form in its purest and most authentic expression.

'When my guru Kittappa Pillai from Bangalore passed away, I thought it would mean the end of my dance,' Hema tells me, nostalgia writ on her face. Luckily for her, after Kittappa Pillai, she met Professor Deepak Mazumdar who ensured that her 'taalim' continued uninterrupted. Today she is grateful to Professor Mazumdar for being a constant source of guidance. The duo had first performed together on stage in Bangalore – opening their association with the rendition of the *Tulsi Ramayan*. They had been invited by renowned Carnatic vocalist P. Ramaa, who had also lent her voice to the dance recital. Profits from that show were assigned for building a temple in Mysore.

It had always been Hema's dream that her daughters should share her passion for dance. But not one to thrust her aspirations on them, she had left it to fate. When both Esha and Ahaana took up dance as a career choice, it seemed the heavens were on her side. Esha's maiden solo Odissi performance was held in Mumbai at a cultural festival called Rimjhim. Trained under the revered Guru Ravindra Adhibudhi, she proved herself as an artist with vast potential.

But what seemed like the perfect culmination of a long-awaited dream took place in 2003 and I feel privileged to have been a witness to it. The Bengali film magazine *Anandolok* was felicitating Hema with a Lifetime Achievement Award, and as a tribute to her passion she, along with both her daughters, presented their latest classical composition, *Parampara*, a jugalbandi between Odissi and Bharatanatyam. A performance that lasted an hour, it was an evening none present would forget. '*Parampara* is for my satisfaction,' an

Jagannath with Raj Kapoor and Hema during the shoot of *Sapno ka Saudagar*

With her guru Kittappa Pillai in USA

Celebrating her birthday at Juhu Hotel with Dharmendra and Raaj Kumar, among others

With (L to R) Prem Chopra, Navin Nischol and Dharmendra

With Dharmendra and Gulzar on the set of *Devdas*, a film that ultimately didn't get made

Stills from *Abhinetri* (top left),
Razia Sultan (top right) and
Seeta Aur Geeta (left)

The cast of *Satte Pe Satta*

With Ramesh Sippy while shooting for *Sholay*

During the Moscow International Film Festival

Top and left:
Photos from the
audio release of
Dil Aashna Hai,
with Dharmendra,
Shah Rukh Khan
and Divya Bharti

At the mahurat of
Dil Aashna Hai
with Dilip Kumar
and Saira Banu

Hema's different avatars during her dance performances. With Esha and Ahaana in the third photo from left, top row

With director Vikas Desai during the shoot of *Terah Panne*

A still from *Ek Thi Rani Aisi Bhi*

A still from *Tell Me O Kkhuda* featuring Farooq Shaikh, Dharmendra, Esha Deol, Vinod Khanna and Rishi Kapoor

emotional Hema professed after the show. 'I feel good when I share the same stage with my daughters. It's a feeling that can't be expressed in words.'

More recently, in 2012, the three performed together once again – this time in Oslo, Norway, at the tenth Annual Bollywood Festival. The performance was a tribute to mark hundred years of Indian cinema. But what followed left the three of them completely stunned. The Norwegian government felicitated India's 'Dream Girl' with a stamp in her name!

'I am proud of being an Indian, and this only depicts how rich Indians are in culture and arts,' Hema responded with delight. Talking about Esha and Ahaana, she added, 'Both my daughters are happy for me. We did not know anything about the stamp. After our performance, the announcement came as a pleasant surprise for the three of us.'

For a person who has had controversies chase her like a recurring nightmare, one would have hoped that Hema's tryst with dance was the only chapter where she would be spared. Unfortunately for her, it wasn't.

Hema had always been vocal about her dream of building a dance institution in Mumbai. She felt that it was the lack of facilities, not interest, that had led to a decline in the participation of the younger generation in classical dance. When the Maharashtra government finally allotted a piece of land to her, it fell under the purview of the Coastal Regional Zone (CZR). She decided to wait for an alternate allocation.

In 2016, a 2,000-square-metre plot, in the heart of the suburban neighbourhood of Oshiwara, was given to Hema Malini for her dance institute. But before long, she was accused of 'land grabbing' by a Right to Information activist, Anil Galgali. He alleged that a plot worth Rs 70 crore was given to Hema for as little as Rs 70,000. Details of the allotment from the Mumbai Suburban District Collectorate showed that she had been given the land at a paltry Rs 35 per square metre. Eventually, Hema refused to take possession, and that is where the matter ended, but not before creating enough noise and allegations of the government's partiality towards her.

Disappointment rife in her voice, Hema says, 'I don't want to talk about it. I have been asking for a piece of land to build the Natyavihar Kalakendra Dance Academy for the last twenty years. As an artist and a senior member of this film industry, my credentials were questioned by everyone. I wasn't asking for that land for my personal use. The institute would have encouraged the youth to take up classical dance and singing. I wanted to bring teachers from all over India under one roof, to help inculcate the Hindustani tradition among the younger generations. As part of the deal I was supposed to develop a garden and hand it over to the Bombay Municipal Corporation. But I guess everyone suddenly wanted to know why and how Hema Malini was getting that land at such a low price. I was extremely hurt to see senior journalists like Arnab Goswami accusing me on his show without even knowing the facts. For them, it was just another controversy, but for me it was my long-cherished dream. I had applied for a piece of land, and as a performing artist, I think I have some credibility to be able to run an institution on dance. But it seems people had issues with that, and they politicized it.'

16

'Abhi-netri': Hema's Political Journey

Hema was nervous. Her mind went back to the day of her first screen test for *Sapnon ka Saudagar*, when she was all of sixteen. Today, however, the role she had to play was a vastly different one. Having agreed to campaign for her dear friend and colleague, BJP MP Vinod Khanna, she had to address a crowd of a few lakh people. The people of Gurdaspur apparently weren't very pleased with his performance so far. That made her job considerably more difficult, adding to her anxiety. 'Frankly speaking, I never wanted to be a politician. I am an artist, and I would like to maintain that forever,' she tells me, remembering her first-ever public appearance in a political role.

Rediff journalist Neena Chaudhury, who covered the campaign in 1999, wrote:[1]

> It was the mood in favour of the Akali–BJP alliance and his own image as a film star which had helped Khanna trounce five-time winner Sukhbans Kaur Binder in the 1998 elections. On promises to convert this extremely backward border area on the extreme northern tip of Punjab into the Paris of India, Khanna had managed a victory margin of over one lakh votes. But things have changed since then. Now the voters in his constituency, with as many as 1600 villages, including some very difficult to access, look upon him as any other politician. People expect results and seek a

---

1. Neena Chaudhary, 'Unsuccessful with the Moon, Vinod Khanna takes stars to Gurdaspur', rediff.com, 26 August 1999. Source: http://www.rediff.com/election/1999/aug/26punjab.htm

balance sheet of his performance in response to their confidence in
him. Formidable potholes on long stretches of the highways narrate
stories of neglect. Realising his changed image among the people,
Khanna managed to secure the support of 'Dream Girl' Hema
Malini to canvass for him last weekend. The heartthrob of many a
Punjabi, she was specially flown in from Mumbai.

By nature, Hema is an introvert. She has often confessed how, just
because of her body language, she ended up not making too many
friends. For her political role, however, she realized early that she
would have to change many things about her to appeal and connect
to the masses. One of the toughest jobs was to master the art of public
speech and communication.

'I was not sure at all if I would be able to address the crowd. When
Vinod requested me to help him in the campaign, I readily agreed, not
knowing the consequences. But after giving him my word, I developed
cold feet. I was sitting in my house and contemplating my decision. I
remember Amma sitting at a distance. Sensing my predicament, she
called out and asked what was bothering me. After hearing me out,
she told me that I was doing the right thing. She said that as actors,
we have certain social and moral duties too. People had showered
me with love and respect for so many years, and now was the time to
do something for them. In fact, the first speech I had delivered at the
Gurdaspur campaign was written by my mother.'

Hema had clutched onto that paper like her life depended on
it. When Vinod Khanna introduced Hema Malini to the crowd at
Gurdaspur, they broke into loud cheers of 'Hema Malini zindabad!'
'Basanti zindabad!' By then Hema had shed all her fears and was
raring to go. Her opening lines were a winner. *'Mujhe Dharam-ji ne
bheja hai aap sab ke beech. Main Punjab ki bahu hoon…* (Dharam-ji
has sent me here amidst all of you. I am Punjab's daughter-in-law…)'
After a moment's silence, the crowd broke into thundering applause.
Hema knew she had passed the acid test. What she didn't realize then
was that the moment marked the beginning of her political career.

Film stars coming to the rescue of political parties during elections
is not a new phenomenon in India. Going by the craze they command,
election meetings, rallies and voters are driven by their charisma.

The possibility of getting a glimpse or a close encounter with an actor is enough for the people of this star-crazy nation to turn up in hordes. Amitabh Bachchan, Govinda, Preity Zinta, Poonam Dhillon, Reena Roy – many a Bollywood star has flirted with politics, but like everything else she does, Hema took her involvement seriously and soon found herself at the deep end.

One of the most remarkable things about Hema Malini is the extraordinary breadth of her accomplishments. An enduring screen diva, a producer and director for films and television, dancer and choreographer, creative collaborator, magazine editor, a public officer, not to mention her many personal roles – I can think of no other industry name who can match the spectrum of her achievements. At an age when most people would prefer to rest on their laurels, Hema keeps finding something new to engage with and dedicate herself to.

Many of Hema's endeavours have centred on the need to make women's issues relevant. After heading the editorial board for *Meri Saheli* magazine for close to a decade, she was given charge of its English edition, *New Woman*, in 1996. Her maddening schedule didn't allow for too many visits to the office, but she ran a tight ship, ensuring a steady churn of hard-hitting, decisive content. Currently, she also writes a column, 'Meri Zindagi, Mere Anubhav', for a bilingual magazine, wherein she shares anecdotes of her life. 'I had been thinking for many years that I should write a column. But I needed a platform that would give me enough space to tell my story, the way I want to tell it. When my publisher from Pioneer Book Company wanted me to write a column, I readily agreed,' says Hema.

One of her more prestigious roles came to her in 2000, when the NFDC decided to make her its chairperson. The institution had been working without a chief since D.V.S. Raju's retirement in 1993, and the appointment, decided by then Union Information and Broadcasting Minister Arun Jaitley, left Hema pleasantly surprised. 'Heading the NFDC has been a learning experience,' she tells me. 'It was a different kind of experience. I guess I am more relaxed now as compared to when I travel with my dance troupe.'

Hema's term at the NFDC is something she remains proud of and deeply satisfied with. It was one of her first public office posts and she gave it every effort and all the time it warranted. Under her leadership, the NFDC went on to produce six feature films in 2002, providing a major boost to regional cinema: *Hemanter Pakhi* (Bengali), *Tiladaanam* (Telugu), *Vaastupurush* (Marathi), *Maguni Ki Bailgadi* (Oriya), *Bub* (Kashmiri) and *Jameela* (Tamil). *Hemanter Pakhi* won the Best Film Award at the National Awards.

Hema also played an important role in opening avenues to take Indian cinema to the international market. With a focus on non-traditional foreign markets, her efforts paid off handsomely. In an extensive interview to *Screen*, she elaborated,

> The Film Museum in Frankfurt, Germany, has expressed its intention to buy prints of 24 Indian films. We are also planning a Bengali film festival in North America. Japan and Korea have expressed an interest in Indian films. We recently sold twenty-five films to Star Gold. But when it comes down to sheer demand and supply, I must say that *Pather Panchali*, the first from Satyajit Ray's Apu Trilogy, is our best bet so far as our sales in foreign markets go. Richard Attenborough's *Gandhi* and Mrinal Sen's *Bhuvan Shome* also have a very good international demand. But no film can beat *Pather Panchali*.

Hema also fought hard to revive the defunct quarterly publication *Cinema in India*, inviting film-makers and journalists from Hindi and regional cinema to come forward and contribute to the legacy. The then managing director of NFDC, Deepankar Mukhopadhyay, feels that Hema at times went out of her way to promote and help the institute with her presence. 'Once, we wanted to shoot a short promotional film on the NFDC; it was fixed within an hour and without any prior notice,' he tells me. 'When we approached Hema-ji for her cooperation, she happily agreed. Not only that, whenever she used to come to the NFDC office, she would stay throughout the day and sort out all the problems. I was very impressed with Hema-ji's attitude.'

She was also one of the few chairpersons who took an active

interest in the organization's internal workings. With a comprehensive roadmap in hand, Hema played a considerable role in overhauling many of its departments and clearing a lot of the clutter.

Subsequently, Hema joined Pritish Nandy Communications as an honorary member, along with noted film-maker Sudhir Mishra. 'Pritish Nandy and his daughter Rangita used to make good cinema. I knew Pritish since his journalism days. I connected with him because Gulzar saab would often talk about PNC and their films. In fact, his daughter Meghna (Bosky) had directed Esha in the film *Just Married* (2007). So, when they asked me to be a part of their board of members, I agreed. They were the first amongst the corporates in Bollywood. But then they stopped making offbeat films a couple of years back. I really wish they would make such content-driven films again. I remember how Gautam Rajadhyaksha had wanted to direct a cute love story with me and Amit-ji (Amitabh Bachchan). But somehow that film never happened, and he (Gautam) passed away. I still feel that film could be made even today.'

Talking to me about her various roles, Hema admits that it wasn't until her stint as chairperson of the Cine Artistes Welfare Fund of India (CAWFI) that she finally found faith in her capacity to be a manager. The CAWFI is the largest charitable trust in the country, established by the NFDC, providing pension and other benefits to retired cine stars. As its chairperson, Hema put to rest any doubts she may have had in her managerial abilities.

The experiences were well-timed, because soon after, she stepped into a role that pretty much defined the next phase of her life.

For someone who has faced controversies all her life, it is not surprising that her political journey has been marked by several of them.

In Gurdaspur, Hema branded herself as their very own 'Punjab ki bahu' (being Dharmendra's wife). But soon there were protests and complaints questioning the legitimacy of her canvassing for votes while holding office at the NFDC. The Election Commission and the Ministry of Information and Broadcasting were asked to clarify if Hema's campaigning was in contravention of the NFDC charter and the service rules. The Communist Party of India and the National Federation of Indian Women's Delhi unit joined the fight. Under election laws, a government servant holding an office of profit could not participate in electioneering.

Later, in August 2003, Hema was nominated as a Rajya Sabha member, when the BJP government was at the Centre. Immediately after taking oath, Hema declared, 'I shall do all the work for the BJP ... I am here only because of them.' Her nomination didn't go down well with everyone. Some like classical singer Girija Devi mocked her credentials, doubting her ability to be able to do more than a 'Durga pose'.

Hema's oath-taking ceremony at the Rajya Sabha was another episode altogether. She arrived late, after the swearing-in had already started. She had to be back in Mumbai the same day as it was her birthday and I remember her telling me all about it. 'I entered late and immediately rushed inside the House. The oath ceremony had already begun. As soon as I entered, all other members of Parliament looked at me. I felt like Jaya Bachchan in *Guddi*. Remember the prarthana scene, where she was always late? I quickly took the piece of paper and started reading my oath. Once I finished, Sushma Swaraj hugged me. Only then did I begin to relax!'

In her maiden speech in Parliament, Hema laid out her elaborate plans as a bearer of public office. 'I wish to share my long-nurtured dreams with the House today. I have been a witness to the evolution and growth of the Hindi film industry for the last thirty years. This industry is now at the peak of its performance. Our films have been nominated for international film festivals. To further the popularity, I propose that a film museum be set up in Mumbai. In fact, we want to expose our new generations to the great veterans who had contributed immensely in building our film industry in India,' she said.

Her sense of discipline shone through ever since she became a member of the Rajya Sabha, although it did take her a few sessions to get used to the new role. 'I was scared initially,' she says. 'I have never been in politics and when I joined the Rajya Sabha, senior members like Laloo Prasad Yadav, Maya Singh, Pramod Mahajan and Arun Jaitley encouraged me a lot. I didn't even know what I was supposed to do in Parliament. But it was Lal Krishna Advani-ji who used to tell me, "*Aap aate rahiye, achha lagega aur aap khud-ba-khud seekh jayengi* (You just keep attending, you'll like it and automatically learn what to do)." And he was right.'

In the early days, Lalitbhai Mehta, member of Parliament from Gujarat, would help Hema in taking notes. Gradually, she started attending the question-and-answer sessions and emerged as one of the most regular members of the House. Hema has utilized her tenure ever since and has built several auditoriums, schools, roads and hospitals across Bihar, Gurdaspur, Odisha and Mumbai.

Not only did Hema complete her tenure successfully, she remains the most enthusiastic Rajya Sabha member from the Bollywood fraternity. Though Lata Mangeshkar and Dara Singh were also nominated as Rajya Sabha members during her tenure, it was only Hema who made it a point to attend Parliament on a regular basis. She tells me, 'I would take part in the question-and-answer sessions. I would even prepare my speech and deliver it in Parliament. Sushma Swaraj-ji and L.K. Advani-ji were very supportive. They would always tell me that I was probably the most regular MP from the celebrity quota!'

As part of her first project, Hema allocated huge funds towards the development of Juhu beach. 'Different organizations in the Juhu area have been working on various plans for years. It is just that I was lucky to be able to use my MP's fund. I'm glad that I could do something for Juhu where I belong,' she says. She had the food stalls removed so that residents of Juhu could enjoy an unrestricted view of the sea. She also ensured that basic facilities like public toilets for women were in place. A resident of Juhu since 1971 herself, she points out, 'Juhu beach is so famous, but it was being spoilt with hawkers and filth.' According to her, the most difficult task was relocating the hawkers.

When asked what her other projects for Mumbai would be, Hema says, 'I want to do something for the Borivali park (Sanjay Gandhi National Park) problem,' referring to the leopard attacks along the park's periphery. Incidentally, Hema's Goregaon bungalow was once attacked by a leopard that travelled all the way from the National Park. Thankfully, neither Hema (she was in USA) nor any member of her family or staff were home at the time. The security guard spotted the wild cat and immediately informed the police. Meanwhile, the leopard escaped and went into the nearby forest by jumping off the bungalow's compound wall before the forest officials could reach the site.

When Hema was called by her office staff, she gave strict instructions not to harm the animal and to let it go back to the forest. 'We are the ones who encroach on animals' space and then say that they (animals) are attacking us. I want to support the Maharashtra government's project of building a wall around the National Park. Mumbai is the only city with such a large forest space. We have to preserve its beauty,' she feels.

I ask her to share her thoughts on her journey as a Rajya Sabha member. She reflects, 'It was a great experience. We used to get funds worth almost Rs 2 crore annually for development and social work (under MPLADS). The benefit of getting nominated to the Rajya Sabha is that we can disburse the amount for any constituency. I have helped in developing schools in Patna, in Gujarat and contributed towards artistic and cultural activities as well. The problem is that unless someone comes and asks for funds, we cannot use them. But the Government of India does give us the privilege of using our funds for social welfare, which, sadly, hardly any Rajya Sabha MP does.'

Recently, when her former colleague Rekha (who is also a Congress-nominated Rajya Sabha member) helped Hema renovate two schools in Mathura – Hema's constituency – it led to a furore in Parliament. People claimed that Rekha was helping Hema out only because they were friends. Hema tried her best to clear the air: 'It's true that I got Rekha to give a huge sum of money, Rs 47 lakh, for the renovation of two girls' schools in Mathura, but it's not her own money. This is the money from the Members of Parliament Local Area Development Scheme (Rs 5 crore per annum at present, allotted to all MPs) for public welfare. Since I had used up all my funds for Mathura and Rekha was not using her funds, I decided to ask her for some money. The girls' schools are in a very bad condition, and no child can be expected to seek education in a place so shoddy. It's a shame that we are not able to provide decent educational facilities for underprivileged children.'

Even though Hema and Rekha have shared a lasting friendship, getting the funds wasn't a smooth process. She elaborates, 'Though she is my friend, I couldn't call her directly. I had to convince her secretary about the urgency of the situation. Rekha then gave Rs 35 lakh for the Raman Girls' Degree College and another Rs 12 lakh for the Kasturba Gandhi Girls' Residential School.'

On 19 February 2004, less than a year after being nominated to the Rajya Sabha, Hema Malini officially joined the Bharatiya Janata Party. Party President Venkaiah Naidu and general secretaries Pramod Mahajan and Mukhtar Abbas Naqvi were present on the occasion. 'The whole credit of getting me into politics goes to Vinod Khanna and Lal Krishna Advani-ji. My mother genuinely liked the kind of work they (the BJP) were doing for the nation. Personally, I admired Atal Bihari Vajpayee-ji a lot. In fact, in all my campaigns I used to talk about his work and his contribution,' she says. One fine day she realized that she hadn't ever met Mr Vajpayee. 'I told one of his office-bearers that I have not even met him, I should meet him once. When I finally met Atal-ji at his office, he was hesitant to talk. I asked one of the party members why he was not really talking to me. The lady informed me, "Actually, Atal-ji is a huge admirer of your work. He has seen *Seeta Aur Geeta* almost twenty-five times. He has always imagined you as a star, and today, when he is seeing you for the first time in person, he is feeling hesitant!" I felt really good that even someone like Atal-ji admires my work and appreciates it. My respect for him grew much more that day.' Mr Vajpayee particularly remembered watching Hema in *Razia Sultan*. Free from the demands of high security in the days before he became PM, it is believed that Mr Vajpayee, along with fifty or sixty of his family members, would gather at their ancestral home in Shinde-ki-Chavni and watch Hema's films. 'I remember sixty-two of us from my family went to the theatre to watch Hema Malini's *Razia Sultan* at a local movie hall,' the statesman had once said. 'I still recall that while watching the film I had changed diapers of my sister's son!'

Most of us who knew her closely were, in fact, surprised by her decision to join active politics. Once again, the move was mired in controversy. How could a member nominated to the Rajya Sabha by the President of India join any political party? This was against the norms, alleged the Congress. They even threatened to approach the then President A.P.J. Abdul Kalam to address the issue, but the BJP stood its ground in support of Hema. Then party president M. Venkaiah Naidu clarified, 'A nominated member of the Rajya Sabha can join any political party within six months of being nominated.'

True to her character, Hema remained unaffected. Her rallies would be packed. From Dharavi to Goa, wherever she went, the crowds would follow in droves. At the time, she had described her schedule thus, 'I step out for campaigning only after I complete my puja at home, which is something I do every day. But I no longer practise dance and yoga, which are also part of my normal morning routine, because I have to join my team at the helipad by 9 a.m. We use the helicopter every day so that I can cover the maximum number of places. I have a very hectic campaign schedule and I have to be on time or the whole programme will be disturbed. I don't get a chance to speak much. The minute I start my speech, the crowd cheers so loudly that I don't get an opportunity to say much. I find it difficult to speak in remote places because it is so hot and dusty that I tend to choke. I am doing this for the first time. Campaigning is a very tough job for me, but I am managing. I prefer to travel by jeep, because you can see everyone and everyone can see you. Huge crowds, numbering in lakhs, come to see me wherever I go. In Aurangabad, I travelled in a private helicopter. I had four more meetings to attend, but some of them had to be cancelled because when we tried to take off, the crowd came too close to the helicopter. Some of them even caught hold of its rotors so the pilot refused to take off.'

In March 2004, Dharmendra too joined the BJP as a Lok Sabha candidate from Bikaner in Rajasthan. Not just that, he won by 55,000 votes. As it turned out, his victory ended up being fodder for yet another controversy. Reporters started speculating whether Hema would agree to make public appearances with her husband, following the massive controversy the Congress had stoked before the start of the elections regarding their marriage.

To put an end to the rumours once and for all, Hema and Dharmendra sat together for President A.P.J. Abdul Kalam's address to a joint sitting of Parliament. Though they arrived separately at the Central Hall, Hema, looking resplendent in a grey-blue sari, left her seat in the third row to join her husband in one of the rear rows as soon as he walked in.

There is no doubt that Hema's political journey, albeit rocked by controversies, has been a success. Made general secretary of the party in 2010, in the 2014 general elections, she defeated the Mathura incumbent, Jayant Chaudhary (of the Rashtriya Lok Dal), by more than three lakh votes, storming her way into the Lok Sabha.

The idea of taking part in the elections came to Hema Malini as she kept visiting Mathura with her fellow ISKCON members. 'Each time I would visit the place and see the pathetic condition of the people, I would feel bad. Soon the local people and the media started insisting that I should become an MP and change the city for good. That thought stayed with me. So, when I was asked to stand for elections, and given a choice between three constituencies, I selected Mathura,' she explains. 'There was also my love for Krishna – what better way to express that love than to work for the people of Mathura. On a lighter note, another reason for my joining politics was Ahaana. I knew that after her marriage, Ahaana would settle in Delhi with her in-laws and I was thinking of ways to be able to spend more time with her in Delhi. I knew that I was getting into a space that would require me to devote time in Mathura. But I have always taken on challenges in life. Now Ahaana is settled in Mumbai with her son and husband, but my dedication towards Mathura is intact.'

From being a superstar with an entourage at her disposal to slogging it out in the scorching summer heat, visiting village after village for her campaign, it wasn't an easy shift. What didn't help were the many comments that came from her detractors on how she was on a fashion parade and travelled in fancy well-stocked air-conditioned cars. 'What rubbish!' she fumes. 'Just because I am campaigning for the elections doesn't mean I have to roam around without any protection. In summer, if I am carrying glares, umbrellas and water, that's not a luxury. The party provides a car and I have travelled in whichever car I have been provided. In Mathura, after winning the elections, I was the one to buy a Tata Nano, because I felt it would help me travel locally. I have never had airs. But yes, as an artist I need to take care of my body and skin. I am very particular about that and it is no one's business to tell me whether I should maintain myself or not,' she says vehemently.

Hema devoted a total of thirty days for her campaign. She knew that anything more than that would be too much for her to take and she made it a point to let her party workers know this early on. Her presence ensured an almost unprecedented number of women in the audience. 'The star value definitely helped in pulling the crowd. But after that they wanted to hear me out to see if I was making any sense. They would not have voted for me if they had thought that I was only glamour and no substance,' she states.

Winning, however, was only the beginning of Hema's challenges. The Opposition soon started speculating about how much time she would be able to devote to her constituency, given her schedule as a film star. While she was touring the US for her dance concerts, posters declaring the Mathura MP 'missing' began to spring up everywhere. Hema tells me candidly, 'I don't give this too much importance. Those in opposing parties will always say negative things, no matter what you do. What's the point in my just sitting here? I have to go and work, right?'

I decide to follow her on one of her trips to Mathura, to get a first-hand experience. After a 160-km drive in her white Audi SUV from Delhi, Hema heads straight to the BJP office in the small temple town. There is a huge crowd jostling to get a glimpse of the star. Greeting them quickly, she makes her way into a cramped room with a single ineffective air conditioner that rattles loudly. The next few hours are packed with people and their demands and complaints. As she tackles each one meticulously, I watch her, suitably impressed.

This was Hema's first trip to Mathura after her US dance tour. The tour had kept the first-time Lok Sabha MP away from the Budget session of Parliament; she had had zero attendance so far in the new House. 'I had already informed my party that I had a prior commitment for the US dance tour. I had the maximum attendance as a Rajya Sabha MP. Nobody can criticize me for that. I was always there,' she clarifies. During her election campaign, Hema Malini had called Mathura her spiritual home and had promised to spend considerable time there. She is clearly exasperated that despite her efforts for her constituency, she is already being rebuked for her absence. 'It has only just begun. Why are people so restless?' She adds, 'Wherever I went in the US, I spoke to a lot of people who are keen to be connected with Mathura. They have already formed a trust in the US and they want to send money here for a number of projects.'

Ever since her resounding victory in Mathura, Hema has been a diligent custodian of her constituency, visiting the temple town frequently.

Hema's daily routine in Mathura starts with meeting the locals and listening to their grievances. Most of them are about roads, water and electricity. 'Honestly speaking, the condition of Mathura was in the negative when I became an MP,' she says. 'In the last three years, I have brought it to level zero. Now in the next two years you will see growth. In the past sixty years, nothing had been done in Mathura. People thought they would have to live like that for the rest of their lives.'

Talking about her initial days, Hema remembers a particular instance. 'I was travelling in my car in Mathura when I noticed eight to ten old men running behind my car and screaming, "*Gaadi roko, gaadi roko* (Stop the car)." I asked my driver to stop the car. I met them and realized that they wanted to reach out to me to build a small bridge that had broken many years ago. Because of that, children had to take a detour and travel a long way to reach their schools. That was the first thing I got repaired when I came to power, and now I have identified almost 500 such bridges across Mathura which need renovation and reconstruction. I have decided to do fifty bridges every year, so that by the end of my tenure I manage to reach at least

250.' Hema's manager, Janardan, keeps a strict watch over each of their projects and keeps her updated.

As MP, Hema also had to adopt a village under the BJP campaign that asked every political leader to do so. She selected Rawal village in Mathura, known to be Lord Krishna's consort, Radha's birthplace. She has been working hard for its development, but it has not been easy. She recalls how, as part of the Swachh Bharat campaign, she got 100 toilets installed at Rawal. She had put Mr Bindheshwar Pathak, the owner of Sulabh Shauchalaya, in charge of the construction. After the inauguration, when Hema visited the site, she saw that all the toilets had been converted into storerooms. Horrified, when she asked around, a local resident informed her that the men of the village preferred to defecate in the open, since that was the practice they were used to.

When she talks about the incident today, Hema emphasizes the irony of the situation. 'I asked that fellow why they were not using the facility and recorded his response on my phone. He explained how they were having a hard time using the commode as the "pressure" wasn't enough! Which is why they preferred to squat in the outdoors! I told him, "*Arey bhai, tum ko toh bahar achha lagta hoga, par tum ne kabhi ghar ke mahilaon ko poochha unko kya achha lagta hai?* (You might like to defecate in the open, but have you ever asked the women of your house what they like?)" The man kept staring at me in silence. This is the real story of our country. Even if you want to give them a better life, they will not take it.' Hema now visits Mathura every month, just to keep a close check.

The Radha Rani temple in Rawal is in a particularly dismal state. Hema tells me how the head priest has taken over the premises to stay there with his family. Once a tourist spot for pilgrims, today it stands desolate and crumbling. There is a school nearby but its condition is as decrepit. Instead of attending classes, kids are found begging outside the temple. 'It hurts me the most when I see such sights,' Hema tells me despairingly. 'I am reconstructing a school nearby at Rawal for the kids and also getting them a three-week free computer course, as well as free medical check-up. I will soon set up a fully functional healthcare centre, but for that I need good doctors. Now where do I get good doctors in Mathura? Everyone wants to practise in the city because they get to earn more. As an MP, I have limited funds, so I am seeking help from NGOs and corporates that are keen on social work.'

Like most of India, scarcity of clean drinking water is the biggest problem in this region. Hema decided to take it up on priority and installed Kent RO water purifiers (the popular brand she endorses) in the villages of Khaira, Tainte and Rawal. The installation of each machine cost her eighteen lakh rupees. She also needed access to land and electricity – something she had to fight with the village pradhans to get. 'Every day is a learning experience for me. I thought that after fighting with the pradhans everything would be settled and people would now get pure drinking water. But things were not that easy.' These machines operate on smart cards. To get access to water, one needs to swipe their cards. 'They need to pay a bare minimum amount for the water, because that money is used in the maintenance of the machine and for electricity. But people are not educated enough to understand that. Some of them don't know how to use the card. Now I will have to conduct a crash course on this as well. I was shocked when someone from Mathura called and informed me that instead of using the water for drinking purposes, people are bathing buffalos with RO-purified water. Can you imagine?' she says, horrified. It was the thought of village women walking miles with pots on their heads to collect water that had driven Hema to do something for them. But she didn't quite realize the enormity of the challenge.

'People call me up for various things ... they have issues with monkeys, issues with garbage ... they call me for anything that bothers them,' she sighs. 'Some people in Rawal don't even know about the existence of a neighbouring village like Akbarpur, while those in Khaira don't know of Farah, for instance. I have made it a point to understand the workings of each and every village and I personally visit those sites to ensure they function properly.'

In the last few years she has met all kinds of people. While some are naïve and cut off from the world, there's also a fair share of bullies. Talking about the people she encounters on a daily basis,

Hema recollects, 'An old man from Akbarpur, Chitthar Singh, once came running to me. He said he was not getting water, was poor and would die soon at this rate. I asked my office to solve the problem immediately. Then my secretary found out that he was a well-to-do man who owned a dhaba. Moreover, he wasn't experiencing a scarcity but a connectivity issue. Now this was in the gambit of the municipal corporation and not in my power. Yet, they come to me. Some people call me directly and tell me, "*Madam, light nahin jal raha hai* (The lights are not working)." I ask them, *Kaunsa light nahin jalta?* (Which lights are not working?)" The lights that I have installed have my name on them. I asked if he could spot my name and he said no. Then I explained to him that those malfunctioning lights are not installed by me. They are innocent people. They don't understand the difference,' she explains.

'The other day someone called me and threatened that he would commit suicide if he didn't get water for farming. He complained about how the Agra canal water supply had been stalled. I immediately called the agricultural ministry and the minister in charge explained that they hadn't stopped the supply but were cleaning the pipes. So I learn something every day,' she adds. One of the biggest lessons has been not to react before gathering all the facts.

An artiste at heart, Hema has also gone out of her way to provide some form of entertainment to the people of Mathura. 'I am a Bollywood artiste, I wanted the people of Mathura to get a glimpse of the glamour world that I am associated with. I hosted the Mathura Festival there, which was free for all. The two-day festival was anchored by Sonu Sood and organized by Wizcraft. The industry supported me well. Apart from that we have the Karthik festival that happens in the month of Karthik, where I get local dancers to perform. I would also want Pandit Jasraj and Hariprasad-ji to perform in Mathura one day,' she says hopefully.

Mathura has just one big auditorium, the Muktakashi Rangmanch, which is not in the best of conditions. 'Over the last two years I have been slowly renovating the theatre. I managed to gather some funds to develop the place. I recently met Chief Minister Yogi-ji (Yogi Adityanath) in Uttar Pradesh, who has promised to finish the pending work. It should soon be relaunched. We also have the Haridas Sammelan here, for which they used to make temporary pandals. But now I will request them to host the event inside the auditorium,' she shares with a smile. Hema is also planning to develop a theme park that will be named after Pandit Deen Dayal Upadhyaya, who was born in the village of Farah in Mathura. 'I have also proposed a Mathura Gate and a community centre at Farah,' she adds.

So, is she ready for another election? 'I don't mind,' she says. 'Because I will be initiating so many things, I want to finish the work, for which I need some more time. I don't want someone else to get credit for something I have initiated. I have already worked on developing roads worth Rs 100 crore, some of which are done and some are in the process.'

Hema has also bought a house for herself in Mathura and plans to move in this year. 'Mumbai will always remain my first home, though,' she tells me. 'Actually, when I began visiting this place so often because of my connection with ISKCON, people assumed I that had my own house here. I used to stay in a hotel. Even after getting elected I stayed in that same hotel. But now I have my own house where I can stay as long as I want. I plan to give it out to friends and family as a guesthouse when I am not using it.' At the moment, she is on the lookout for a good interior designer to do up the place. 'I don't want to make it fancy; I want to keep it simple. Just like Mathura is,' she says.

Hema's love for Mathura and its people is evident. I have seen how urgently she treats any issue or distress call that comes from there. But like any good work one takes up, here too, she has had to face flak. 'Mostly these are a misinterpretation of facts,' she explains.

In 2014, Hema was criticized for her comment on how widows from Bengal and Bihar should stop overcrowding Vrindavan, the holy city of Uttar Pradesh and home to thousands of destitute women. 'Vrindavan widows have a bank balance, good income, nice beds, but they beg out of habit. There are 40,000 widows in Vrindavan. I think there is no place in the city anymore. A large population is coming (to Vrindavan) from Bengal ... that's not right. Why don't they stay in

Bengal? There are nice temples there. The same is true for those from Bihar,' she had said at a press conference.[2]

She defended her statement, clarifying how no one had listened to her 'actual interview' to the media. In a series of tweets on Twitter, she wrote:

> I haven't said anything that I should be ashamed of. I stand by my statement that they [the widows] should be allowed to live with dignity. It is traumatic to see these poor widows begging on the streets even for their daily existence. Have all of you ever witnessed their plight? Of course, I intend doing what I can to improve their condition but Vrindavan has a space limitation too. State government too should contribute.
>
> For no fault of theirs, they are thrown on the streets and are compelled to beg to survive. Is this fair? Do you think these old women deserve this fate? Also, most are from West Bengal, Bihar and Odisha. My request was to these people to have a more humane approach and look after these poor widows properly. These women were abandoned by their families and put on trains to Vrindavan without any money. Most of them find jobs as maids or turn to begging. Younger ones are also exploited and then left to their fate. Out of the 5000, only 1500 have a proper roof over their heads.[3]

Hema clarifies to me that she hadn't made any communal comment. 'I was not aware of the reason why most widows there happened to be from Bengal. It was only later that someone explained to me that in Bengal there is a tradition (established by the pioneer of the Bhakti movement, Shri Chaitanya Mahaprabhu), in which widows are encouraged to spend maximum time in chanting the Hari kirtan and devoting their last years in serving Lord Krishna. I respect their tradition, but all I am asking is for them to live a decent life. Is that wrong? I have observed that though the ashrams have accommodation

---

2. '"Widows from Bengal, Bihar, Stay There. Why Crowd Vrindavan?": Hema Malini', ndtv.com, 17 September 2014. Source: http://www.ndtv.com/india-news/widows-from-bengal-bihar-stay-there-why-crowd-vrindavan-hema-malini-667204

3. 'Hema Malini defends her remarks on Vrindavan widows', *The Hindu*, 18 September 2014. Source: http://www.thehindu.com/news/national/other-states/hema-malini-defends-her-remarks-on-vrindavan-widows/article6422898.ece

facilities for 200 widows, only eighty people live there while the rest are living on the streets. I don't think they want to stay in ashrams because there are a lot of restrictions, just like a hostel. I think they want to lead a free life, which is why they roam the streets. Now what can I say? Many ashrams are also not in a good state. I am willing to redevelop those, provided someone helps.'

Just when this controversy seemed to get resolved, Hema landed herself in another. This time she was targeted by the media for an 'untimely' tweet where she mentioned that she was heading out for the shoot of *Ek Thi Rani Aisi Bhi* on Madh Island. Back in her constituency, Mathura was burning. Twenty-four people, including two police officers, had been killed and over forty people injured in clashes during a drive to evict illegal occupants of a piece of land in Jawahar Bagh. The order for the drive had been passed by the Allahabad High Court. The evictions, carried out by the police, faced severe opposition from the Azad Bharat Vidhik Vaicharik Kranti Satyagrahi. More than 374 people had been arrested in connection with the clashes. News channels didn't waste any time in picking on Hema's 'misplaced sense of priority'. Soon celebrities like Chetan Bhagat joined in the criticism.

Hema's cousin Prabha Raghavan (Pappu) defends Hema's predicament: 'Hema was shooting for *Ek Thi Rani Aisi Bhi* with Vinod Khanna saab. He had not been keeping well, and the director somehow managed to get combined dates from Hema and Vinod-ji. Hema had just returned from Mathura and was about to join the shoot. Whatever happened was unfortunate, but to blame Hema for being insensitive and irresponsible was uncalled for. The moment she started getting calls from Mathura, she immediately tweeted and condemned the act. I accompanied Hema back to Mathura. She was anxious to reach the site at the earliest. But the entire place was cordoned off by the police. Both Hema and I waited outside, for almost an hour or so, but cops didn't allow us in. It was a state administrative issue, but everyone attacked Hema because she is the MP of Mathura. One needs to understand that Hema was shooting for that film because she didn't want the producer to lose money. She also knew about Vinod-ji's health condition. Keeping everything in mind she agreed to finish the shoot.'

17

Experiments with Spirituality

Ever since she was a child, Hema Malini had always been inclined towards religion. Brought up in an orthodox Iyengar family, she, along with her brothers, had been taught to offer prayers and do the aarti every day. Hema makes it a point to take time out for some daily meditation and yoga. Talking about a habit that was inculcated from a young age, she says, 'It was never forced on us. I have been a bhakt of Krishna since my schooldays. I love worshipping God. I have a room for my gods and goddesses in my Juhu bungalow as well as in my house in Madras. They are the source of my energy. I am not a fanatic, but I love my culture and my tradition. I have an amazing collection of Ganeshas and Krishna idols back home.' One can sense the dedication in her voice as she talks about it.

For Hema, dance had always been more of a form of devotion. She believes that much of the love and respect she feels for the divine has been strengthened through her dance recitals. 'I agree,' she says when I asked her. 'Bharatanatyam is mainly based on Hindu shlokas and hymns. The music makes me feel pious. I guess that's the reason why my father insisted on me playing characters based on the gods and goddesses on stage. It gives you a spiritual elevation. Have you ever noticed that most dancers are religious? Because dance is as good as offering prayers to God. So, I don't devote much time on puja, but on something constructive like dance, which is as good as puja.'

On my first visit to her Juhu bungalow (twenty years ago), I remember noticing her temple. It was a neatly done puja-ghar – a sacred space Hema has always been very particular about. If you hadn't had a bath you were not allowed inside. The fragrance of sandalwood incense and ghee is still fresh in my memory. Spirituality has always been an important part of Hema's life. 'The need for it comes in everybody's life and one has to work very hard towards it,' she says, going back in time to 1974, when she was the number one actress in the industry. The pressures were unforgiving and life seemed to be moving at an impossible pace.

She recollects, 'I used to feel like crying when producers would come to my house. My only reaction used to be: another year of my life gone. Also, being at the top is never easy. You realize your life is not your own, your fans expect so much from you and you have to deliver, it becomes a responsibility. I was shooting two to three shifts a day, day after day, dubbing at the same time and I had no life. It was then that I met my Guru Ma, Indira Devi, and she gave me a lot of strength. I can't express how my interaction with her made me see life in the proper perspective. I could live without letting things outside of me bother me. I got direction in my life. Today I enjoy my work, the creativity that goes into it and I am at peace with myself. I think everybody needs a guide.'

Hema always carries Ma Indira's photograph with her at all times. 'Sometimes I feel close to God, maybe because of my guru. She taught me a lot. She became the greatest influence on me and helped me become what I am today. When you are in films you're caught in a situation where you have nowhere to go. You're young, you are restless, there are so many things happening around you. Someone has to put you on the right track and that is something only a guru can do – a perfect guru. I believe everyone needs a master to guide him or her. What else is there to life? It is all so temporary and meaningless. After a guru comes into your life, you are able to withstand everything and you keep moving forward with happiness. You feel thankful to the Lord for whatever happens.'

She tells me a bit more about her Guru Ma: 'Guru Ma Indira Devi met her guru, Sri Dilip Kumar Roy, in October 1946. She was drawn to him by his innate power of truth and sincerity. The first time she laid eyes on him, a current shot up from the base of her spine to her neck. She knew at once that he was her guide, with the same conviction that she knew that God exists. It was in Pondicherry, where she met Sri Aurobindo (Sri Dilip Kumar Roy's guru) for the first time, that she had realized that meditation came naturally to her. She just sat still and closed her eyes and peace entered her mind. The art of meditation, which I still practise, has been inculcated by my Guru Ma.'

Hema's sister-in-law, Prabha Chakravarti, elaborates on Hema's tryst with spirituality. 'She is extremely spiritual. She always carries her idols for puja, lights an agarbatti and does her puja even if in a hotel room. She makes it a point to recite the Hanuman Chalisa and a few other shlokas. We are disciples of the Hari Krishna Ashram of Ma Indira Devi in Pune. She started going to Pune regularly and sometimes I've had the privilege of going with her to meet Ma. Even her children are into the same practice of praying. Whenever Hema travels alone or with her family, she chants "Jai Hanuman-ji ki jai and "Satguru Dada-ji Ma Ki Jai". It is something that is integrated into her lifestyle. It is her spiritual strength that actually keeps her going even during adversities.'

Anyone who meets Hema is particularly astonished by her level of mental and physical strength, especially during her complex dance performances. Watching her on stage – a tornado of energy and vitality – is a lesson in how far commitment and dedication can take you. Apart from learning the long-term benefits of yoga and meditation at the Sri Sri Ravi Shankar ashram, Hema is also a second-degree Reiki master and a regular at Art of Living courses. All these have played their part in bringing a rare equanimity to her inner self. Hema quotes Sri Sri Ravi Shankar, 'In life, strength comes along with challenges. If we focus on the strength instead of the problems, we will become stronger. All the problems of the world are due to narrow-mindedness – a lack of a broad world vision and stress or lack of personal peace. A truly stress-free person will never harm anybody.'

Knowing her to be a devout follower of Krishna, I am not surprised to learn that Hema is also a life member of ISKCON (International Society for Krishna Consciousness). She tells me of the time she had performed her ballet, *Radha Krishna*, at the ISKCON auditorium on Janmashtami. 'Dancing on that day is a spiritual experience. Onscreen, I have to play so many roles, but in front of Krishna, I can be myself.'

Hema's association with ISKCON began with its cultural wing, the Bhakti Kala Kshetra. Founded in 1978, its purpose was to promote the arts and Vedic culture. Since its inception, the Bhakti Kala Kshetra has hosted some of the most revered names in classical dance and music, including Pandit Bhimsen Joshi and Pandit Hari Prasad Chaurasia. And, of course, Hema Malini.

The vice-president of Bhakti Kala Kshetra, Surdas Prabhu, tells me more about Hema's involvement with the organization: 'Hema-ji is born with the calibre to portray the strongest women characters from the Vedic history of India. She performs her ballets based on Krishna and thus imparts knowledge of the Bhagavad Gita to those who are unaware of this text. All her ballets – at the script level – are flawless because learned persons from ISKCON guide her. Hema-ji has performed charitable shows all over India and in countries abroad, like New Zealand, Nairobi and Australia. We even had a six-day Hema Malini Dance Festival in Mumbai, where she presented all her ballets. Being a Vaishnavite, she understands the meaning of devotion. She has been associated with ISKCON for the last twenty-five years.

'Hema-ji would stage her ballet during Janmashtami every year as her offering to God. Once, I had asked her about this and she replied, "Some offer agarbatti, some coconut and some flowers. I am a mere dancer and what better can I offer to my Lord other than myself and my dance?" She maintains her sanctity through her work. She selflessly serves Lord Krishna, so she gets everything on a golden plate.'

Hema has kept up the tradition of performing her ballet at the ISKCON auditorium every year on Janmashtami. 'I don't even remember how long I have been doing this as a ritual,' she says. 'In fact, I still remember that the first time I wanted to do *Radha Krishna* as a ballet, I faced a financial roadblock. I had just finished *Meera* and *Ramayan*, and I didn't have enough money to record songs for *Radha Krishna*. But somehow, people came forth and I managed to finish the production work on time. While you might say it was my destiny, I feel it was divine intervention that made it possible. Since then, I have continued to do something or the other on Krishna.'

Hema visits the ISKCON temple regularly. From relishing the special 'prasadam' served there to chanting the Krishna Mala to taking part in social service activities, the Rath Yatra and the 'Food for Life' programmes, she does it all. 'I remember her visit to Kolkata during the Rath Yatra in 1996,' says Surdas Prabhu. 'Our idea was to present the most popular idol of Indian cinema in front of Lord Jagannath. It was a conscious effort to encourage people in the path of Krishna Consciousness. When they saw Hema-ji and Indian cricket captain Sourav Ganguly on the chariot of Lord Jagannath, they started screaming "Basanti, Basanti." But when they saw how Hema-ji was also cleaning the path of the chariot with a broom, like any other servant of the Lord, they fell silent. That's when they understood the value of devotion.'

Hema is not the first from the world of Bollywood to be associated with ISKCON. Actors such as Vyjayanthimala, Meenakshi Sheshadri and Rani Mukerji are followers too, but none have matched her level of participation. 'Not just her ... her mother, brothers, bhabhis, Dharam-ji and her daughters also visit the temple,' Surdas says. 'In fact, Esha and Ahaana had their maiden stage performances at the ISKCON auditorium during the Rath Yatra. This reminds me of the Bhagavad Gita, where the Lord says, "*Evam parampara praptam imam rajasrayo viduh*", which means, "The supreme science flows from one generation to another". Hema-ji's belief and bhakti in the form of dance has wonderfully flown in her daughters' veins. Even Dharam-ji comes with Hema-ji. He is not a regular visitor, but he is also religious. He is a believer of the Arya Samaj.'

Hema's association with the temple and the organization has only grown over the years. When Esha was to get married to Bharat Takhtani – her childhood friend – Hema decided on ISKCON as the main wedding venue. 'I wanted a temple wedding for Esha; that was what I had dreamt of for my marriage. I wanted to fulfil my dream through my daughter's wedding, and why not?' says Hema. 'I wanted Krishna and Radha to be a part of the wedding, so we had the

traditional shehnai, along with the beautiful flute.' A song, 'Krishna
Rukmini', was specially composed and sung by a group of singers at
the venue. For her younger daughter Ahaana's wedding with Vaibhav
Vohraa, Hema did the same but on a smaller scale. 'Ahaana wanted
a bigger venue because Vaibhav's family members and friends were
coming from Delhi. So, we had the garland exchange ceremony at
the temple, and they were blessed by Surdas-ji, after which the rituals
took place at the ITC Grand Maratha,' she says.

Hema Malini follows a strict and austere lifestyle. Her sense of
discipline spills into every aspect of her life, her diet being one of
them. I ask her about her eating habits. 'It is a misconception that I
survive on idlis and dosas,' she tells me emphatically. 'Well, idlis are
fattening so I prefer poha and vadas. I have maintained my father's
tradition of keeping an Iyengar cook. The bhog for my bhagwan is
also prepared by a Brahmin cook. In spite of all this, I am not a fanatic.
I am very flexible; in fact, I have to be. In our profession, you can't
afford to be so fastidious. I love dahi, dal, one cup of rice, chapattis.
I believe in eating and not dieting. Your body is your temple, why
pain your body? I used to fast once a week because it used to keep
my entire system under control. Actually, I saw most of my dancers
observing the Santoshi Mata and Vaibhav Laxmi Mata fast on Fridays.
Even I wanted to keep a fast on Fridays. I did that for many years.
Recently my doctor asked me not to fast, and to have small meals at
regular intervals, so I had to stop.'

Not a party person, on the rare occasions when she does make a
brief appearance, Hema sticks to salads and desserts. 'Those are my
favourites and it stops me from gaining weight. At this age, if you put
on weight, it is very difficult to reduce. Your body metabolism changes
and it is an effort to lose weight. So, I am quite conscious. Fruits and
juices are like medicine. If you don't want to end your life with doses
of tablets, it's better to have fresh fruits for breakfast. I take care of
my health, because that's my profession. I don't believe in anything
artificial. Whatever I did, whatever I am doing and whatever I will
do is natural. My mother used to say, "Don't work on the mastery of
God. Just keep it clean and pure." I still maintain those words.'

While most vegetarians tend to get judgemental about the eating habits of non-vegetarians, Hema, has never had those hang-ups. Bhushan Lakhandri tells me, 'Hema-ji is a strict vegetarian but she would never fuss if someone ever had non-vegetarian food around her. I am a hardcore non-vegetarian and love fish. She would never grumble on that issue.' He also shares an interesting episode when Hema practised Reiki on him: 'It was just before the show of *Draupadi*. I had a severe headache. I was feeling very irritated. Suddenly I felt two palms being placed on both sides of my head. I looked up and saw that Hema-ji was chanting something under her breath and I also closed my eyes for a couple of minutes. Thereafter she went away and I soon realized that my headache had gone. I think Hema-ji has learnt Reiki to that level where she can teach it and practise it on others. She also introduced me to her Reiki guru-ji, a young man from Manipur, in Kolkata, after the *Draupadi* performance.'

Hema's spiritual outlook to life also extends to her compassion for animals. A few years ago, a police station in Mumbai found its ground-floor office flooded with bouquets. They were gifts from Hema Malini to some of the officers who had rescued a truck-full of pregnant buffaloes, headed to a slaughterhouse. A few hours after the rescue, almost all the buffaloes delivered their calves. A die-hard animal-lover, Hema has always been vociferously campaigning against the illegal slaughter and trade of animals. She speaks animatedly about another time when a similar raid had been conducted at multiple locations simultaneously. 'More than 250 goats were crammed into a single truck permitted by law to hold only forty. The animals had broken legs and severed spinal cords. My heart goes out to these poor animals and I am deeply grateful to these wonderful officers for their actions.'

Following her mother's footsteps, Esha Deol is also a staunch vegetarian. Hema is extremely excited when recalling the time Esha was voted the 'Hottest Vegetarian Alive' in a contest conducted by the People for Ethical Treatment of Animals India (PETA), in August 2003. During her promotional tour for *Koi Mere Dil Se Poochhe*, Esha had spoken fondly about her first pet: a lizard! She had caught a baby lizard, put it in a jar and had been very possessive about it. Hema, on the other hand, had constantly tried to get rid of it, but had failed. When she finally did, the little girl was not happy. It took a lot of explaining on Hema's part about how lizards were not meant to be pets before Esha finally relented. To make up for her loss, she was gifted her first puppy.

Years later, while in Bangkok for a shoot, Esha spotted a stray puppy and sneaked it into her hotel room. 'She was dirty and I spotted her on the street, where they were selling puppies. I fell in love with her and wanted to bring her home. She was so tiny that I managed to hide her inside my long leather jacket and took her to my room. I would bathe her, clean her and take her with me on my shoot. Finally, when we wrapped up our shoot and I had to come back to Mumbai, I realized that it would be difficult to take the puppy on a flight. That's when I called Mom, and she was so taken aback! Her instant reaction was anger, because she knew how difficult it was to get pets on international flights. But I convinced her and then I almost begged at the immigration counter, and after all that drama I finally managed to get Piccola home!'

Hema, on her part, has always kept pets at home. 'I don't like caged birds. I always set them free. Dogs are free and they stay with you like family members. I always used to have a dog, since my early days in Mumbai. Even Dharam-ji is very fond of animals. Now, when most of the time he is resting in the farmhouse in Lonavala, I visit him and we spend time with all the ducks, hens, birds, dogs, cows and horses. It's so nice to see them running around in a free space,' she says with a smile.

Dharmendra, in fact, has been encouraging people to take up organic farming. He grows his own fruits and vegetables in his farmhouse. 'The milk that we consume every day comes from the Lonavala farmhouse,' Esha tells me. 'Can you imagine that someone actually drives all the way from Mumbai to Lonavala every day just to get fresh cow's milk? This system was started by my papa when we were kids. Now that I am pregnant and Ahaana has had her baby, he insists that we should drink only pure milk and not the (packaged) ones with preservatives.'

Listening to Hema talk about her life, I almost feel a sense of calm. Perhaps it's the energy she radiates; perhaps it's her innate sense of peace. 'How do I maintain serenity?' She smiles at my question. 'Well, frankly speaking, I have no answer for that. Many people tell me that. I think I'm a little different in a sense that a lot of things don't affect me. Many things happen around me but I don't let myself be affected. I continue living my life. Maybe my guru guides me…'

It is perhaps this sense of self that helped her through a difficult phase in the latter part of her career. Though she had agreed to switch to character roles with films like *Himalay Putra* (1997) and *Hey Ram* (2000), Hema realized that these films were doing nothing for her. 'I was not getting the kind of roles I was expecting. I did those films mostly out of less or no choice. I could never say no to certain people, and Vinod Khanna was one of them. When he wanted me to play Akshaye's mother in the film (*Himalay Putra*), I agreed. Even in *Hey Ram*, when Kamal Haasan narrated my role, I knew the length would be minuscule. But I agreed to do the film because it was a period drama. I wanted to experiment as an actor. But unfortunately, these films didn't work and my work in them went unnoticed. That's when I decided to take a break from Bollywood,' she explains.

When Hema went on a break, nobody knew what to make of it. But what she was planning was a comeback to beat all others … and in 2003, she kept her promise.

18

Still at the Top

A close look at box-office numbers will tell you how Hema Malini still holds the record for retaining the top slot amongst Hindi film actresses for the longest duration. Her career graph is proof of how one star bucked every trend to stay on top of her game. In 2012, news channel NDTV conducted a poll amongst 30,000 people from across the country, asking them to name the top five greatest Bollywood actresses of all time. Hema Malini emerged a clear winner, leaving behind the likes of Kareena Kapoor, Katrina Kaif, Madhuri Dixit, Kajol and Rekha. Veteran journalist Prannoy Roy of NDTV said, 'Hema-ji has been voted by the public, and that says it all.' And yet, despite the number of films she has starred in and their phenomenal success rate, Hema has won the Filmfare award only twice – for *Seeta Aur Geeta* in 1973 and the 'Lifetime Achievement' award in 2000. The year 2000 also saw her being conferred the fourth-highest civilian award in the country – the Padma Shri.

Hema was characteristically candid in her speech after receiving the Lifetime Achievement award:

I think I deserved awards for my roles *in Sholay, Prem Nagar, Lal Patthar, Khushboo, Meera, Rihaee* and *Ek Chadar Maili Si*. I guess I should look at this trophy as an all-in-one for my work in films. I still have a large fan following all over the world and am often asked why I'm no longer working in films. But there's no inclination to make time for ordinary mother roles in movies. Give me something worthwhile and I'll go out of my way to accommodate it ... Though some may look at this award as a signal for retirement, I still have a long way to go. It's certainly not over for me.

Her words were prophetic. It was only a matter of time before Hema Malini returned to the big screen with one of the biggest hits of the new millennium.

The script for Ravi Chopra's *Baghban* (2003) was thirty years old. His father, the legendary film-maker and producer B.R. Chopra, had wanted to make the film with Dilip Kumar and Waheeda Rehman, but it didn't work out. Decades later, his son took over the project, knowing well how dear this one had been to his father. In an interview to rediff.com (1 October 2003), Ravi had shared,

> I was shooting for my debut film, *Zameer*, with Amitabh and Saira Banu. I needed a big garden and we just couldn't find one. That's when Dilip [Kumar] uncle loaned us his garden. During the shooting, Dad and Dilip uncle were sitting and chatting. That's when he narrated the script to Dilip uncle, who loved it. But Dad was busy with other films and Dilip uncle wanted to start another film first ... Dad was supposed to direct it but he fell ill. Then, we got busy with the television series, *Mahabharat*. Later, I decided *Baghban* should be our comeback film. Since Dad was still ill, he asked me to direct it ... I guess I was fated to direct it.

A family drama that struck a chord universally, *Baghban* explored the dynamics between ageing parents and their grown-up children. Raj Malhotra and his wife Pooja (played by Amitabh Bachchan and Hema Malini respectively) have been ideal parents – their lives revolving around bringing up four children, often at the cost of their own dreams and ambitions. In the autumn of their lives, when they find themselves emotionally and financially dependent on their offspring, their children have no time for them. The disappointment is heartbreaking; the pain is real. In the end, it is their adopted son who rises to the occasion.

For Hema, this was her second film with Ravi Chopra after *The Burning Train* in 1980. About Hema's performance in the film, he had said in the same rediff.com interview, 'When I told Hema-ji I wanted to do a film with her again, she was surprised. I narrated the subject and she said she never thought she would get a role like this. It's a role of a lifetime! It is difficult to get it when you are young. To get it when you are old is even better. No actor could have refused it. She has improved tremendously. I couldn't believe it. I thought Amit-ji might leave her behind as he is such a fantastic actor. But she walked with him step-by-step throughout the film.'

One of the main reasons why Hema had stayed away from the arc lights for so long was her refusal to conform to set trends. She had always been vocal about her reservations against taking up the stereotypical 'mother' roles just because her age, according to industry belief, warranted it. She was waiting for an offer that would be deserving of a comeback and with *Baghban*, she got just that.

One must give credit here to both Ravi and Hema for putting an end to a prevailing screen stereotype. Pooja Malhotra was a refreshing departure from the self-sacrificing, pitiful mother figure Hindi cinema had been selling from time immemorial. Here was a woman with a spine of steel, unafraid to speak her mind or shake a leg, all the while looking like a million bucks.

Baghban was a mega hit and Hema got most of the accolades, bagging a Best Actress nomination at the Filmfare and Screen awards. Manjula Negi of the *Hindustan Times* wrote:

> Hema Malini not only imbues her character with believable traits, but also carries forward the plot alongside Bachchan. Not for a moment in the tearjerker does she let one feel that the role is overdone. While Bachchan cries at the drop of a hat, Malini takes her time about it and is more convincing as a woman who understands her family better than her husband … She is finally the one to convince her husband that it may be the wisest decision as well … Hema Malini is the only actress of her time (apart from, say, a Rekha) who has defied conventional aging. Despite her dismal accent – even after all these years – Hema Malini hasn't lost her loyal fan following and remains one of the very few stalwarts of Indian cinema whose fans haven't moved on to other heroines. In fact, she has simultaneously gained a few more even in the current

generation. And that's saying a lot for short public memory for an industry, which churns out more than 900 films annually.

Hema, naturally, was thrilled with the response to the film. Asked about how she has managed to maintain the image of a still-glamorous star, she retorts, 'What image? I don't have to live up to some image which someone has built. What I am is my natural self. So, I don't have to fake anything. I wish other actresses too would do that. I neither worry about my age nor my wrinkles. I don't have worry lines because I don't keep looking at the mirror worrying when I am going to get them.'

Baghban put the spotlight back on well-conceived meaty roles for senior actors and actresses. The following year witnessed two senior actresses nominated in the Best Actress category at the Filmfare 2004 awards – Hema Malini for *Baghban* and Shabana Azmi for *Tehzeeb* – quite a feat for an industry that relegates actresses to bit or mother roles the moment they cross a certain age.

But life as always has its way of balancing out joy and sorrow. Close on the heels of the triumph of *Baghban*, came the death of Jaya Chakravarthy, who passed away in 2004. For Hema, life would never be the same. Throughout the greater part of Hema's life – and through her years as the number one star of Hindi cinema – Jaya had wielded an influence and control that was absolute and unquestioned. For the outside world, the dominance might have seemed excessive but for Hema, it was a manifestation of the solidarity and instinctive understanding they shared. She never had any reservations in obeying Jaya, not even when she became a mother herself.

Jaya had been an accomplished artist in her own right. A professional painter, writer and film producer, her death brought together the worlds of art and cinema in shared grief. Hema stayed composed for days and allowed the floodgates to break only after the last guest had left.

'*Amma, it was your dream to see me where I am today. I know that you are not with me physically, but you are with me always … as mothers never die.'* This was her first public statement after her mother's demise and the only time we saw in her a trace of vulnerability.

No matter how imminent, one is never really prepared to face the loss of a loved one, especially parents. Jaya had been suffering for a while, so Hema was more prepared for her demise than V.S.R. Chakravarti's death in 1978 that had left everyone visibly shaken. Hema had taken years to fully come to terms with it.

Prabha – Kannan's wife – shares with me the circumstances of his passing away, something the family still finds difficult to talk about. 'A fan from Pakistan sneaked into Hema's make-up room and a girl spotted him there. He took out a knife. The girl screamed and my father-in-law got very upset and started calling the police. He did not know who it was. Hema was doing three shifts then and was out for a shoot. My father-in-law, who was a heart patient, suffered a heart attack after this incident and collapsed. We informed Hema. She rushed home. Hema was totally heartbroken that just someone wanting a glimpse of her had resulted in such a loss in her life. That was the first time I saw Hema crying. Now I realize why Hema used to keep telling me: "You don't know of the sacrifices I've had to make to be a star."'

Hema speaks to me about the incident. 'It was like a nightmare for me. Now that I think about it, I don't even know who that person was or what was his name. The police arrested him, but I don't know if he was finally released or jailed. You think I should find out?' she asks.

Hema was extremely fond of her father. She remembers how, during his last days, he would often tell her, 'I had a dream where I am pressing Lord Vishnu's feet and telling him to take care of my chinni (little girl).' Those words would make her quickly change the subject, after reassuring her Appa that nothing untoward would happen.

As fate would have it, Hema's father wasn't around to see his daughter tie the knot. Two years after his death, when Hema married Dharmendra, Jaya went through a lot of turmoil, knowing that her husband had never really approved of the relationship. Hema urged her mother to seek advice from Indira Ma. 'Amma asked Guru Ma, who told her that Dharam-ji would be ideal for me and that Amma should not think that I was going against anyone's will. Nothing happens without His divine intervention, so I should follow the course of life, as it comes,' she says, adding that she has never spoken about these incidents to anyone till date.

It was around this time that Hema decided to redo her bungalow in Juhu, which she had built and moved into in the early 1970s with her parents. The refurbishing had been long overdue especially after its lower floors had got damaged in the deluge in 2005. 'All my valuable papers, awards and even my Padma Shri certificate were damaged. The first floor was flooded with water, the electrical lines were damaged too,' Hema recollects.

Hema fondly remembers how Jaya had been emotionally attached to the house. 'She'd say, "This is my house, I'm going nowhere."' Hema stayed on with her mother, watching the house decay around her. It was only after Jaya Chakravarthy passed away that work on redoing the house could begin in earnest.

'I miss my mother a lot here,' Hema says. 'You need your own people to help you with everything. At one time the house used to be bustling with so many people…' Her voice trails off as her mind goes back to fond memories of the old days. 'But I'm happy with how life has shaped up for me. Every time I am done with one part of my life, another door, another opportunity, opens up on its own.'

19

Esha's Tale

'I was a little slow as a kid,' says Esha Deol, when asked about her earliest childhood memories. Growing up in a family that would often make headlines wasn't easy. She remembers how Hema's make-up room, often bustling with hairstylists and make-up dadas, used to be right opposite her room. Some of her most vivid memories are of the early mornings when she would get ready for school while Hema would simultaneously ready herself for a day of shooting. 'That section of the house would be the busiest in the mornings. Mom would come with me in the car and drop me till the school gate. I used to go to Besant Montessori then. She would religiously drop us almost every day till the tenth standard, irrespective of her professional engagements. I would notice other mothers dressed normally and how mine was always with these rollers (in her hair) or half-done make-up. She would obviously not get out of the car, because that would create chaos outside the school gate. I think those were my earliest realizations that my mom was not a "regular" mom,' she says.

A little girl trying to wrap her head around these strange things, Esha didn't particularly like the word 'shooting'. 'I would stare at her long hair and her wig for hours,' she continues. 'I always wanted a wig for myself and I remember she actually got one made for me when I was little. I used to love her lipsticks and often ended up breaking a few while playing with them. When I used to ask her, "Where are you going, Mamma?", she would tell me that she was going for "shooting". I didn't know what that (the word) meant but I knew it meant she wouldn't be back before 8 at night. It meant she wouldn't be home when I got back from school. So obviously, that word didn't mean happy things for me!'

Hema had reduced the number of films she was working on by then, more out of compulsion than choice. The roles on offer were not the best and she realized that her position at the top of the charts was getting slippery. Esha recalls, 'Obviously, there were days when she didn't have to go for shooting. These were rare because I remember she was working all the time. But even on the days she was not shooting she would have some party or some social commitment in the evenings. As a kid, I learnt to predict her schedule through her nails. Whenever her nails were painted, it meant she would head out in the evening! I remember a rather funny incident. She had a guest over and she was talking to that person when she suddenly felt something cold on her feet. When she looked down she saw me sitting there with a nail-polish remover. I was quietly taking off the paint from her toenails, hoping that no nail polish would mean she wouldn't end up going out!'

Growing up with two superstars as parents, it is not surprising that she wanted to be one too from as early as she can remember. Esha's friends' circle also had its share of 'star kids' – almost every one of them with similar aspirations. But for Esha, there was one more factor that played a deciding role in her career choice – the film *Seeta Aur Geeta*!

'In her (Hema's) room she used to have a huge collection of VHS tapes,' she remembers. 'When I grew a bit older she asked me to watch *Seeta Aur Geeta* to understand more about her work and what she did during shoots. I got completely hooked to that film and ended up watching it every day! Even now I can tell you every scene and dialogue from that movie backwards. I would make our house help and caretaker dress like Raka and Chachi and I would dress up like Geeta. From playing "house-house" we moved on to playing "Seeta Aur Geeta". That's when I gradually started understanding what shooting meant. I used to watch some of her other films too but I didn't like watching her with other actors. I used to avoid those films. While watching *Chitrahaar*, if they played any song starring my mom along with a co-actor, I would ask Amba (Jaya) to turn the TV off.'

Esha studied at Besant Montessori School, Juhu, till the second standard. She failed her class that year and was transferred to Jamnabai Narsee, from where both sisters completed their school finals. 'Besant Montessori was a very nice school and the best part was that they didn't give us any "bhaav"' as star kids,' she recollects. 'I repeated second standard, because I failed in my earlier school. Actually, I used to travel a lot with my parents and would miss my classes. Mom would always take me for outdoor shoots. I was too young to even understand what failing a class meant. That was the first time my father shouted at me. I didn't even realize what had happened or why he was yelling. I remember crying a lot because my father had never shouted at me till that day. Our caretakers use to try and scare us, though, by saying, "*Khana nahin khaogey toh papa ko bol dungi!* (If you don't eat I'll tell your papa)."'

While children don't usually like changing schools, for Esha it was different. Not only was Jamnabai Narsee a bigger school, it also allowed parents to enter the premises during lunch hours and spend time with their children. 'It was here that people started to point me out and I realized that they were talking about me being so-and-so's daughter. I would often hear them say, "*Ärre, yeh woh hai* (Look, that's her)." I never wanted that attention.'

It wasn't always easy, however, to ignore the attention. When I ask her about the unpleasant incidents, Esha is quick to point out, 'You know I am five months' pregnant, and whatever I say now, the child will be able to hear. So, I am only going to tell you positive things!'

However, she does share one story. Esha was in the fourth standard when one day a classmate asked her, 'You have two moms, right?' Completely unexpected, that question almost shook the ground beneath Esha's feet. It left her troubled for the rest of the day till she finally reached home and confronted her mother.

'I immediately snapped back at my classmate, saying, "What rubbish! I have only one mother,"' Esha tells me. 'But the moment I reached home, I told my mom that a friend was asking me this question. I think it was at that point of time that my mom decided to tell me the truth. Imagine, we were in the fourth standard and had no idea about anything! Nowadays kids are much smarter. So, that was when I understood that my mother had married someone who was already married to another lady and that they also had a family. But frankly speaking, I never felt bad about it. Till today, I don't think there is anything wrong with it. And I give full credit to my parents for not making us ever feel uncomfortable.'

Hema's daughters are particularly proud of growing up in their mother's house. Speaking about her father's presence in their lives, Esha tells me, 'My dad comes home every day. He has one meal with us. It's true that he doesn't stay with us, which we are fine with. In fact, if he stays, we wonder why and end up asking, "How come Dad is staying back? Is he all right?" Nowadays Dad is mostly in Lonavala. When I was younger, I used to go to my friends' houses where I would see both parents being around. That's when I realized that it's normal to have dads around too. But somehow, we were groomed in a way that it didn't affect me much. I was very content with my mother and I loved my father. But it wasn't the same for Ahaana. She would demand that Dad go out with her for a coffee and spend quality time with her. I think Dad gave more time to Ahaana because she would want that from him.'

Hema has always lived in her own house. That also meant that she never really had to deal with Dharmendra's parents. I ask Esha if the kids ever miss their paternal grandparents. 'No, I never missed my grandfather or grandmother (paternal) because we had an overdose of relatives in our house from my mother's side,' she tells me. 'Amba was more than enough! She was very actively involved in our growing-up years. She would give me Hindi tuitions and wake us up at 6 a.m. to study during exams and give us company. It was a lovely house. Pappu (Hema's cousin, Prabha Raghavan), Mohan, Shanta (Jaya's sister) nani would fill up the house. Papa would come, meet us and go ... and at night it used to be Ahaana, Mom and me in her bedroom. She would tell us stories till we fell asleep. Only after joining films did I move to a different room because of my schedule. My cousin Chinni, from Chennai, would also join us during vacations. Chinni and I used to sleep on a mattress on the floor while Ahaana and Mom would sleep on the bed. I think I understood their (her parents') relationship perfectly. All credit for it goes to my mom. My mom has been the picture of dignity.'

I realize I am venturing into sticky territory when I ask Esha about her stepbrothers. She, however, remains characteristically unflustered. Both Esha and Ahaana have been vocal about their fondness for Sunny, Bobby and Abhay Deol but somehow, the brothers have never publicly returned the gesture. 'We don't believe in a public display of affection,' she tells me. 'Look, I don't even expect Sunny bhaiya and Bobby bhaiya to show their affection publicly because some of the family members on "that side" are still a little uncomfortable. What we share in private is no one's business. People can say what they want but the fact remains that Sunny bhaiya and Bobby bhaiya are a part of my life in a very active sort of way. Just because we are public figures doesn't mean that the world needs to know how well we bond or don't bond as siblings.'

But the public expects them to make an appearance together at least once. 'But why? I was not getting married for the public, and why should we display our emotions? Moreover, why do or force someone to do something they are uncomfortable with? That respect is there from both the sides,' she says.

On her relationship with Sunny, she says, 'He is like a father figure to me – an innocent and lovely human being. There are very few men like that. He has a wonderful temperament. We tie a raakhi on all our brothers every year. Thankfully, the media didn't know about this but now after this book, I won't be surprised to see the paparazzi outside my house! Bobby is more reserved. At one point when we were both working in the industry we would bump into each other at parties and award shows.'

With Abhay, it is more of a warm and friendly camaraderie. 'Abhay and I are very close. We met for the first time in school! He walked up to me and said, "I am your elder cousin brother ... your Ji chacha's (late Ajit Deol) son." So, we introduced ourselves instead of our families introducing us! I used to tie him a raakhi in school. He was like the cool dude brother! Later, even when he went abroad, we stayed in touch. During my wedding, he was very much around, doing all that a brother is expected to do. Abhay and I talk to each other every second day. He is also very fond of Bharat. He has in fact always been a little abstract in his thinking. He would take off abroad quite often ... do a course in caricature (he is an amazing artist) or in carpentry or something. His quirkiness also reflects in the kind of films he chooses. He joined the industry much later and would often tell me to work on films that had unique content. In fact, he wanted me to act in a film called *Exchange Offer* made by Shivam Nair, with Rahul Bose, but unfortunately that film never got released.'

Always a sensitive child, Esha sensed the kind of challenges her mother faced in raising both her daughters early on. With that realization came a special kind of love and respect. She made it a point to never let her parents feel that she missed a regular home environment. Instead, she focused all her energies on her own little world – filled with happy schooldays and friends. In fact, it was at an interschool competition, 'Cascade', that she met her now husband, Bharat Takhtani.

'I was in the arts section and he was also in the same section. I already had a boyfriend then, you know, those teenage crushes. But Bharat didn't know about my crush, maybe when he reads this book he will come to know! And then I saw Bharat and we immediately clicked. I slyly wrote my number on a tissue paper and gave it to him. We used to have a landline in those days. This was a private number which my mother used and it had an extension in her bedroom. To use that phone was a huge task! So, whenever she would be on an outdoor shoot we would spend hours talking on that phone. Even now Bharat knows that number by heart,' Esha gushes.

From amongst the star kids, Shatrughan Sinha's twins Luv and Kush were Esha's earliest friends outside of school. 'I think Luv and Kush were my first "boy" friends. I guess I had more boys as friends rather than girls because I understood boys better. We (Luv, Kush and she) were literally "diaper buddies". Sonakshi was born much later. I remember how she used to dress up like a doll and always wore lots of kaajal. She would love to sit with my father and complain to him about me. "Uncle, she didn't give me this and she didn't do that," she would say. Then there were Sonam and Rhea who would also join in. I used to conduct a fashion show as a kid and I remember all of them would come dressed up beautifully for it. Our parents used to be our audience. We even did a play once on my parents' anniversary, in which Luv and Kush also participated.'

Hema being an Iyengar Brahmin, non-vegetarian food was never allowed in her kitchen. As a kid, Esha craved eggs and there were only two places she could indulge herself – the homes of Shatrughan Sinha and Anil Kapoor. 'Poonam aunty and Sunita aunty make the world's best anda curry,' she says. 'They always knew how much we (Ahaana and Esha) loved it and would inevitably make that dish for us. For a vegetarian kid that was a very big thing!'

Many would think that being born to star parents would make it easy when she decided to take the plunge as an actor. For Esha, though, the going was tougher than most would imagine. Moreover, Hema and Dharmendra made it a point never to interfere in her life, ensuring that she dealt with challenges her own way. 'I have had to face a lot of politics. I have never been the kind to take the initiative and network with directors and production-house heads. It didn't even occur to me. Till today I am pathetic at networking. Whatever I am doing today is because of Bharat and his ability to network and connect with people. Being a businessman, he understands its importance and has a wide circle of friends. I am happy with the way things are. I consider it my weakness – and kudos to those who are good at it.'

After a moment's reflection, she adds, 'When I joined the industry, it was different. We had shoddy costumes and make-up. None of us was groomed. Now everyone has a stylist and a personal trainer, with a dedicated manager. Slowly things got more corporatized. Then the "camps" were formed. If you were not a part of a camp, you were left behind.'

Then there is the issue of being constantly under one's star parent's shadow. For those like Esha and Abhishek Bachchan (as she points out in particular), born to two superstars, the pressure would have been immense. She confesses, 'Abhishek and I faced the maximum pressure. It seeped in much later though, when I was not actively involved any longer in films. I realized that they kept comparing me with Mom, just like Abhishek was compared with his parents. I was eighteen when I did *Koi Mere Dil Se Poochhe* (2002). I was raw, and I must admit I wasn't groomed in the way actresses like Alia Bhatt or Deepika Padukone are today. I also had quite a mind of my own and insisted on looking "natural". So, I refused things like make-up and false eyelashes! But later, of course, I had to give in because in films like *Dhoom* (2004), I wouldn't be allowed in front of the camera without make-up!'

'I remember my first review,' she continues. 'Besides writing about my baby fat, they wrote things like, "She is not even a patch on her mother." Obviously, I won't be a patch on my mother! I had to live up to the pressure of being Hema and Dharmendra's daughter. I still feel it was very unfair.'

I remind her that outsiders would argue that, despite the challenges, a lot of other things must have fallen into place when you were the daughter of Hema Malini and Dharmendra. She jumps in before I can finish. 'I am not denying that I never had to go knocking on doors with my portfolio. There was a big production house that wanted to cash in on the fact that it was launching Dharam–Hema's daughter. For them it was a huge deal. Today, Tiger Shroff and Shraddha Kapoor are launched in a bigger and better way than any other newcomer, and why not? There are advantages and disadvantages to every situation. But today when I look back ... and maybe this book on my mother has helped me with the realization that acting was only a part of my life, it was never my entire life. My life has always been beyond cinema. Cinema was one chapter. I enjoyed it while it lasted and now I have moved on.'

I am not surprised when Esha tells me about how vehemently Dharmendra had fought against allowing his daughters to join the industry. It always seems particularly ironic to me that those who have got the best out of Bollywood end up trying to protect their loved ones most fervently from it. Perhaps they have seen too much from too close. Perhaps they want to shield their offspring from the industry's fickleness. Dharmendra never requested any producer or director to cast his daughters in their films. Esha actually lost out on working with many top-ranking producers and directors because they didn't want to miff Dharmendra by casting her. 'He never supported my decision to join films. He stopped talking to me for almost six months,' she tells me. 'I don't know how my mom convinced him. I remember when I was growing up he would constantly tell me and Ahaana – "No dance and no acting". And then I go ahead and do both! But when Papa sees me today, he is proud. It is only now, at this stage in life, that I understand why he didn't want me to become a film heroine. As a father, I feel he was completely right. He knew that it is a world of vultures out there and he was only being protective.'

Interestingly enough, Esha and Ahaana being trained Odissi dancers is something that makes their father particularly proud. 'He gets all teary-eyed when he sees us dancing on stage,' Esha says with a smile. 'He is proud of the fact that we chose Indian classical dance over the more contemporary styles of the times.'

I ask Esha about her relationship with Ahaana. 'As a kid, I was very protective of Ahaana. Now when I see Ahaana's son Darien he reminds me of Ahaana as a kid. Our fights as kids started much later when she stared fitting into my clothes! She used to be the innocent kind in school while I was quite the "dada". I remember, during lunch break, once I saw she was been asked to kneel by some teacher, hold her ears and apologize. I was fuming. I went up to her, asked Ahaana to go back to class and gave that teacher a piece of my mind! Kids are not supposed to be physically tortured or punished like that. I told her that our mother doesn't talk or punish us like that so who the hell was she to? Later she actually called home to say sorry!'

She continues, 'When I started acting in films I would take her along with me to the sets, but Ahaana would always end up doing her own thing and wasn't really interested in what was happening on the sets.'

Incidentally, both Dev Anand and Shoojit Sircar had wanted to launch Ahaana but she wasn't keen. She didn't much care for the limelight. 'She is too shy to become an actress,' Esha says. 'I remember as a kid she would tell me, "I want to get married and have my own child." Just because you are Hema Malini's daughter doesn't mean you can't have a simple life.'

In her younger days, there was a phase when controversies seemed to follow Esha wherever she went. From link-ups with multiple men to accusations of keeping dangerous company and cultivating even more dangerous habits, the yellow pages had a field day at her expense. For most people who knew Hema, reports of how Esha was turning into a 'wild child' seemed as unbelievable as it was ludicrous. 'I would like to say that I am dead against drugs and I have never touched it,' Esha emphasizes. 'When that article (about her being a drug addict) came out, I was so depressed and hurt that I told my mom she could get my blood test done to check. I would have never done anything that would put my parents to shame. Yes, I would party, I would have a few drinks with my friends, I had my share of fun and why not? That was the right age and time. At that age, everyone parties and drinks; the only issue was that I was in the public eye. Today if you ask me, I hate going to pubs. Bharat sometime forces me to join him because he loves to party. But I like to sit back with my friends and family in our terrace.'

Today, she is content being a homemaker – a job that keeps her on her feet. 'Financially I am not in a situation where I have to work to make money, thankfully. But I would like to be a part of something creative, not necessarily acting. I am a hands-on wife and I will be a hands-on mother till my child turns two,' she tells me.

While Dharmendra wanted Esha to get married as soon as she turned eighteen, it was Hema who insisted on waiting for the right time. 'As a girl, it's a nice thing to settle with the right partner at the right time. Some of my friends have missed out on the right time and are now finding it difficult to find the right match. Also, every actress has a shelf-life. Although I admire those like Rani (Mukerji) who fought that concept. But in most cases, the public is interested in an actor only till a particular time. I feel a lot of people are delusional when they ignore this (family) side of life, which is equally beautiful. You need to have a family, kids and live up to your duties along with your career. I was very sure I didn't want to grow old alone. I wanted a family to be around me. In fact, I look forward to having two or even three kids and bringing them up!' she says, reminding me of how similar she is to her mother.

Esha has been living in a joint family since she got married. 'It is a very demanding job by itself,' she admits. 'I went through those phases of being a working woman and often looked down upon housewives, thinking how boring their lives were. But when you become one, you get to know how tough it is.'

So, did she learn to multitask from her mother, I ask her. Esha laughs. 'Yes, she is the epitome of multitasking – a dancer, an actor, a director, a production person and a politician. But ask her where the sugar is kept in the kitchen or how much ration is required for next week to run the house, and she will quickly change the subject or hide her face in the pillow! My mom is not a terrible cook. In London, during vacations, she would make us good meals. But she has never enjoyed cooking. Neither have I. That way my mother was very lucky. It was as if God knew that this beautiful human being needed to focus on the arts and do something for the world – and that's how her life was designed. I am glad she married Papa. If she had married some Iyengar Brahmin, she would have been a housewife today! After marriage, she took on lead roles, which I think was a first for those times. After Ahaana's birth, Bhushan Lakhandri came into Mom's life, and that was a huge turn in her career as well. After two daughters, she focused on dance and took it to a new level. And now, with grandkids around, she is busy with her political career and has started learning music. If you ask me, there is and can be only one Hema Malini. Even her daughters will never be able to emulate her.'

So how does she plan to take the legacy of Hema Malini ahead, I ask her. 'Right now, I am planning to do it by having a baby! I often visit this beautiful place in Chennai called the Oneness University where I attend meditation sessions because they say that when your child is in your womb, his or her brain starts developing. I want to be around positive people so that the child is born with lots of positivity in life,' she tells me, smiling.

20

Dawn and Darien

'Mamma is very persistent, and that can be annoying,' Ahaana Deol starts off by saying. Hema's younger daughter, and probably her dearest, was born on 28 July 1985.

'When the nurse handed over Ahaana to me and I held her, I knew she was going to be my world,' Hema remembers. 'I named her Ahaana, a Sanskrit word that means "dawn". Her smile won my heart that very instant. It's true that I had wanted a boy that time but when I saw her, I forgot everything else. She is God's gift, and probably the best I could ever ask for.'

Of all the family members, Ahaana is the only one who is a media recluse, fiercely protective of her privacy, preferring to stay away from the limelight. 'Why should I talk to people or be in the news?' she asks. 'Because I am Hema Malini and Dharmendra's daughter? Please! That's just too silly!'

A school teacher and a costume designer, Ahaana has also studied film editing, first at the New York Film Academy and then at the Whistling Woods International Academy. Her life has invariably skirted the world of glamour, though she has been careful about not venturing into it headlong. 'I like it that way,' she says simply.

It was quite a Herculean task to get an interview with her. For her, opening up her life to a stranger is out of the question. 'I've known you for a long time, so there is a comfort factor which puts me at ease,' she tells me, referring to the decades-long association I have shared with her mother.

'I knew I was born into a celebrity household because I would see Mamma with her rollers and make-up since I was a kid,' Ahaana continues. 'It was very normal for us to see her decked up all the time. But she would never create an environment that would make us feel different. In fact, she would sit in our Maruti 800 and drop us to school right till our teenage years.'

Ahaana was quite a sports enthusiast, playing handball as left inner at the state and national level and travelling to places like Sholapur, Satara and Latur in Maharashtra for it. In fact, she led the team at her school, Jamnabai Narsee. Her coach, Cyril, was her inspiration, she says. 'Papa was very proud of the fact that both Esha and I were so good at sports,' she remembers with a smile.

It was because of Hema's persistence that both daughters learnt the value of discipline early in life. 'She was very particular about studies. We could never get away in that department. The only person who pampered us was Amba, who would just let us be. In fact, Mamma would often have arguments with her over how strict she used to be with her and how lenient she turned out to be with us,' Ahaana laughs. 'Without Mamma's guidance and support, I wouldn't have been able to face the world the way I do now. I have learnt most things from my parents, because the apple doesn't fall very far from the tree. While self-restraint and romanticism were Papa's forte, Mamma taught me dedication and discipline.'

Hema, however, was never one to thrust her decisions on her children, even if she hoped they would take up classical dance. Like Esha, Ahaana too chose Odissi, but only because she thought Bharatanatyam would be too difficult. 'I came from a sports background, so for me to take up a dance form that required permanent squatting was a bit much!' she explains.

'Since I was five, I used to see Esha doing Odissi. Personally, I also thought that Odissi was more graceful ... no offence to any other form of dance or culture! But it's not true when people say that because we chose a different form of dance, Mamma was not involved in our dance lessons. She was and still is. We have our guru (Ravindra Adhibudhi), but Mamma is always around when we are composing new tracks for our performances. I also realized that when you are onstage, no one cares if you are so-and-so's daughter. You can't make a fool of yourself onstage. I knew that I was facing the public and I had to hone my skills.'

She admits that the demand for classical dance is slowly on the decline. While Hema often gets to perform on stage because of her ballets, the Deol sisters barely get an opportunity to perform solo these days. 'Barring corporates and foreigners, no one wants to watch pure classical. The audience is niche and I can see the change. When Esha and I started off, we used to get invited to several solo shows, but these days everyone expects something different. That's the reason I went ahead and did a crash course in contemporary dance, and would like to do some sort of fusion to revive the classical dance form. We can't be rigid; any form of art goes through evolution. The one who can keep up with time and tide is the one that survives,' she feels.

Apart from dance, Ahaana also tried out other vocations like setting up her own designer boutique, Rabbit Hole, and teaching toddlers at Kangaroo Kids. 'Just to break the monotony, I would often pick these jobs. It was therapeutic. I seriously want to do something in clothing. Maybe in the future.'

Was it her protective upbringing, perhaps, that played a part in her wanting to shun the limelight, I ask. She denies this and continues: 'I was a ziddi kid, but I wasn't like Esha. She was the pampered one, though she feels it's the other way around! I remember seeing Esha, as a kid, sitting on the floor, thumping her feet and crying till she got what she wanted from my parents! It's pretty evident, isn't it?' says Ahaana, chuckling. But she also admits that it was her elder sister who invariably protected her from any harm that might have come her way.

So, what was Ahaana stubborn about, I ask. 'Only when it came to clothes,' she replies. 'I did not like someone else deciding my clothes. As a kid, I would select my clothes myself. On my birthdays, Mamma would get those frilly frocks made, and I would think to myself, "Oh no!" But eventually when she realized I didn't like them, she let me be. I guess my love for clothing eventually drove me towards opening my first boutique. I think I always had it in me.'

Playing with her mother on the latter's off days, or when she got back from work, remains one of Ahaana's most vivid childhood memories. 'Mamma would tell me these stories which she used to cook up. I still remember this story about a lion that she would often tell me ... and now she tells the same story to Darien! I also remember this game she had come up with where we would play hide-and-seek in the room, and she would also sing a song "*Mamma and baby, we make a love pair*"!'

While most mother–daughter relationships turn tumultuous during the child's teenage years, Ahaana and Hema went on to discover each other as confidantes and friends. 'I was completely different from other kids,' she admits. 'In fact, when Mamma caught me dating my first boyfriend, I told her that this was the age for people to fall in love! Of course, I was scared of her, but I began to share things with her that girls usually keep away from their mothers. I could also see that Mamma often lived her own teenage years through me. I used to tell her openly that I wanted to live my life, and that we shouldn't be deprived of the things she missed out on as a teen. She realized then that these things were part of the normal growing-up process.'

While Esha travelled a great deal with Hema during her shoots, Ahaana, during her younger days, barely joined them. In fact, she doesn't remember a single shoot schedule of her mother's, except for *Dil Aashna Hai*. 'I remember interacting with Shah Rukh Khan and Divya Bharti as a kid, but that was a different experience because Mamma was directing the film. So, she was around whenever she wasn't directing. But I don't remember her taking me for her shoots otherwise. Later, when I did go with Esha for a couple of shoots, I ended up getting very bored! Of course, initially you enjoy it, but after a point it's the same dialogue and the same scene that they shoot for days! I found it a bit tedious.'

Was growing up as Hema and Dharmendra's daughter a bed of roses, considering the difficult times her parents had been through? 'Of course, there were nasty comments,' she says instantly. 'I read a few and those used to annoy me no end. None of these people knew anything about them but they still had such staunch opinions. It's good for them, and God bless them all, but as a kid, I used to get very irritated with all the irresponsible "news" that would go around. Esha and Mamma would have to calm me down. I finally realized that I couldn't go knock on every door and correct their opinion, so it was better to let it go.'

It wasn't till Ahaana was in the sixth standard that her friend, Neeti, told her about her father's first marriage. It is a subject she rarely talks about and even today, she hesitates before finally opening up. 'Can you imagine?' she tells me, traces of astonishment still evident on her face. 'I would often come across friends in school who would ask about my parents but I never indulged them, because I felt they were asking for the sake of their entertainment. But then I felt confused, wondering why so many people were asking me about my parents. Gradually, I realized that something was not "normal". I was also old enough to understand that because I wasn't living in a fairy-tale world. But I didn't want to put Mamma in a spot and never asked her directly. I was, of course, hurt by the fact that no one shared the truth with me, and I had to finally hear it from a friend. Till then, I vaguely remember asking Mamma questions about why Papa didn't stay with us, or how Sunny bhaiya and Bobby bhaiya were related to us. As a kid, I was curious. But Mamma would tell me some nice, happy stories and deviate from the topic. I had to then learn things on my own, as no one spelled it out for me.'

To deal with so much as kids would not have been easy. When she thinks back, does she regret those days or the fact that, even though born into privilege, their childhood had had its share of difficulties? 'Not even once in my life,' she vehemently says. 'If you ask me, I would like to be born as their kids in all my births. I am very lucky to have a father like him. He is a man with a huge heart. Today, my father has two families and has given unconditional love to both. He has been there for each and every member of his family. Whenever I needed him, I would call him and he would be beside me. We would often go out for lunches and dinners to the Marriott and the Sampan – just me and Papa. He never ever said no to me. I am sure that the other side of the family feels the same about him. If I have a knack for writing poems, it's because of Papa. He is a wonderful shayar, and has penned many poems for Mamma. I write poems too. As a kid, I had written a few for both. I have to give full credit to Mamma for keeping the atmosphere at home so calm. I remember how she would leave an imprint of her lipstick for me every time she would go out on a long schedule. I have preserved them all.'

As much a daddy's girl, Ahaana's memories with Dharmendra are all joy and sunshine. 'We used to have this long pillow on which we would plonk ourselves and ask Papa to drag us all across the floor! We used to jump on his shoulders, dance around him, make him go mad with all our antics!' she remembers fondly. 'I remember Esha would not get up from her bed in the mornings till Papa or Mamma gave her a piece of chocolate!' she says. 'During one of our vacations in London, I remember, Papa lost Mamma and Esha in a huge department store He panicked and asked the store manager to make an announcement. (This was the pre-mobile phone era.) So, the manager announced, "Ms Hema Malini, your husband is waiting with your daughter at the enquiry counter, kindly visit us!" They were both superstars and that announcement didn't help much because a huge crowd gathered at the enquiry counter to take a look at their favourite stars!'

Of late, Ahaana and her husband, Vaibhav, spend a lot of their time with Dharmendra at his Lonavala farmhouse, while little Darien has a field day playing with the ducks, hens and other animals at the farm.

Like Esha, Ahaana too is close to both Sunny and Bobby. 'Sunny bhaiya stays in touch with us, while Bobby bhaiya is a bit shy. But we often connect over phone. Abhay is Ji chacha's son and we get along really well. In fact, I still remember how I had met Abhay in Juhu while I was walking on the street. He came and introduced himself as my brother! I already knew about him because Esha had mentioned him. In fact, we have a cordial relationship with all (the Deols). I recently read that Karan aka Rocky (Sunny's son) is making his acting debut. I am very happy for them. I am sure he will make us all proud. Sunny bhaiya is also very fond of Darien.'

Unlike the rest of the family, Ahaana doesn't seem to be too much of a careerist. In fact, as Esha says, Ahaana always wanted to get married to a prince. 'Esha is kidding.' Ahaana says, laughing. 'Of course, I wanted a family, but that didn't mean I didn't want a career. I want to direct or produce a film someday. There are lots of ideas stuck in my head. I need to tell those stories, but I never wanted to act in movies. I had seen Mamma and Esha, and neither of them had a private life. They were always in the public eye. Same goes for my Papa and brothers.'

Incidentally, Dev Anand had been very keen on launching Ahaana's career in films. 'Dev saab saw Ahaana with me during a shoot and kept asking me if he could launch her,' Hema recollects. 'But Ahaana was too young at that time. Even later many directors approached her with films, but somehow she stayed away from acting.'

'This industry is full of fake people,' Ahaana adds vehemently. 'I wanted to stay away from all of them. I can't handle fake people. That's how I am by nature, and maybe that's the reason I have very few friends. I keep reading articles written on star kids and I see how comfortable they are talking about being star kids. But I am not like that. I'd rather talk about my work.'

Ahaana, however, did not reject all offers that came her way. Shoojit Sircar wanted to launch her with Aditya Roy Kapur, and she agreed, but somehow the project never took off. 'The project became more and more commercial and I kept asking myself if I really wanted to act. I didn't want to sell my soul for a movie, so I politely excused myself from the project. But I adore Shoojit Sircar and his kind of cinema,' she says.

She is also hugely inspired by her cousin, Abhay Deol. 'I can completely relate to his kind of movies. But I think even Abhay understands that to connect with the masses one also needs to focus on commercial films. By working in experimental films alone, you will not be able to hold on to your fan base.'

Moving on to how she met Vaibhav, Ahaana tells me it was Esha and Bharat who played cupid. 'Bharat was annoyed with me and stopped talking to me because he would insist on me meeting Vaibhav and I would pay no attention! Finally, to keep his word, I met Vaibhav. My first thought was, "Wow! He looks good!" We went on to date for two years and finally decided to get married. No one put a gun to our heads; it was a mutual decision and I am glad that I took it. All credit though goes to Bharat and Esha!'

Ahaana had wanted a quiet temple wedding in a small town somewhere, with only a handful of people. But both Hema and

Vaibhav's family wanted a 'big fat Bollywood wedding'. Finally, she had to give in. 'I still can't believe that instead of it being a private affair, my wedding became national news, with Mr Narendra Modi and Mr Shah Rukh Khan attending my reception.'

Today, Ahaana is a proud hands-on mother. 'I don't like to be dependent on maids and nannies. I never had an entourage for myself; that's for Mamma – she loves to be around people.' It is Ahaana who chose her son's name. Darien is a Greek word that means 'the gift of God'. 'I call him Mowgli at home because he is adventurous and keeps hopping from one place to another,' she says dotingly.

'I always wanted to adopt,' Ahaana says, talking about her plans once she has had two biological children. 'In fact, there was a phase when I used to think that if I didn't get married, I would adopt babies. I have discussed this with Vaibhav and he is as keen.' The alarm on her phone goes off. 'Oh! I have to leave right now,' she says, jumping up. 'Darien will be waiting for me in school!' She reminds me of her mother in that instant. Three decades ago, Hema would have reacted just the same way.

21

An Accident on the Highway

Hema Malini could barely see anything outside her car, beyond the gathering crowd. Startled shouts of 'Accident ho gaya (There's been an accident)' could be heard. She hadn't realized it, but her manager, Pramanik, began to panic, seeing a deep gash on her face near her right eyebrow.

While driving back from Mathura to Delhi after a hectic schedule, Hema had decided to pay a visit to the Mehendipura Balaji (Hanuman) Temple in Jaipur. It was late evening when her Mercedes Benz was crossing the Dosar highway. She was exhausted and couldn't wait to catch the flight to Mumbai, where she would meet Ahaana and her grandson Darien. She had just taken a quick nap when all of a sudden there was a massive collision with another car. In a state of complete shock and disarray, she tried to compose herself, but all she could see were the people gathering outside her window, trying to click pictures of her in that sorry state.

The impact of the collision had caused Hema to hit the screen of the LED TV placed between the rows of seats, leaving her with a broken nose and grievous injuries on her head, neck and face. Her first realization was a partial loss of hearing, after which she found herself bleeding profusely. In severe pain, all she could think of was to hold her handkerchief tightly to the cut to control the bleeding.

Outside, on the road, a five-year-old girl, Sonam, lay dead. Six of the passengers in the other car had been badly injured, including Sonam's father, Hanuman Mahajan.

Fortunately for Hema, help arrived shortly. Dr Shivkumar

Sharma, who was driving by, rushed her to Fortis Hospital in Jaipur, a few hours away. In the meantime, the other victims were rushed to SMS hospital in Dausa. Mahesh Chand Thakur, the driver of Hema's car, was arrested and found guilty under Section 304 for culpable homicide not amounting to murder. Subsequently, he was let out on bail.

At Fortis, Hema had to undergo surgery that lasted two hours. According to P. Tamboli, the facility director, she had suffered lacerations to her forehead and in the para-nasal area. It took Hema almost sixty days to recover completely.

It didn't take time for news of the accident to spread. Accusations flew thick and fast as the media did its best to whip up a frenzy. Sonam's father, it was said, had made a statement that his child might have been saved if she had been taken to Jaipur along with Hema Malini. But at a time when Hema herself was injured and at the mercy of those around her, was she in a position to take those calls? She may have been completely unaware of the fact that a five-year-old was lying some metres away, critically injured. Incidentally, while everyone put the blame on Hema's car, senior police officer Rajinder Tyagi mentioned in a press statement, 'The Alto (the car the other family was in) driver may not have paid attention while entering the section of the highway where the collision took place.'

At the time of the accident, Esha was cooking dinner in Mumbai while Ahaana was trying to put her son Darien to sleep. When Dharmendra called them, he was in a state of shock, but concealed it from his daughters. Esha recalls, 'I was cooking at home when Papa called to say that Mom had met with an accident and that they were showing it on TV. It took me a long time to get back to cooking. The incident left me so shocked that I began to think that each time I would cook, something bad would happen.

'I was appalled at the behaviour of the public,' she continues. 'They were constantly clicking pictures of Mom in that state, and it didn't stop there. They went and posted those pictures on social media. Who takes photographs of a lady in such a state and posts them on social media? It's so disrespectful to take photos at a time like that. Bharat and I took the first flight out to Jaipur. Vaibhav was in Delhi, so he drove down immediately and was the first to reach the hospital. Mom was attacked by everyone only because she is a celebrity. It was an accident, and an accident is an accident. I was shattered by the behaviour of people. Even learned journalists like Arnab Goswami went on ranting on national television without knowing what exactly had happened. It was extremely upsetting for both the families, and we have all expressed our heartfelt condolences for the child who died that day. But instead of helping the victims or figuring out the truth, the media turned it into a political circus.'

Two days after the accident, Hema was discharged from the hospital. Accompanied by Esha and Bharat, she made her way back to Mumbai in a hired chartered plane. While the media was relentless, hounding her for a statement, Esha stepped up, as always. Hema – hardly in a state to face a barrage of questions – let her elder daughter do what was needed. '*Jab accident hua tab Mummy ki jo condition thi, wo kisi aur ke baare mein kaise soch sakti thi … koi bhi nahi soch pa raha tha … par hame afsos hai ki uss parivar ne koi apna khoya hai* (When the accident took place, neither my mother nor anyone else was in a condition to think about anything or anyone. But we are saddened that that family has lost a dear one),' Esha said.

'This incident shook us badly,' Esha tells me. 'You cannot imagine that this could happen to your own mom. I mean, not just for the world but even for us, she is a superwoman. I fondly call her Tinker Bell! Her feet are never on the ground, she is constantly travelling. So, when I met her at the hospital, I jokingly asked her, "How did this happen to our Tinker Bell?"'

Soon after recovering, Hema, along with a group of people from her office, made it a point to meet Sonam's family. 'They were nice people. They were not at all the way they were being portrayed by the media,' Esha declares. In fact, she is certain that most of the drama that was whipped up had been politically motivated.

'Panel discussions were conducted, and none of us were even invited or asked to voice our opinion on the issue. I have nothing against the media or their role in our society, but all I am expecting from them is a fair report. There were television channels that went on a rampage and almost forced people to say that my mom was responsible for this accident,' Esha says. 'And who were these people who were judging her anyway? They don't even know of the kind of work she does or her contributions. The only agenda they have is to humiliate people who are doing genuine, good work. Recently, a man who wanted publicity made a nasty public statement on how my mom consumes alcohol every day. I was so angry that I wanted to bash his face! People can stoop to any level for publicity.'

She pauses for a few minutes. 'I liked it when she was a Rajya Sabha member because she was working for the country and it was a prestigious social duty. But I am not very happy about her being so actively involved as an MP in Mathura. Just like the film industry, even in politics there are vultures, waiting to pull you down.'

Hema, who had refrained from talking about this incident all this while, finally decides to share her thoughts on what had undoubtedly been a distressing episode for all of them. 'It was disappointing,' she tells me. 'Before I say anything else I would like to convey my condolences to the family and my prayers for the little girl. I think, for any parent, losing a child has to be the biggest loss.'

Since that day, Hema has been unable to use the Jaipur–Delhi highway. She still gets a shiver down her spine at the thought of that fateful night. 'I get flashbacks from that night. It's very difficult to forget. By the time I realized something major had happened, I was being taken by a gentleman in his car to the nearest hospital. I remember being able to walk, but in a daze. I realized that the media was everywhere, and they were constantly shooting and perhaps playing the footage. You won't believe it if I told you that I came to know that a little child had died in the accident almost twenty-four hours later. The moment I reached the hospital, the doctors rushed me to the operation theatre because I was bleeding profusely. I don't remember anything once I was taken inside the operation theatre.'

The allegations of Hema being 'inhuman' and refusing to help the victim's family left her deeply disturbed. Her silence on the matter was further misinterpreted. It was assumed that she was refusing to apologize and take responsibility for what had happened. 'It was Esha who told me the next day that a child had died in that accident. I immediately asked Pramanik to figure out their details and do whatever was possible. But you have to understand that when the accident happened, I was not in a state to figure out the situation,' Hema explains.

When Hema finally decided to speak up, she used her Twitter account to explain her side of the story. But that backfired as well. In one of her tweets, she mentioned how Sonam's father should have been more careful. The child had been sitting in the front seat and not wearing a seatbelt. If he had taken the necessary precautions, she might have been saved.

Her words were misconstrued and made to sound as if she was blaming the victim's father for the child's death. 'Everyone in my family had asked me not to meet or talk to the media. I was almost locked up, and wasn't allowed to interact with any media person. That's because they all felt that the media wasn't really interested in my story. All they wanted was to play judge. They had, in fact, already decided who the villain was, so there was no point in discussing anything with them.'

When I ask physiotherapist Dr Shivkumar Sharma about the incident, he reveals that he got a shock when he spotted Hema Malini sitting inside her car, bleeding profusely. 'I could see people taking pictures while her secretary was making frantic calls for help. I saw that the Alto was badly damaged, and an ambulance was already there for the victims. I thought that Hema-ji needed immediate medical treatment, so I requested her to shift into my car, and I drove her along with her assistants to Fortis Hospital. In the car, Hema-ji enquired about the accident, but she was not in a state to understand what had happened. I could see from the rear mirror that Hema-ji was in deep pain; she had closed her eyes, covered her face with her handkerchief, and kept asking how far the hospital was.'

Incidentally, Hema showed her gratitude towards Dr Sharma by inviting him home for dinner with her family. Hema also gave him a handwritten note after the dinner: 'Dear Shivkumar Sharma, It was indeed a pleasure meeting you today at my residence. I take this opportunity to thank you for your timely help when I had met with an accident, at Jaipur highway on 2 July 2015. You took me to safety and (the) most suitable hospital in Jaipur, without even thinking about the distance or other possibilities. I truly appreciate that. Thank you.'

In the two months that Hema took to recuperate, she had a regular visitor. Sunny Deol – who had also been the first one to visit her once she was back home – made it a point to check on Hema's health every day.

'Yes, Sunny is a wonderful boy,' Hema says warmly. 'Poor fellow would come every day to ask about me. I had stitches on my face, and Sunny organized the best surgeon to come home and cut my stitches so that it didn't hurt me or leave me with scars on my face. Sunny has been extremely fond of Esha and Ahaana. Bobby is not that expressive, but even he is protective about them. Sunny's son (Karan) is now making his debut in films and I am always happy for him! In fact, he makes it a point to always call me for his trials and take my feedback.'

22

Playback Time

In Prakash Mehra's 1974 release, *Haath Ki Safai*, there is a scene in which Hema Malini plays the role of Chandramukhi. Part of a comic sequence, it has Randhir Kapoor playing Devdas. Kishore Kumar was doing the playback for Randhir and Hema had to lip sync her bit. '(But) Kishore-da insisted that I sing the "bol" of the song. I thought it would be fun doing a song with Dada!' Hema says. And that is when Hema unwittingly took her first formal steps into playback singing.

Immediately after this, Kishore Kumar was about to record a Bengali song, *'Goon goon kore je mon'* for HMV in 1973. The Hindi version of the song had been sung by Lata Mangeshkar in *Suhana Geet*, but it was never released. When he suggested Hema for this, she was naturally a bit surprised.

'Kishore-da used to come up with these weird ideas! He wanted me to sing this song for a private album for Durga Puja, but I wasn't a trained vocalist. He kept encouraging me with words like, "Hema, you have a pretty face and a pretty voice. Just feel the words, I will manage the rest." That's when I decided to try my hand at music. My brother Kannan worked with the State Bank's foreign department in Kolkata for many years and lived in Alipore. He is very fluent in Bengali, Hindi and Urdu. So, for this song, I rechecked the pronunciation with my brother. On the day of recording, I still remember how impressed Kishore-da was with my homework, and after a few takes, we recorded the song.'

It couldn't have been an easy job because that was still the era of live music recordings. Singers had to be meticulously in tune, unlike today when they have the option of correcting vocal errors through a host of technical support systems. 'I wasn't nervous but I was sceptical. In fact, I remember telling Dada, *"Agar achha nahin hua recording toh hum isey release nahi karenge*. (If the recording is not up to the mark, I will not let it get released.)" But he had complete faith in me. He had set the tune of the song in a way that would suit my capabilities,' she remembers. The album was finally released with elaborate publicity in West Bengal, and did reasonably well – Hema's first foray into music and yet another feather in her cap!

After that first attempt, Hema continued singing the odd song in films like Pramod Chakraborty's *Dream Girl* and, much later, even a full-fledged number for *Indira* (1992). 'My God! Both were equally bad,' she says, laughing.

'I never really wanted to be a singer,' she emphasizes. 'But being a dancer, I would eventually end up singing the taals and maatras during rehearsals. So, I won't say I was completely off-tune, but yes, I was not the best in the business!'

Hema's love for shlokas eventually drove her to record an album – her first – *Soundarya Lahari* in 2013. 'In *Noopur*, I had danced to one particular shloka of "*Soundarya Lahari*". It was then that I started learning to chant the "*Soundarya Lahari*". Till then, people knew me as an actor and a dancer, but more recently, I thought to myself – why not do this album?' she says. It was to be her debut album in Hindi, and she requested Amitabh Bachchan to render the introduction. 'I wanted someone to introduce the work to the public, and who better than Amit-ji? When I asked him if he could do a little introduction, he promptly agreed.' Noted playback singers Shankar Mahadevan and Suresh Wadkar also sang a few shlokas for the album. 'There are a hundred shlokas and I have chanted some of them. But this was more for spiritual and meditational purposes,' she adds.

The album was launched at the Juhu ISKCON temple amidst much fanfare. Hema, though, was sure this had been a one-off experiment, unaware of the number of windows it would open for her.

During her days of political campaigning, Hema had to travel extensively with fellow party members. One of them was popular playback singer and BJP minister Babul Supriyo. On one such trip, Hema casually shared some of the songs she had sung during her early years, including the ones with Kishore Kumar. 'After hearing the songs, Babul insisted that I rerecord them with a new music arrangement and release them again,' says Hema. After turning him down several times, Hema finally relented. 'I was apprehensive because I hadn't been in touch with music for so many years. *Soundarya Lahari* was more like spiritual chants, but Babul wanted me to record two Bengali songs and one Hindi duet with him. So, I started practising again and recorded '*Goon goon kore mon*' and '*Kande mon piyashi*'. But, to be honest, I didn't like the pitch he had chosen for the songs. I still prefer the one Kishore-da had recorded. But I am grateful to him and to Saregama for taking the initiative and bringing back old memories and melodies. He also recorded a Hindi duet, "*Aaji suniye zara*", with me, which was a fun song for Valentine's Day.'

Apparently, Hema had been so anxious about these songs that she had made a desperate call to Kavita Krishnamurthy! 'Hema-ji is very sincere about her commitments. I got to know later that Kavita had been helping her with her riyaaz regularly. When I called Kavita to congratulate her on her new student, she laughed and said that Hema-ji was so charged up all the time, it was difficult to ever say no to her. The only difference between singing for Kishore-da and me was that with him, she had to do a one-take recording, while with me, she had the privilege of retakes,' Babul elaborates.

The launch of this music video was again a grand event, attended by the likes of Amitabh and Jaya Bachchan and Dharmendra. At the event, Amitabh jokingly said, 'Everyone questions me at this age about how I manage to do *Kaun Banega Crorepati* and so many films at the same time. I just want those same people to ask Hema-ji how she manages to act in films, television, attend Parliament, contest elections, perform her ballets on stage and now also sing!' Everyone present must have agreed with Mr Bachchan wholeheartedly, as Hema received a standing ovation following his words. Jaya Bachchan delivered the closing lines, 'Hema Malini means multitasking; that's the meaning I have deciphered from her in these years!'

Immediately after the launch, Hema was flooded with offers from music companies, but her political career left her with little time for other pursuits. 'But deep down I had started enjoying the attention and adulation I was getting for my music,' she confesses.

When Hema decided to gift her music album to Prime Minister Narendra Modi, she was stunned to hear him say that he already had a copy of the CD. 'Modi-ji mentioned that he had already acquired the CD and listens to the '*Soundarya Lahari*' during Navratri. He also complimented me on my Sanskrit pronunciation.'

Incidentally, Hema's association with the prime minister goes back to his days as chief minister of Gujarat. 'I had campaigned for him during that time. He had in fact called me to thank me during his swearing-in ceremony, and had wanted to invite me, but I couldn't make it. Later, when he became the prime minister, he had called me again to thank me for my contribution. I felt a bit uncomfortable because it's the people who had voted for him and I had barely made any contribution to his victory. To that he had said, "*Nahin, Hema-ji, boond boond se sagar banta hai, aap ka yogdaan utna hi mahatvapoorn hai.* (An ocean gets filled drop by drop; your contribution is equally important.)" That was really sweet of him, to acknowledge me for whatever little I had done for him and for the party.'

Hema has shared a good equation with the prime minister ever since. 'I meet him directly to address issues related to Mathura. He appreciates my enthusiasm for doing good work,' she says. In fact, he had attended Ahaana's wedding reception and, more recently, the Indo-Georgian Sukhishvili dance festival that Hema had organized in loving memory of her mother.

More recently, when ISKCON's Narayan Agarwal – the man instrumental in launching several of Jagjit Singh's bhajan albums – approached Hema Malini for a bhajan album, the thought, at first, didn't seem daunting. 'I have been singing for albums, so initially I thought that I would be able to pull it off.' Only once she began to delve deeper did she realize the scope of the challenge. Narayan Agarwal wasn't hoping for one or two numbers from Hema – he wanted her to deliver all eight tracks. Not just that, when he walked in one day with the tunes and the lyrics, he informed her that Pandit Jasraj, Pandit Shiv Kumar Sharma, Rajan and Sajan Mishra and Pandit Hariprasad Chaurasia had each composed two tracks for the album, and they were keen that Hema sing them all. 'I got a shock,' Hema exclaims. 'I had cold feet and knew I wouldn't be able to sing such difficult classical, raga-based songs. I told Narayan Agarwal-ji, "*Aap toh mujhe marwa doge!* (You will get me into trouble.)" These were all stalwarts of Hindustani classical music. I was a nobody in front of them! Forget singing, I couldn't even have hummed properly in their presence!'

While that might have been her first reaction, nobody loves a challenge more than Hema. Having given it some thought, she finally decided to go ahead. 'When Narayan Agarwal-ji played the "dhun", I realized that this was not easy. But I didn't want to give up. I immediately decided to find a teacher who would be able to train me in classical music and help me with my riyaaz. That's when I met this singer called Gagan Singh, who agreed to train me. I have to give him credit for working hard on my vocal skills.'

For the new album (yet untitled), Hema recites a few lines as a prelude to every track. Of all the tracks, Hema's personal favourite is '*Palna jhule Nand Gopal*'. 'When I was rehearsing this song, Darien was born, so I used to sing this as a lullaby for him. When I finally went to record it, I kept imagining his face! I remember recording this one at the Lata Mangeshkar Studio in Andheri. This bhajan has been composed by Pandit Jasraj-ji and he was assisted by his disciple Tripti-ji. The lyrics were written by Narayan Agarwal-ji and the music coordination was by Vivek Prakash. I am discovering a new me – one I didn't even know existed! Singing is such an enthralling experience and I'm thoroughly enjoying my new avatar. For this album, I had to use the Brij language; the dialogue had been written by the late Ravindra Jain.'

Next on her wish list is a recording of the *Durga Saptashati* and the Bhagavad Gita. She hopes to finish both by the end of 2017. 'I don't get time to rehearse, which is why I have to keep recording so that I can keep up my riyaaz. Recently my brother Kannan gave me a few lines from the Bhagavad Gita to recite at a BJP rally, but I wasn't prepared enough, so I didn't recite them. But it kept bothering me. So eventually I made it a point to learn those lines and now I start my speeches with them. Every time I start my speech with a song like this, I get undivided attention from the crowd; a "dry" speech from netas otherwise gets boring for them,' she explains.

Even when she was rehearsing for her devotional album, Kannan kept requesting Hema to try her hand at ghazals. 'I had never sung ghazals in my life but he would keep sending me different tracks from various singers,' she tells me with a smile. 'Finally, I chose Farida Khanum-ji's evergreen *"Aaj jaane ki zid na karo"*. On the last day of the recording of the bhajan album, I requested the studio to give me some time so that I could record a ghazal. Everyone was taken aback, because till then I hadn't told anyone that I was practising for one! Finally, I recorded it, without music and in one go. Vivek Prakash liked it so much that he fixed a tune for it and even mixed it for me. I shared the song with Pankaj Dheer and he loved it so much that he now wants to do a music video and release it on YouTube.'

When Hema shared the recording with Dharmendra (a great fan of ghazals), he fell in love with it. 'In fact, Dharam-ji wants me to record Mehdi Hassan saab's *"Ranjish hi sahi, dil hi dukhane ke liye aa"*. That's yet another timeless track. I have been working on the song and will soon record it and surprise Dharam-ji,' she says, blushing.

Hema's earliest association with music started way back, with legends like Shankar–Jaikishan, Laxmikant–Pyarelal, Rahul Dev Burman and Gulzar. The composers had always been very fond of her and admired her skills as a classical dancer. It was through them that Hema developed a warm and enduring association with the Nightingale of Indian cinema, Lata Mangeshkar. 'I am so fond of Lata-ji,' she tells me ardently. 'She has given me the maximum number of hit songs in my career. I am eternally grateful to her for immortalizing those sequences with her voice. I am still regularly in touch with her.

She would often send me gifts – a pen or a coffee mug or a sari, out of love. She would always wish me on my birthday! I have always wanted to invite her for one of my dance ballets, but she is sweet enough to admit that she wouldn't be able to sit through a ninety-minute production. I want to gift her my bhajan album. I hope she likes it.' Over the years, Hema has carefully preserved every handwritten note she has ever received from Lata Mangeshkar, admitting that these are far more precious than any trophy. In an interview to veteran journalist Subhash K. Jha, Lata too spoke very fondly about Hema Malini. 'Hema is a wonderful lady,' she said. 'I admire her courage when she ventures into something. I have always admired her body of work. She is truly an ideal image of a Dream Girl.'

Coming back to the world of films, Hema is waiting patiently for roles of substance to come her way. She made a stupendous comeback with *Baghban*, but even that didn't guarantee offers that were good enough. 'Yash-ji (Chopra) came to meet me after *Baghban* with a DVD of *Ek Chadar Maili Si* and wanted me to play the role of a typical Jat woman in his film *Veer Zara* in 2004. That was a guest role, but I agreed to be a part of that film only because of Yash-ji, Amitabh Bachchan and Shah Rukh Khan, even though I didn't have much of a role in the film. But they had a beautiful Lohri song sequence where I got to dance with Amit-ji, Shah Rukh and Preity Zinta,' she says.

In 2006, Hema took up Ravi Chopra's *Baabul* – a film that eventually left her disappointed. 'I didn't even ask Ravi-ji about the story when he wanted to make *Baabul*. I knew that after *Baghban* he would want to capitalize on Amit-ji and me as a screen pair. But the film eventually turned out to be Amit-ji and Rani Mukerji's story. I was like a prop in the background. That was very disheartening, especially because I have always shared a very good relationship with Ravi-ji.'

Regarding the dearth of good roles in Bollywood, Hema doesn't hesitate to speak her mind. 'Journalists often ask, if someone like a Meryl Streep can do such challenging roles even at this age, why can't we (senior actresses) in India get such roles? I have always replied that they should really ask the studios and the established producers the same question. Look at Amit-ji and Rishi Kapoor – they are doing such fantastic films because they are being offered those roles. But will anyone write a role for Jaya (Bachchan) or Rekha or me?' she asks. 'Scripts (in Hollywood) today are conceived keeping Meryl Streep in mind. She is not an option but the only choice for that role. That's the difference.'

I ask her about the present generation of actors. After Madhuri Dixit, Sridevi and Rani Mukerji, Hema feels that Vidya Balan and Kangana Ranaut are the only other names that have been able to create a substantial impact at the box office. 'I think Vidya and Kangana both are doing good films. I liked *Kahaani* (2012) and *Queen* (2014); not many actors of this generation would have been able to deliver such powerful roles. I also admire Deepika Padukone for her performance in *Bajirao Mastani* ... she was gorgeous. I think Sanjay Leela Bhansali makes an ordinary story look extraordinary,' she says. In fact, not many know that Manmohan Desai, in 1975, had wanted to make a film on Bajirao and Mastani with Rajesh Khanna and Hema Malini in the lead. The first look as well as the poster for the film had been released in trade magazines, but somehow the film never took off.

Having worked with almost every top name in the industry, is there any director today with whom she would like to work? 'Sujoy Ghosh, because I like his narrative,' she replies. '*Kahaani* is one of my favourite films of recent times. I would also like to work with Sanjay Leela Bhansali, Mani Ratnam, Rajkumar Hirani, Shoojit Sircar, Zoya Akhtar, Gauri Shinde and Karan Johar. Directors like Basu Chatterjee, Gulzar, Ramesh Sippy, Hrishikesh Mukherjee and Shakti Samanta would all make heroine-oriented films and producers would invariably support their vision. But things have changed now. I have heard that now people make films backwards. First, they fix the release date, then the distributor, then they sell the satellite rights, plan the publicity and marketing, and only after that do they make the movie. It's a completely different scenario,' she says.

If you visit Hema's office, you will still find producers making a beeline for her. But most of these offers are for the typical mother and grandmother roles – something Hema has always vehemently refused to accept. 'I don't demean those who take up such roles on-screen. It's a personal choice. But if you ask me, why would I play the role of a mother in a movie where I would have nothing to contribute? I don't have to work in films for the sake of it. I will only work in a movie when I know that the role will give me some sort of creative satisfaction.'

Hema agreed to be a part of *Bbuddah Hoga Terra Baap* in 2011 – a film that was a virtual Amitabh Bachchan fan-fest. She also did a strong cameo in Prakash Jha's *Aarakshan* the same year. 'I think people can only imagine Amit-ji as my hero when they write or conceive a film today. I don't blame them, considering that none of the heroes of my generation are working in films. So, there are no other options,' she says. Hema admits that the two of them make a great on-screen pair even today. 'I want to produce a film which Pankaj Dheer wants to direct. It's tentatively titled *Mera Pati Ganpati*. I want Amit-ji to play the lead. Unfortunately, he's been so busy that he is yet to hear the script,' she tells me.

In the last few years, it is not as if Hema has completely stayed away from the arc lights. In 2006 and 2007, we saw her in *Ganga* and *Gangotri* (Bhojpuri) respectively, again with Amitabh Bachchan. In 2007, she also did an item number for Pradeep Sarkar's *Laga Chunari Mein Daag*. Raj Kanwar's *Sadiyan* with Rekha and Rishi Kapoor followed in 2010; *Barbareek* – a mythological film – in 2013 and, finally, *Ek Thi Rani Aisi Bhi* and the Telugu film *Gautamiputra Satakarni* in 2017. In 2016, Dev Anand's last release, *Aman Ke Farishtey*, had Hema in a guest role, playing a cop and beating up goons with a flourish. But the film tanked, with almost no shows whatsoever. Hema is also excited about Ramesh Sippy's romantic comedy, *Shimla Mirchi*, with Rajkummar Rao. In it, she finally gets to play the central character. 'I don't know when they are going to release the film,' she says wearily. 'It's such a cute love story, but whenever I ask Ramesh-ji, he tells me, "very soon". I have now stopped asking.' She adds that she tends to lose interest if a project stretches on for too long.

For the Telugu film, *Gautamiputra Satakarni*, Hema was apparently offered a whopping Rs 2 crore to play the role of Rajmata Gautami. A costume drama directed by Krish, Hema had agreed to be a part of the project because it marked the hundredth film of Telugu superstar Nandamuri Balakrishna (son of the legendary N.T. Rama Rao). The film was projected as epic on the lines of *Baahubali* (2015). Telugu was an alien language for Hema and she found the whole experience challenging. Eventually, her lines had to be dubbed by a local artist.

'They helped me a lot and were extremely cooperative. It was wonderful working with Balakrishna and Shriya. But I wish they had used me a bit more in the movie, considering they paid a decent amount for the role,' she says on a lighter note.

With this film, Hema apparently set a record for being the highest-paid female actor in a character role across regional and Hindi cinema. 'I don't want to comment on that,' she tells me. 'But I think people should get well paid for their work; at least they shouldn't be denied what they deserve.'

It is interesting to note that Hema had once worked with Balakrishna's father, the iconic N.T. Rama Rao, in a mythological film. It was a 1971 production called *Shri Krishna Vijayam*. She recalls, 'Those days I used to be very busy with my Hindi film commitments. I was shooting round the clock, and barely had time to breathe. Around then, NTR wanted me to do a song sequence in his film that starred Jayalalithaa as the female lead. Just as I was about to turn down the offer, my guru, Vempati Chinna Satyam, mentioned to me that he was choreographing the song sequence. Without saying another word, I immediately took time out from my schedule for it! I am so glad I did that song, because it was so beautifully choreographed.' Hema ended up spending seven days on that song sequence because it wasn't an easy one to do.

So, does she have any regrets as an actress? 'No, not really. Barring the fact that I never got a chance to act in a Hrishikesh Mukherjee film. He was very nice to me, and he made some brilliant films with Dharam-ji. We would often meet at social dos. He praised me for my performance in many a film, but somehow I never got a chance to work with him,' she says, a hint of sadness in her voice.

23

Bliss

'*Ghar kahan dekha maine?* (When have I had the chance to enjoy time at home?)' Hema Malini asks, sitting in her easy chair in the sprawling balcony of her New Delhi apartment. Since she was a child, she has constantly been on the move; one apartment to another, one city to the next, one studio to the other. Sipping on her green tea with Ayurvedic honey, she reflects, 'It's a strange feeling; I started my childhood in Delhi, and now that we are on the last chapter of this book, we are sitting here in my Delhi apartment! It's literally been a full circle. Here I am today, looking at the Parliament and wondering how that shy little kid from Gole Market, who could barely talk to anyone, can today deliver a public speech even in her sleep!'

Hema's living room is tastefully done up with photographs of Dharmendra, Esha, Ahaana, Bharat and Vaibhav on the walls. I notice that Darien's pictures are missing. 'Those are in my bedroom,' she says with a broad smile. '*Nazar lag jaati hai* (It's inauspicious to keep them on display).'

So, does she think that most of her childhood was lost somewhere in the by-lanes of Gole Market?

Before she can answer my question, her phone starts to ring. What follows is the first of a hilarious round of frantic calls from the locals of her constituency. '*Arre lekin main Delhi mein hoon, aapke ghar mein bandar aa gaya hai toh main kya kar sakti hoon? Aapko main Janardan-ji ka number deti hoon, aap unko phone kijiye, okay?* (I am in Delhi right now, how can I help you if a monkey has entered your house? Please call Janardan [her secretary] and he will connect you to

210

With Kishore Kumar, recording her first playback song, '*Goon goon kore je mon*'

At Gurdaspur with Vinod Khanna, where Hema took her first steps into politics

With Zeenat Aman and Dharmendra on her sixtieth birthday

In a still from *Sadiyaan*, with Rekha

With Pandit Jasraj

With sarod maestro Amjad Ali Khan and his wife Subhalakshmi

With Amitabh Bachchan and Shatrughan Sinha

Holidaying with Dimple Kapadia in London

With Shah Rukh Khan at the Synergy show, Mumbai

At Esha's reception with Jeetendra and Shobhaa Kapoor

With Dharmendra and Markand Mehta (her secretary since the *Haath Ki Safaai* days)

A still from *Gautamiputra Saptakarni*

With the Sukhishvili and Indian dance troupes at the Synergy show in Mumbai

With one of Hema's first co-stars Tanuja and her daughters Kajol and Tanishaa

Salman Khan arrives at Esha's reception

Abhishek Bachchan with Esha and Bharat at Esha's wedding

With Rashmi Thackeray, Jaya Bachchan and Esha at Esha's godh bharai

With Minister for Women and Child Development Maneka Gandhi

With Minister of Finance and Corporate Affairs Arun Jaitley and External Affairs Minister Sushma Swaraj

On the campaign trail in Mathura

After her Rajya Sabha nomination with former Prime Minister Dr Manmohan Singh, Sushma Swaraj and others

With Esha, Bharat, Dharmendra, Esha's in-laws and L.K. Advani

Participating in the Holi Mahostav in Mathura

Always at the people's service

At Mathura's tallest Krishna temple with former President Pranab Mukherjee

With Baba Ramdev

With Kokilaben
and Nita Ambani at
Esha's wedding

With the vice-
president of Bhakti
Kala Kshetra, Surdas
Prabhu, at ISKCON

Receiving an honorary doctorate from Udaipur Singhania University

Receiving the Padma Shri from former President K.R. Narayanan

Hema and Esha at Advitiya. *Photo credit: Avinash Gowariker*

With Prime Minister Narendra Modi and Narayan Agarwal at the launch of her first bhajan album *Gopala Ko Samarpan*

With Prime Minister Narendra Modi in Mathura celebrating her victory after the elections

the right person).' As she disconnects, she notices the amazed look on my face. 'I am used to it,' she says casually, and picks up from where we left.

'Yes, I used to miss my childhood, but I did get a chance to relive it through Esha and Ahaana. Now that they are becoming mothers, I will get yet another chance to relive my childhood, this time as grandmother! God has been kind to me, so I really should not be sitting and complaining,' she says.

Her phone rings once again. '*Ji yeh bilkul galat hai ki kisi ne aapke ghar saamne kacchra dal diya hai, par main Delhi mein hoon abhi, toh kya aap kisi local karyakarta ko phone kar sakte hain? Woh aapki madad karenge!* (It's absolutely unforgivable that someone has dumped their garbage right outside your house. But I am currently in Delhi, so it would be better if you could seek help from some local administrator).'

I'm amazed at the patience with which she handles these calls. This is certainly a new Hema sitting before me. Meeting, connecting and sharing life with people at the grass-roots has been a humbling experience for the superstar. 'I cannot be expected to behave like a film star when I have decided to serve my people. They have voted for me with expectations and I cannot take them for granted,' she reiterates.

Going back to her younger days, she tells me, 'When we sold our first car – a green Ambassador (bought by her father in Chennai) – we all got emotional and cried! I had learnt to drive in that car. Once, I ended up driving all the way to T. Nagar, where my dance school was. I remember getting quite a firing when my father got to know, but I was a good driver and he didn't know that. I guess those are middle-class emotions – honest and naïve. Nowadays we don't get attached to things so easily. We dispose of everything so casually, from relationships to mobile phones. That was a time and a generation that valued memoirs. I am still attached to my wedding sari, and preserve it with care. There are so many little things I have kept as loving mementos of my father and mother. My daughters too have done the same. But I doubt if the next generation will. Maybe they will preserve everything on a USB, to keep their own memories light.'

Hema's Juhu bungalow is up for renovation again; this time to welcome Esha's autumn baby. Esha's friend Noorien Jumani has been working on brand new interiors for Esha, Bharat and their first-born. 'I am also getting Ahaana's and my floors renovated,' Hema tells me before pausing. 'I have never shared this ... but I remember how one day, while I was shooting in Mumbai, I got a call from my dad saying that I needed to get to Walkeshwar for a puja. I never questioned my parents, so during the shoot break I went over. There I saw a sprawling sea-facing apartment that my father had just bought for me. He asked me if I liked the flat. That was perhaps the first time I told him that I didn't fancy staying in town (south Bombay) but wanted instead a house with a lot of trees, just like the one we had in Chennai. It was then that he started looking for a bungalow in Juhu.

'I still remember it was after Subodh Mukherji signed me on for *Abhinetri* (while I was still shooting for *Sapno Ka Saudagar*) that we shifted from Ananthaswami's house to Manavendra Apartments in Bandra. It was a tiny flat which Bhanu Athaiya used to visit for dress trials. Finally, when we did move to a bungalow in Juhu, on 7th Road, it turned out to be haunted.'

She pauses. Her phone is buzzing again. '*Haanji boliye. Paani aayega. Aap thoda wait karo, sabko time-time pe milega, aap tension mat lo!* (I assure you, you will get water, it's being distributed by turns. Have patience!)'

She picks up the thread again. 'Every night I would feel someone was trying to choke me; I used to have difficulty breathing. I would sleep with my mummy and she noticed how restless I used to be. If this had happened only once or twice we would have ignored it, but it happened every night. That's when we decided to buy our own apartment. Actor Biswajit Chatterjee became my neighbour. I converted the garage into my dance rehearsal hall. I remember Dharam-ji would drop by for coffee, but back then I had no idea I would fall in love and get married to him.'

Finally, in 1972, while she was shooting for *Seeta Aur Geeta*, Hema bought a bungalow in Juhu. 'It was a five-year-old bungalow that belonged to a Gujarati. We constructed extra rooms in the house later. I loved that house because it had lots of trees around it.' Incidentally,

Hema was amongst the first heroines to settle in Juhu. Today the large, leafy neighbourhood is touted as the Beverly Hills of Bollywood.

Hema and Dharmendra's marriage took place at her brother's house. It was a quiet, traditional Tamil wedding. That's how the couple had always wanted it. Dharmendra's father, Kewal Kishan Singh Deol, was very fond of Hema and her family. She recollects fondly, 'He would drop by and meet my father or brother for chai. Instead of shaking hands he would arm-wrestle them, and after defeating them he would jokingly say, "*Tum log ghee-makkhan-lassi khao, idli aur sambhar se taqat nahi aati* (Have butter, lassi and ghee. Idli and sambhar will not make you strong)." My father would join in the laughter. He (Dharmendra's father) was a very jovial person. Dharam-ji's mother, Satwant Kaur, was equally warm and kind-hearted. I remember how she came to meet me once at a dubbing studio in Juhu, after I had conceived Esha. She hadn't informed anyone in the house. I touched her feet, but she hugged me and said, "*Beta, khush raho hamesha* (I give you my blessings)." I was happy that they were happy with me.'

Hema has never visited Dharmendra's house. She was always clear that she didn't want to disturb the 'other' family. She had met Dharmendra's first wife, Prakash Kaur, on several occasions, most of them social gatherings, but after her marriage their paths never crossed. 'I didn't want to disturb anyone. I am happy with whatever Dharam-ji did for me and my daughters. He played the role of a father, like any father would do. I guess I am happy with that. Today I am a working woman and I have been able to maintain my dignity because I have devoted my life to art and culture. I guess, if the situation was even slightly different from this, I wouldn't be what I am today. Though I have never spoken about Prakash, I respect her a lot. Even my daughters respect Dharam-ji's family. The world wants to know about my life in detail, but that is not for others to know. It's no one's business.'

Esha is probably the only one (from Hema's family) to step into Dharmendra's house. Dharmendra's younger brother, Ajit Singh Deol (Abhay Deol's father), was very unwell and bedridden. Keen on meeting her Ji chacha, Esha paid him a visit. 'I wanted to meet him and pay my respects. (He passed away in 2015.) He had been very sweet to both me and Ahaana and we have always been very close to Abhay,' Esha shares. 'There was no option of him visiting us, because he was bedridden, and neither was he in a hospital where we could visit him. So, I called Sunny bhaiya and he organized everything.'

Hema's bungalow Advitiya is five minutes away from Dharmendra's 11th Road house, but it took almost three decades for Esha to traverse it. On her way out, she also met Prakash for the first time. 'I touched her feet, she blessed me and I walked away…' she tells me after a prolonged silence.

Meanwhile, as Hema says, life for her keeps 'happening' at a frenetic pace. 'I want to do so many things in life,' she says. 'I have a lot to do for Mathura; I am also planning a new ballet; I am reading scripts, and … oh yes, I have to start my dance academy.' After a brief pause she adds, with a hint of scepticism, 'Though I sometimes think it might be too late to build a school. I have been following up with government officials for almost twenty years. Maharashtra Chief Minister Mr Fadnavis has assured me that he will give me land, but now I am contemplating if I should take up the project at all. I am now turning seventy, where is the time? It's a lot of responsibility, maintaining an academy. The dancer in me says that I must do something for art and dance. Subhash Ghai started Whistling Woods at the right time; today, Meghna and Rahul (Subhash Ghai's daughter and son-in-law) are taking good care of the institution. I don't know if I should leave this mammoth responsibility to Esha and Ahaana. Maybe I should consider making a state-of-the-art auditorium instead that would promote Indian culture and dance. I want to invite international dancers to perform, but we don't have the right infrastructure in Mumbai and Delhi. They don't maintain it, and it becomes difficult for artists to perform.'

Hema confesses that ever since she has entered politics, things have been different. 'I am always criticized even if I want to do something good for society. This academy has been my dream because I have been pursuing classical dance since I was six years of age. And when on national television a certain journalist tries to malign me without knowing my credentials, it's hurtful. I have no issues answering questions from the media or facing trials, because I haven't done anything wrong. I still remember how during the Mathura massacre incident, there was a local TV reporter who stood outside my house, focused his camera on my room and ran a live show, saying, *"Yeh dekhiye Mathura ki sansad Hema Malini araam ki neend le rahi hai, aur Mathura le log aspatal mein maut se joonjh rahe hai* (Look at Mathura MP Hema Malini, peacefully sleeping at her residence, while victims are struggling for life in the hospital)." Now, I wish I could ask this journalist – is trespassing allowed in journalism? How did he know if I was sleeping or talking or doing anything else? Also, what did he expect me to do in the middle of the night? Is it a good idea to disturb patients at the hospital in the middle of the night? They are targeting me because they want sensationalism in television. Similar things have happened to me on several occasions. During the Jaipur highway accident, there was a local channel who wanted to bribe the victim's father and force him to say that I was drunk and driving the car. Who are these people, I want to know.'

So, do these repeated incidents and being constantly under the public scanner leave her bitter? 'Never!' she says vehemently. 'If I become bitter and withdraw, "they" will win. That's their purpose – to corner me. But I have followed the words of Lord Krishna in the Bhagavad Gita – don't work with expectations, work without any vested interest and the result will be the by-product of your good deeds. Each time they tried to malign me, I have emerged stronger, with more will power to fight against all odds.

'People ask me if I am sad,' she continues, going back to her personal life. 'I tell them I am very happy in whatever I am doing, and they should also be happy and not bother about others. It's a very sad situation in our country where women are perceived to be happy and secure only when they are with their fathers, husbands, brothers or sons. I have felt most secure with my mother, aunt and daughters. Unless we think beyond (these stereotypical notions), nothing is going to change. I could have stopped working, but I didn't. Yes, there was a time when I thought that it was "pack-up" for me. That's when Gulzar saab met me and said, "Hema, you have reached the peak. Don't look down, because between one peak and another lies a deep valley. You need to keep walking." Being a mentor and friend, I think he has the knack to simplify the most difficult things as lucidly as possible. The day I feel I am done, I will fail. There are always newer mediums to explore and I would like to explore them all. I would like to work with younger talents and probably do a film that Darien and Esha's baby would someday be able to relate to.'

Most of Dharmendra's time nowadays is spent at his farmhouse in Lonavala, where Hema and her daughters often join him. 'Far from the madding crowd, we chat about life. He indulges in shayari, which he claims he writes only for me, and I know that is not true! But I record them on my phone because of his voice and his Urdu pronunciation. Then he asks me to sing a song, and he records that on his phone. Later, whenever we are away from each other, we listen to each other's voices on our phones. I guess that's love ... an emotion not many people will be able to relate to.'

She plays the latest sher Dharmendra has written. It is a beautiful Urdu couplet, delivered impeccably. I ask her if I can use it in this book and she promptly tells me, 'I'll have to seek his permission first, and if I ask him, I will have to tell him the purpose. Then he will want to decide only after reading the entire book. He will never find the time to read it, and you will eventually be waiting eternally to get it published! I would suggest, after writing this book, you write a book on Dharam-ji. I really feel someone should write a book on him, because by default it will become a chronicle of Bollywood since 1950...' Before she can finish, she receives a call from Dharmendra.

As I excuse myself immediately, she smiles at me. I take my leave but can still faintly hear her asking Dharmendra about his health and if he has been eating his meals on time. This is the world that Hema has created for herself – a space built painstakingly over thirty-eight years with love, passion, dedication, sacrifice and dignity. A space that no one, apart from these two, can ever understand or should even try to. Hema is a stronger woman today because of Dharmendra. She knows that he is always around, but she has never misused her shield.

Shobhaa De had once written in her column for *Bombay Times*, right after Esha's wedding, 'It takes guts to do what Hema did. Today Esha and Ahaana are known as Hema's daughters, while Sunny and

Bobby are known are Dharam's sons. In a patriarchal society, human beings like Hema reassure hopes for every woman in our society!'

I remember the late Farooq Shaikh telling me once about the television show he used to host, 'While I was hosting a celebrity show, *Jeena Isi Ka Naam Hai*, there was a segment in which we used to show photos from albums. The background music would be that of a violin. Hema-ji promptly remarked on the show, "*Yeh sad music kyon dala?* (Why are you playing this sad music?) What is so sad about [the] past?" I looked at her and smiled; she would often say such meaningful things so casually.'

So, is Hema Malini, on the brink of her seventieth birthday, a truly happy person? My guess is that she is beyond such transient feelings, and onto something far more blissful.

Afterword

Hema Malini-ji and I started our careers almost together, way back in the 1960s. I signed her on for the first time in 1969 for *Andaz*, after which we went on to do films like *Seeta Aur Geeta* and *Sholay*. Strangely, after *Sholay*, we didn't work together for a long, long time. I continued making movies, while she got busy with her share of commitments. In fact, immediately after *Sholay*, I had approached her for *Shaan*, but things didn't work out. I remember reading somewhere how she had once said, 'Uss role mein kuch khas nahin tha karne ke liye.' But I can now say, 'Agar woh yeh role kar leti toh shayad wohi role kuch khas ho jata!' It took another forty-two years for us to work together again, but neither time nor distance has managed to diminish my friendship with Hema. She's someone I have always admired for her sincerity and dedication towards everything she sets out to do.

After three blockbuster movies, both Hema-ji and I wanted to make a film that would be especially remembered by her fans – which is probably why it took us four decades to collaborate! *Shimla Mirchi*, our upcoming film, will be released by Viacom18 later this year. If you watch the movie, you will understand why we waited this long to reunite for a film!

I still remember, after *Andaz*, I immediately wanted to start work on *Seeta Aur Geeta*. We released *Andaz* in May 1972 and I was keen on starting another film by July 1972. I had approached Mumtaz for the film, because I knew she would be able to bring about the zing in Geeta's character. But when she turned down the offer, citing non-availability of dates, I immediately approached Hema-ji. But Hema-ji was reluctant to take up a double role that would draw comparisons with a thespian like Dilip Kumar (he played a similar role in *Ram Aur Shyam* in 1967). The challenge seemed too daunting for her, but I somehow managed to convince her. The rest was history. The film broke all possible records at the box office. Mumtaz's refusal, if I look back now, was a blessing in disguise. In those action scenes, Hema Malini proved to be a big surprise for the audience.

When I approached her for *Sholay*, I remember Hema-ji telling me, 'If you want me to do this role, I will do it.' She hadn't even read the script or asked any questions before saying 'yes' to *Sholay*. In fact, while playing the character of Basanti, she was simultaneously playing Kusum in Gulzar saab's *Khusbhoo*. I would jokingly tell her how she was once again playing *Seeta Aur Geeta*, only this time in two different films! In *Sholay*, I wanted to cast Hema-ji as a tangewali, because I felt we had to do something that would be bigger than our last outing. Everyone had seen a tangewala but never a tangewali. The streak of 'Geeta' in 'Basanti' was overwhelmingly apparent, and it worked like magic for the audience.

My wife Kiran and I have always shared a warm and cordial friendship with Hema-ji. I have always considered her a unique person – someone who reflects the qualities of both Seeta and Geeta! I remember her as shy and an introvert at first, who, with the years, went on to become a confident and fine actor. She married the person she loved; she went on to produce movies, and direct serials and films. Today she is a proud and happy grandmother with a successful political career, not to mention her role as India's cultural ambassador in promoting Indian classical dance and music.

As a star and as an individual, Hema-ji has managed to bring about a balance in her world beautifully. It isn't an easy thing to do, especially when you are a public figure. No one has ever spoken ill of her because she never speaks ill of anyone. She has always focused on self-improvement and the best thing about her is that she never boasts about it. She has made her own choices in life and has stood by them. She is not a feminist, she is an individualist. To my mind, she is an individual who proved that you can live your life the way you want to, and need to, and make the world respect you for it. I don't think there is another person in this industry who holds the same kind of position as her. There is a lesson one needs to take from her life story.

Being the 'Dream Girl' was only the beginning of her career ... she went way beyond her dreams to achieve so much more. She became a woman of substance, in her own right. A book on her life, when Hema-ji is completing fifty glorious years of her acting career in Hindi cinema, is very well deserved. I congratulate publishers HarperCollins and author Ram Kamal Mukherjee for putting together this authorized biography. We have enough chronicles on great films, great heroes and film-makers, but we rarely write about heroines. I hope this encourages many more books on the great leading ladies of Indian cinema.

I have always been proud of my professional association with Hema-ji – an association that continues even today. She had once mentioned how I help bring out the best in her as an actor, but the truth remains that she needs to have it in her for me to bring the best out of her. She has scaled some extraordinary heights over the last fifty years – not many women can say that about their professional lives. In fact, how many women in our industry have worked for fifty years in the first place?

When I asked Ram Kamal Mukherjee why he wanted to write a second book on Hema Malini, he said, 'Hema-ji has achieved so much in life after *Baghbaan* that I feel this is the right time to retell her story.' I couldn't disagree with him. I have never seen Hema-ji sitting idle. I have never seen her satisfied. The hunger to do something bigger and better makes her an unstoppable achiever – a fact that the book's title probably validates.

Ramesh Sippy

Filmography

SOUTH

Ithu Sathiyam (1963)
(as a dancer); Starring: Asokan, Chandrakantha; Director: K. Sankar; Producer: Saravanaa Pictures

Pandava Vanavasam (1965) (as a dancer); Starring: N.T. Rama Rao, S.V. Ranga Rao, Savitri; Director: K.K. Rao; Producer: Anjaneyulu Adusumilli

Shri Krishna Vijayam (1970); Starring: N.T. Rama Rao, Jayalalithaa; Director: K.K. Rao; Producer: Kaumudi Productions

HINDI

Sapnon Ka Saudagar (1968); Starring: Raj Kapoor, Tanuja; Director: Mahesh Kaul; Producer: Screen Gems

Jahan Pyar Mile (1969); Starring: Shashi Kapoor, Nadira; Director: Lekh Tandon; Producer: LRT Films

Waris (1969); Starring: Mehmood, Jeetendra, Prem

Chopra; Director: Ramanna; Producer: Vasu Films

Abhinetri (1970); Starring: Shashi Kapoor, Nirupa Roy; Director: Subodh Mukherji; Producer: Subodh Mukherji Productions

Sharafat (1970); Starring: Dharmendra, Ashok Kumar; Director: Asit Sen; Producer: Madan Mohla

Johny Mera Naam (1970); Starring: Dev Anand, Pran; Director: Vijay Anand; Producer: Gulshan Rai

Aansoo Aur Muskan (1970); Starring: Ajay (Parikshat) Sahni, Jagdeep, David; Director: P. Madhavan; Producer: B. Ananthaswami

Tum Haseen Mein Jawan (1970); Starring: Dharmendra, Rajendra Nath; Director: Bhappi Sonie; Producer: Bhappi Sonie

Lal Patthar (1971); Starring: Raaj Kumar, Vinod Mehra, Raakhee;

Director: Sushil Majumdar;
Producer: F.C. Mehra

Andaz (1971); Starring: Rajesh
Khanna, Shammi Kapoor;
Director: Ramesh Sippy;
Producer: G.P. Sippy

Naya Zamana (1971); Starring:
Dharmendra, Pran; Director:
Pramod Chakraborty;
Producer: Pramod Chakraborty

Paraya Dhan (1971); Starring:
Rakesh Roshan, Balraj Sahni;
Director: Rajendra Bhatia;
Producer: Rajendra Bhatia

Tere Mere Sapne (1971);
Starring: Dev Anand, Mumtaz;
Director: Vijay Anand;
Producer: Dev Anand

Babul Ki Galiyaan (1972);
Starring: Sanjay Khan, Shatrughan
Sinha; Director: S.D. Narang;
Producer: S.D. Narang

Raja Jani (1972); Starring:
Dharmendra; Prem Nath; Prem
Chopra; Director: Mohan Sehgal;
Producer: Madan Mohla

Seeta Aur Geeta (1972); Starring:
Sanjeev Kumar, Dharmendra;
Director: Ramesh Sippy;
Producer: G.P. Sippy (Hema
Malini in a double role)

Gora Aur Kala (1972); Starring:
Rajendra Kumar, Rekha, Prem
Chopra; Director: Naresh Kumar;
Producer: Raj Kumar Kohli

Bhai Ho To Aisa (1972): Starring:
Shatrughan Sinha, Jeetendra;
Director: Manmohan Desai;
Producer: A.K. Nadiadwala

Shareef Budmaash (1973):
Starring: Dev Anand, Ajit;
Director: Raj Khosla;
Producer: Dev Anand

Jugnu (1973): Starring:
Dharmendra, Prem Chopra, Pran;
Director: Pramod Chakraborty;
Producer: Pramod Chakraborty

Joshila (1973); Starring: Dev
Anand, Raakhee; Director: Yash
Chopra; Producer: Gulshan Rai

Chhupa Rustam (1973); Starring:
Dev Anand, Vijay Anand, Ajit;
Director: Vijay Anand;
Producer: Vijay Anand

Gehri Chaal (1973); Starring:
Jeetendra, Amitabh Bachchan;
Director: Sridhar;
Producer: Chitralaya

Patthar Aur Payal (1974);
Starring: Dharmendra, Vinod
Khanna; Director: Harmesh
Malhotra; Producer: N.P. Singh

Amir Garib (1974); Starring: Dev
Anand, Tanuja; Director: Mohan
Kumar; Producer: Mohan Kumar

Haath Ki Safaai (1974); Starring:
Vinod Khanna, Randhir Kapoor,
Simi Garewal; Director: Prakash
Mehra; Producer: I.A. Nadiadwala

Prem Nagar (1974); Starring: Rajesh Khanna, Prem Chopra; Director: K.S. Prakash Rao; Producer: D. Rama Naidu

Kasauti (1974); Starring: Amitabh Bachchan, Pran; Director: Arvind Sen; Producer: Arvind Sen

Dost (1974); Starring: Dharmendra, Shatrughan Sinha; Director: Dulal Guha; Producer: Premji

Pratiggya (1975); Starring: Dharmendra, Ajit; Director: Dulal Guha; Producer: Dharmendra

Dulhan (1974); Starring: Jeetendra, Ashok Kumar; Director: C.V. Rajendran; Producer: B. Ananthaswami

Khushboo (1975); Starring: Jeetendra, Sharmila Tagore (sp. app.); Director: Gulzar; Producer: Prasan Kapoor

Dharmatma (1975); Starring: Feroz Khan, Rekha, Prem Nath; Director: Feroz Khan; Producer: Feroz Khan

Sholay (1975); Starring: Dharmendra, Amitabh Bachchan, Sanjeev Kumar, Amjad Khan, Jaya Bachchan; Director: Ramesh Sippy; Producer: G.P. Sippy

Sunehra Sansar (1975); Starring: Rajendra Kumar, Mala Sinha; Director: A. Subba Rao; Producer: Vadde Sobhanadri, A.S.R. Anjaney

Sanyasi (1975); Starring: Manoj Kumar, Premnath; Director: Sohanlal Kanwar; Producer: Sohanlal Kanwar

Do Thug (1975); Starring: Shatrughan Sinha, Danny Denzongpa; Director: S.D. Narang; Producer: S.D. Narang

Jaaneman (1976); Starring: Dev Anand, Prem Nath; Director: Chetan Anand; Producer: Dev Anand

Maa (1976); Starring: Dharmendra, Nirupa Roy; Director: M.A. Thirumugam; Producer: M.A.A. Chinnappa Devar

Mehbooba (1976); Starring: Rajesh Khanna, Prem Chopra; Director: Shakti Samanta; Producer: Mushir Riaz

Charas (1976); Starring: Dharmendra, Amjad Khan; Director: Ramanand Sagar; Producer: Ramanand Sagar

Dus Numbri (1976); Starring: Manoj Kumar, Prem Nath, Pran; Director: Madan Mohla; Producer: Madan Mohla

Aap Beati (1976); Starring: Shashi Kapoor, Ashok Kumar; Director: Mohan Kumar; Producer: Mohan Kumar

Kinara (1977); Starring: Jeetendra, Dharmendra; Director: Gulzar; Producers: Pranlal Mehta, Gulzar

Dream Girl (1977); Starring: Dharmendra, Ashok Kumar; Director: Pramod Chakraborty; Producers: Jaya Chakravarthy, Gulshan Rai, J.K. Behl

Chacha Bhatija (1977); Starring: Dharmendra, Randhir Kapoor, Yogeeta Bali, Rehman; Director: Manmohan Desai; Producer: Baldev Pushkarna

Dhoop Chhaon (1977); Starring: Sanjeev Kumar, Yogeeta Bali; Director: Prahlad Sharma; Producer: S.N. Jain

Sharafat Chhod Di Maine (1976); Starring: Feroz Khan, Neetu Singh; Director: Jagdev Bhambri; Producers: Damodaran Menon, V.M. Shah

Palkon Ki Chhaon Mein (1977); Starring: Rajesh Khanna, Rekha; Director: Meraj; Producers: Nariman I. Baria, A. Khalia

Azaad (1977); Starring: Dharmendra, Ajit, Prem Chopra; Director: Pramod Chakraborty; Producer: Pramod Chakraborty

Naach Uthe Sansar (1978); Starring: Shashi Kapoor, Simi Garewal; Director: Yakub Hussain; Producer: Mohmud Sarosh

Apna Khoon (1978); Starring: Shashi Kapoor, Ashok Kumar; Director: B. Subhash; Producer: S.K. Kapur

Dillagi (1978); Starring: Dharmendra, Mithu Mukherjee; Director: Basu Chatterji; Producer: Bikram Singh Deol

Trishul (1978); Starring: Amitabh Bachchan, Sanjeev Kumar, Shashi Kapoor, Raakhee, Waheeda Rehman; Director: Yash Chopra; Producer: Gulshan Rai

Dil Kaa Heera (1979); Starring: Dharmendra, Sachin; Director: Dulal Guha; Producer: Manian, Vidwan V. Lakshmanan

Meera (1979); Starring: Vinod Khanna, Shammi Kapoor; Director: Gulzar; Producer: Premji

Hum Tere Aashiq Hain (1979); Starring: Jeetendra, Amjad Khan; Director: Prem Sagar; Producer: Prem Sagar

Ratnadeep (1979); Starring: Girish Karnad, Dheeraj Kumar; Director: Basu Chatterji; Producer: R. Kannan, Jagannath

Janta Hawaldar (1979); Starring: Rajesh Khanna, Yogeeta Bali; Director: Mehmood; Producer: Manoharlal P. Chhabria, Manohar P. Jaisingh

Do Aur Do Paanch (1980); Starring: Amitabh Bachchan,

Shashi Kapoor, Parveen Babi;
Director: Rakesh Kumar;
Producer: C. Dhandayuthapani

The Burning Train (1980);
Starring: Dharmendra, Vinod
Khanna, Jeetendra, Parveen Babi,
Neetu Singh; Director: Ravi
Chopra; Producer: B.R. Films

Alibaba Aur 40 Chor (1980);
Starring: Dharmendra, Zeenat
Aman; Director: Umesh Mehra;
Producer: F.C. Mehra

Bandish (1980); Starring: Rajesh
Khanna, Tanuja; Director:
K. Bapaiah; Producer: D. Rama
Naidu

Aas Paas (1981); Starring:
Dharmendra, Prem Chopra;
Director: J. Om Prakash;
Producer: Jagdish Kumar

Kranti (1981); Starring: Manoj
Kumar, Dilip Kumar, Parveen
Babi, Shashi Kapoor, Shatrughan
Sinha; Director: Manoj Kumar;
Producer: Manoj Kumar

Krodhi (1981); Starring:
Dharmendra, Zeenat Aman,
Shashi Kapoor; Director: Subhash
Ghai; Producer: Ranjit Virk

Kudrat (1981); Starring: Vinod
Khanna, Rajesh Khanna, Raaj
Kumar; Director: Chetan Anand;
Producer: B.S. Khanna

Naseeb (1981); Starring: Amitabh
Bachchan, Shatrughan Sinha, Rishi

Kapoor, Reena Roy; Director:
Manmohan Desai;
Producer: Manmohan Desai

Jyoti (1981); Starring: Jeetendra,
Vijayendra Ghatge, Shashikala;
Director: Pramod Chakraborty;
Producer: Pramod Chakravorty

Dard (1981); Starring: Rajesh
Khanna, Poonam Dhillon;
Director: Ambrish Sangal;
Producer: Shyam Sunder
Shivdasani

Maan Gaye Ustad (1981);
Starring: Shashi Kapoor, Pran,
Bindu; Director: Shibu Mitra;
Producer: S.K. Kapur

Meri Awaaz Suno (1981);
Starring: Jeetendra, Parveen Babi;
Producer: G.A. Seshagiri Rao;
Director: S.V. Rajendra Singh

Desh Premee (1982); Starring:
Amitabh Bachchan, Parveen Babi,
Shammi Kapoor, Sharmila Tagore;
Director: Manmohan Desai;
Producer: Subhash Desai

Samraat (1982); Starring:
Dharmendra, Jeetendra, Zeenat
Aman, Amjad Khan, Shreeram
Lagoo, Shashikala, Om Shivpuri,
Kader Khan; Director: Mohan
Sehgal; Producer: Madan Mohla

Baghavat (1982); Starring:
Dharmendra, Reena Roy, Amjad
Khan; Director: Ramanand Sagar;
Producer: Ramanand Sagar

Rajput (1982); Starring: Vinod Khanna, Rajesh Khanna, Dharmendra, Ranjeeta, Tina, Ranjeet; Director: Vijay Anand; Producer: Mushir Riaz

Satte Pe Satta (1982); Starring: Amitabh Bachchan, Ranjeeta, Amjad Khan, Shakti Kapoor, Prema Narayan, Paintal, Sachin, Kanwaljeet; Director: Raj Sippy; Producer: Romu N Sippy

Farz Aur Kanoon (1982); Starring: Jeetendra, Rati Agnihotri, Raj Kiran; Director: K. Raghavendra Rao; Producer: Roja Pictures

Taqdeer (1983); Starring: Shatrughan Sinha, Mithun Chakraborty, Zeenat Aman, Ranjeet; Director: Brij; Producer: Brij

Andhaa Kanoon (1983); Starring: Amitabh Bachchan, Rajnikant, Reena Roy, Prem Chopra, Maadhavi, Danny Denzongpa; Director: T. Rama Rao; Producer: A. Purnachandra Rao

Justice Chaudhury (1983); Starring: Jeetendra, Sridevi, Moushumi Chatterjee, Debasree Roy, Kader Khan; Director: K. Raghavendra Rao; Producer: G.A. Seshagiri

Nastik (1983); Starring: Amitabh Bachchan, Pran, Deven Verma, Amjad Khan; Director: Pramod Chakraborty; Producer: Vinod Doshi

Razia Sultan (1983); Starring: Dharmendra, Pradeep Kumar, Parveen, Ajit, Vijayendra, Tajdar, Shorab; Director: Kamal Amrohi; Producer: A.K. Mishra

Ek Nai Paheli (1984); Starring: Kamal Hasan, Raaj Kumar, Padmini Kolhapure, Mehmood; Director: K. Balachander; Producer: Subba Rao

Ek Naya Itihas (1984); Starring: Bhishnu, Vinod Mehra, Rageshwari, Raza Murad, Ranjeet; Director: B.S.Narayan; Producer: Asha Devi

Qaidi (1984); Starring: Shatrughan Sinha, Jeetendra, Shakti Kapoor, Ranjeet, Maadhavi, Kader Khan; Director: S.S. Ravichandra; Producer: G. Hanumantha Rao

Raaj Tilak (1984); Starring: Raaj Kumar, Dharmendra, Sunil Dutt, Reena Roy, Sarika, Yogeeta Bali, Ranjeeta, Raj Kiran, Kamal Haasan; Director: Rajkumar Kohli; Producer: Anil Suri

Sharara (1984); Starring: Shatrughan Sinha, Mithun Chakraborty, Raaj Kumar, Vijayendra, Shakti Kapoor, Ranjeet, Kader Khan;

Director: S.V. Rajendra Singh;
Producer: R.J. Chakravarti

Aandhi Toofan (1985);
Starring: Shatrughan Sinha,
Mithun Chakraborty, Meenakshi
Sheshadri, Danny; Director:
B. Subhash; Producer: Pahlaj
Nihalani

Babu (1985); Starring: Rajesh
Khanna, Deepak Parashar, Rati
Agnihotri, Paintal, Madan Puri;
Director: A.V. Tirulokachander;
Producer: V.R. Parameshwaram

Durgaa (1985); Starring: Raj
Babbar, Pran, Ashok Kumar, Aruna
Irani; Director: Shibu Mitra;
Producer: S.K. Kapur

Hum Dono (1995); Starring:
Rajesh Khanna, Reena Roy, Mukri,
Johnny Walker, Jagdeep; Director:
B.S. Glaad; Producer: Tony Glaad

Phaansi Ke Baad (1985);
Starring: Shatrughan Sinha, Shakti
Kapoor, Satyen Kappoo, Iftekhar,
Amrish Puri, Ajit; Director:
Harmesh Malhotra;
Producer: Harmesh Malhotra

Ramkali (1985); Starring:
Shatrughan Sinha, Suresh Oberoi,
Sudhir, Ranjeet, Nirupa Roy,
Kader Khan; Director: Shyam
Ralhan; Producer: Ashok

Yudh (1985); Starring: Anil
Kapoor, Tina Munim, Shatrughan
Sinha, Jackie Shroff, Pran, Danny

Denzongpa; Director: Rajiv Rai;
Producer: Gulshan Rai

Ek Chadar Maili Si (1986);
Starring: Rishi Kapoor, Poonam
Dhillon, Kulbhushan Kharbanda,
Dina Pathak, A.K. Hangal;
Director: Sukhwant Dhadda;
Producer: G.M. Singh Nindrajog

Ram Tera Desh (1986); Starring:
Shabana Azmi, Arun Govil, Sarika,
Vijayendra, Prem Chopra, Ashok
Kumar; Director: Swaroop Kumar;
Producer: Tito

Anjaam (1987); Starring: Shashi
Kapoor, Shafi Inamdar, Rajan
Sippy, Parijat; Director: Hariharan;
Producer: Ramesh Tiwari

Hiraasat (1987); Starring: Mithun
Chakraborty, Shatrughan Sinha,
Anita Raaj, Shakti Kapoor, Prem
Chopra; Director: Surendra
Mohan; Producer: Sunil Sharma

Jaan Hatheli Pe (1987); Starring:
Dharmendra, Rekha, Jeetendra,
Shakti Kapoor, Ranjeet, Raj
Babbar; Director: R. Jhalani;
Producer: Sudesh Kumar

Kudrat Ka Kanoon (1987);
Starring: Jackie Shroff, Radhika,
Charanraj, Shafi Inamdar;
Director: K.C. Bokadia;
Producer: Suresh Bokadia

Sitapur Ki Geeta (1987);
Starring: Shoma Anand, Shakti
Kapoor, Raza Murad, Pran;

Director: Shibu Mitra;
Producer: S.K. Kapur

Apne Apne (1987); Starring:
Jeetendra, Rekha, Mandakini,
Kader Khan; Director: Ramesh
Behl; Producer: Ramesh Behl

Mohabbat Ke Dushman (1988);
Starring: Sanjay Dutt, Raaj
Kumar, Pran, Farha, Amrish
Puri; Director: Prakash Mehra;
Producer: Prakash Mehra

Mulzim (1988); Starring:
Shatrughan Sinha, Kimi Katkar,
Jeetendra, Amrita Singh, Kader
Khan; Director: K.S R Das;
Producer: G. Hanumantha Rao

Vijay (1988); Starring: Anil
Kapoor, Rajesh Khanna, Rishi
Kapoor, Meenakshi Sheshadri,
Sonam, Shakti Kapoor, Anupam
Kher; Director: Yash Chopra;
Producer: Yash Raj Films

Sachche Ka Bol-Bala (1989);
Starring: Dev Anand, Jackie Shroff,
Meenakshi Sheshadri; Director
Dev Anand; Producer Dev Anand

Desh Ke Dushman (1989);
Starring: Mandakini, Sadashiv
Amrapurkar, Raaj Kumar, Aditya
Pancholi; Director: Swaroop
Kumar; Producer: Manmohan
Kapur

Paap Ka Ant (1989); Starring:
Rajesh Khanna, Govinda, Madhuri
Dixit, Anupam Kher;

Director: Vijay Reddy;
Producer: Gautam Bokadia

Santosh (1989); Starring:
Shatrughan Sinha, Manoj Kumar,
Raakhee, Sarika, Prem Chopra,
Om Shivpuri; Director: Balbir
Wadhawan; Producer: Balbir
Wadhawan

Rihaee (1990); Starring: Vinod
Khanna, Naseeruddin Shah,
Reema Lagoo, Neena Gupta,
Mohan Agashe, Ila Arun; Director:
Arunaraje Patil; Producer: NFDC

Shadyantra (1990); Starring:
Raj Bundela, Pankaj Kapoor,
Alok Nath; Director: Rajan Johri;
Producer: Shakil Productions

Jamai Raja (1990); Starring: Anil
Kapoor, Madhuri Dixit, Shakti
Kapoor, Satish Kaushik, Anupam
Kher; Director: A.K. Reddy;
Producer: T. Trivikrama Rao

Deshwasi (1991); Starring:
Poonam Dhillon, Manoj Kumar,
Suresh Oberoi, Anupam Kher;
Director: Rajiv Goswami;
Producer: Rajiv Goswami

Lekin (1991); Starring: Vinod
Khanna, Dimple Kapadia,
Vijayendra Ghatge, Amjad
Khan, Alok Nath; Director:
Gulzar; Producer: Hridayanath
Mangeshkar

Hai Meri Jaan (1991); Starring:
Kumar Gaurav, Ayesha Jhulka,

Sunil Dutt, Raza Murad, Nirupa Roy; Director: Roopesh Kumar; Producer: Roopesh Kumar

Indira (1992); Starring: Suresh Oberoi, Rohini Hattangadi, Prem Chopra; Director: Nripen Mohla; Producer: Balram Mohla

Param Vir Chakra (1995); Starring: Navin Nischol, Tariq Shah, Saeed Jaffrey, Raza Murad, Kulbhushan Kharbanda; Director: Ashok Kaul; Producer: Ashok Kaul

Maahir (1996); Starring: Govinda, Raj Babbar, Kader Khan, Farha; Director: Lawrence D'souza; Producer: Harish Barot

Jai Dakshineshwar Kali Maa (1996); Starring: Alok Nath, Ajinkya Deo, Jayshree Gadkar; Director: Shantilal Soni; Producer: Anuradha Paudwal

Himalay Putra (1997); Starring: Akshaye Khanna, Vinod Khanna; Director: Pankaj Parashar; Producer: Vinod Khanna

Hey Ram (2000); Starring: Kamal Haasan, Rani Mukerji, Naseeruddin Shah, Shah Rukh Khan; Director: Kamal Haasan; Producer: Raajkamal Film International

Censor (2001); Starring: Dev Anand, Rekha, Jackie Shroff; Director: Dev Anand; Producer: Navketan Films International

Baghban (2003); Starring: Amitabh Bachchan, Salman Khan (sp. app.), Mahima Chaudhary; Director: Ravi Chopra; Producer: B.R. Films

TELEVISION PROJECTS

Terah Panne (1986); Director: Vikas Desai; Producer: Kiran Shantaram; Channel: Doordarshan; Episodes: 13

Adalat (1991); Director: Dheeraj Kumar; Producer: Dheeraj Kumar; Channel: Doordarshan; Episode: 1

Naam Gum Jayega: Ahankar; Director: Sudipto Chattopadhyay; Channel: Doordarshan; Episodes: 8

Women of India: Amrapali; Director: Hema Malini; Producer: Hema Malini Channel: Doordarshan; Episodes: 8

Rangoli; Producer: NFDC; Channel: Doordarshan; Episodes: 150

Yug; Director: Sunil Agnihotri; Producer: Satte Shourie; Channel: Doordarshan; Episodes: 450

Aap Ki Saheli; Producer: Hema Malini; Channel: Doordarshan; Episodes: 13

Jai Mata Ki; Director: Puneet Issar; Producer: Cinevista; Channel: Doordarshan; Episodes: 56

Sangam; Producer: Sahara; Channel: Sahara; Episodes: 13

Kamini Damini; Director: Ravi Chopra; Channel: Sahara Manoranjan; Episodes: 200

SPECIAL APPEARANCES

Garam Masala (1972, Director: Aspi; Producer: C. Mohan); **Kunwara Baap** (1974, Director: Mehmood; Producer: Amarlal P. Chhabria); **Ginny Aur Johnny** (1976, Director: Mehmood; Producer: Amarlal P. Chhabria); **Tinku** (1977, Director: Parvez; Producer: Navin Pics); **Cinema Cinema** (1979, Director: Krishna Shah; Producer: Shahab Ahmed); **Suraag** (1982, Director: Jagmohan Mundhra; Producer: Jagmohan Mundhra); **Meherbaani** (1983, Director: A. Nairang; Producer: Ajit Singh Deol); **Mrigtrishna** (1984, Director: Rajendra Shukla; Producer: Naheta Films); **Swami** (1977, Director: Basu Chatterjee; Producer: Jaya Chakravarthy); **Tohfa Mohabbat Ka** (1988, Director: Ram S. Govind; Producer: Mukesh Kumar); **Sachhe Ka Bol-Bala** (1989, Director: Dev Anand; Producer: Navketan Films); **Jai Kali** (1992, Director: Nikhil Saini); **Swami Vivekananda** (1996, Director: G.V. Iyer; Producer: Subi R. Reddy); **Veer Zaara** (2004, Director: Yash Chopra; Producer: Yash Chopra);

Mahabharat Aur Barbareek (2013, Director: Dharmesh Tiwari); **Tell Me O Kkhuda** (2011); **Aarakshan** (2011)

GUEST APPEARANCES

Gautamiputra Satakarni (2017); Ek Rani Aisi Bhi Thi (2016); Aman Ke Farishtey (2016); Andaaz (TV Series, as herself); Amazing Women (2014) (as herself); Bbuddah ... Hoga Terra Baap (2011); Sati Behula (2010) Bhojpuri and Bengali dubbed; Sadiyaan: Boundaries Divide ... Love Unites (2010); Gangotri (2007); Laaga Chunari Mein Daag: Journey of a Woman (2007); Baabul (2006); Ganga (2006); Bhagmati (Animation and Feature Film, 2005); Shimla Mirchi (post-production, 2017); Akbar The Great (one episode as Meera); Baje Payal (one episode as herself)

AS DIRECTOR

Dil Aashna Hai (1991, feature film); Starring: Shah Rukh Khan, Divya Bharti, Dimple Kapadia, Mithun Chakraborty; Jeetendra; Amrita Singh, Kabir Bedi, Farida Jalal, Sonu Walia

Noopur (1990, TV); Channel: Doordarshan; Episodes: 13

Mohini; Producer: ZEE TV

Tell Me O Kkhuda (2011); Starring: Esha Deol, Dharmendra, Rishi Kapoor, Vinod Khanna,

Farooq Sheikh, Arjan Bajwa, Sudhanshu Pandey, Madhoo and Salman Khan (Guest)

PRODUCER and PRESENTER

Awaargi (1990, Director: Mahesh Bhatt); **Gardish** (1993, Director: Priyadarshan); **Jhansi Ki Rani** (56 episodes, Director: Ravi Chopra); **Umbhartha** (Marathi Serial); **Songadi** (Marathi Serial)

PLAYBACK IN FILMS

Haath Ki Safai; Dream Girl; Indira

PLAYBACK PRIVATE ALBUM

Gun Gun Gun and *Kande Mon Piyashi* (1973 HMV, remixed in 2016), Music director: Kishore Kumar; *Soundarya Lahiri* (2013); *Aaji Suniye Zara* with Babul Supriyo (2016); *Gopala Ko Samarpan* (2017), Music by Pandit Hariprasad Chaurasia, Pandit Jasraj, Pandit Shiv Kumar Sharma, Pandit Rajan and Sajan Mishra

DANCE BALLETS

Meera; Ramayan; Durga; Radha Krishna; Savitri; Mahalaxmi; Geet Govind; Draupadi; Yasodha Krishna; Rukmini Parinay; Parampara

INCOMPLETE/UNRELEASED FILMS

Devdas (Director: Gulzar; Cast: Dharmendra and Sharmila Tagore); **Chandragupta Maurya** (No information available); **Rakshak** (No information available); **Takrao** (No information available); **Ganga Bani Jwala** (1989, Director: P. Chakravarti; Cast: Suresh Oberoi and Sonu Walia); **Insaaf Ka Suraj** (1990, Director: Sudhakar Sharma; Cast: Shammi Kapoor and Kiran Kumar); **Marg** (1988, Director: Mahesh Bhatt; Cast: Vinod Khanna and Dimple Kapadia); **Jeevan Saat Suron Ka Sangam** (1993, Director: Ashim Bhattacharjee; Cast: Hema Malini, Prasenjit Chatterjee, Mamta Kulkarni and Amrish Puri; Music: R.D. Burman); **Nargis** (1993, Director: Khalid Sami; Cast: Zeba Bakhtiyar, Naseeruddin Shah and Amjad Khan; the film's music created waves); **Insaaf Bhawani Ka** (1990, Director: S.R. Pratap; Cast: Suresh Oberoi, Hema Malini, Sumeet Saigal, Archana Joglekar, Anjana Mumtaz and Raza Murad); **Aazma Kar Dekh Lo** (1998, Director: R.K. Jain; Cast: Govinda, Urvashi, Hema Malini, Satish Kaushik and Sadashiv Amrapurkar; Music: Laxmikant-Pyarelal; the film was later retitled *Engineer No 1* to capitalize on Govinda's string of No. 1 films); Kewal Sharma's **Jhansi Ki Rani** (Shot pilot episode for Zee TV, shelved for financial reasons, Hema played the title role)

Index

Aandhi-Toofan (1985), 85
Aap ki Saheli (tele-serial), 129
Abbas, K.A., 49
Abhinetri (1970), 24, 28–29, 212
Adhiputi, Guru Ravindra, 138, 187
Advani, Lal Krishna, 147, 149
Agarwal, Narayan, 203–4
Agashe, Mohan, 120
Agnihotri, Sunil, 126
Akhtar, Javed. *See* Salim-Javed
Akhtar, Zoya, 207
Aman Ke Farishtey (2016), 208
Amir Garib (1974), 34, 39, 82
Amrapali (1966), 25
Amrapali (tele-serial), 126–27
Amrohi, Kamal, 87–91
Amrohi, Tajdar, 88–89, 91
Anand, Chetan, 73
Anand, Dev, 25, 33–34, 66, 72–73,
    82, 183, 191–92, 208
Anand, Vijay, 34, 73
Anandolok, 138
Ananthaswami, B., 18–19, 22, 23,
    27–28, 30, 36, 49, 212
Andaz (1971), 36–37, 42, 50, 57,
    59
Andha Kanoon (1983), 85
Anjaam (1987), 86
Anuradha, K., 6
Aruna Raje, 118–21

Ashok Kumar, 56, 73, 83
Athaiya, Bhanu, 88, 89, 212
Attenborough, Richard, 92, 127,
    144
Awaargi (1990), 104–5
Azad Bharat Vidhik Vaicharik
    Kranti Satyagrahi, 159
Azmi, Shabana, 46, 59, 92, 172

Baabul, 206
Babu (1985), 37
Babu, S.V. Rajendra Singh, 93, 104
Bachchan, Abhishek, 72, 181–82
Bachchan, Amitabh, 37, 45, 50,
    61, 63, 70–72, 83, 85, 90,
    116–17, 143, 145, 170,
    201–2, 206, 208
Bachchan, Jaya *nee* Bhaduri, 55, 72,
    146, 202, 207
Baghban (2003), 170–72, 206
Bahar (1951), 25
Bahurani (1963), 83
Bajwa, Arjan, 115
Balakrishna, Nandamuri, 208–9
Bali, Geeta, 103
Bali, Yogita, 116
Bbuddah Hoga Terra Baap (2011),
    208
Bedi, Rajendra Singh, 103
Berry, Sudesh, 125

Bhagavad Gita, 204, 205, 215

Bhansali, Sanjay Leela, 60, 87, 207

Bharatiya Janata Party (BJP), 141, 146, 149–54, 202

Bharti, Divya, 111, 113, 115–16, 117, 125, 189

Bhatt, Mahesh, 68, 104

Bhattacharya, Nandita *nee* Ahlavar, 10–11

Birju Maharaj, Pandit, 59

Bobby (1973), 38, 39

Bub (2002), 144

Burman, R.D., 55, 60, 205

Burning Train, The (1980), 170

Censor (2001), 34

Chacha Bhatija (1977), 67

Chakraborty, Mithun, 41, 73, 116, 121

Chakraborty, Pramod, 83, 201

Chakravarti, Jagannath (brother), 5, 6, 14–15, 22, 164, 200

Chakravarthy, Jaya (mother), 1–3, 5–6, 8–17, 18–22, 26–28, 30–31, 47, 74–75, 122, 135, 172–74, 177

Chakravarti, Kannan (brother), 5, 6, 8, 10, 15, 17, 26, 95, 96, 127, 173, 205

Chakravarti, Prabha (sister-in-law), 28, 95–96, 131, 162, 173

Chakravarti, Suchitra, 96

Chakravarti, V.S.R. (father), 2, 5, 11–12, 13, 15–16, 17, 19, 22, 26, 47, 173

Charas (1976), 48

Chatterjee, Basu, 108, 207

Chatterjee, Biswajit, 212

Chattopadhyay, Saratchandra, 57, 60

Chattopadhyay, Sudipto, 59, 127

Chaudhary, Jayant, 151

Chaudhury, Neena, 141

Chaurasia, Pandit Hariprasad, 156, 163, 204

Chhupa Rustam (1973), 34

Chopra, B.R., 65, 170

Chopra, Kailash, 60–61

Chopra, Ravi, 128, 170–71, 206

Chopra, Yash, 54, 206

Cine Artistes Welfare Fund of India (CAWFI), 145

Conran, Shirley, *Lace*, 110

D' Souza, Lawrence, 105

De, Shobhaa, 216-217

Deewana (1992), 111, 112

Denzongpa, Danny, 85

Deol, Abhay, 179, 191, 192, 213

Deol, Ahaana (daughter), 64, 69, 86, 99–100, 138–39, 151, 164–65, 167, 178–79, 181, 183, 185, 186–93, 194, 195, 199, 203, 210, 211, 212, 214, 216

Deol, Ajay, 191, 199

Deol, Ajit Singh (Ji chacha), 179, 191, 213

Deol, Bobby, 179, 190, 191, 199, 217

Deol, Esha (daughter), 25, 64, 69, 72, 86, 94–99, 100, 114, 115, 133, 138, 139, 145, 164, 166–67, 175–85, 187–89, 191–92, 195–97, 199, 210, 211, 212, 213-214, 216

Deol, Kewal Krishan Singh, 213
Deol, Sunny, 41, 179, 190, 191,
    199, 214, 217
Desai, Manmohan, 72, 207
Desai, Vikas, 101, 102, 105, 106
Desh Premee (1982), 72
Devdas (1955), 25
Devdas (2002), 60, 87
Devgn, Ajay, 108
Dhadda, Sukhwant, 103
Dharmendra, 24, 32, 37, 40,
    43–49, 50, 53–54, 58, 60–61,
    65, 68, 71–72, 74–81, 82–83,
    86, 88–90, 94–95, 99–100,
    103–4, 105–6, 108, 113–14,
    117, 119, 123–24, 128, 142,
    145, 150–51, 164, 167, 173,
    178, 181–84, 186, 189, 191,
    195, 202, 205, 209, 210, 212,
    213, 216
Dheer, Pankaj, 127, 205, 208
Dhillon, Poonam, 78, 143
Dhoom (2004), 182
Dhoop Chaon (1977), 46
Dil Aashna Hai (1992), 41, 65, 68,
    109, 110–15, 117, 125, 189
Dilip Kumar, 34, 42, 65–66, 111,
    170
Dixit, Madhuri, 105, 120, 169, 207
Draupadi, 72, 131, 132–33, 134,
    166
Dream Girl (1977), 123, 201
Dulhan (1974), 56, 75
Duniya (1968), 33
Durga (1985), 84, 86
Durga (dance ballet), 106, 134,
    135, 136, 137
Durga Saptashati, 204

Dus Numbri (1976), 66
Dutt, Nargis, 46, 82

Ek Chadar Maili Si (1986), 103,
    206
Ek Nai Paheli (1984), 93
Ek Naya Itihas (1984), 93
Ek Thi Rani Aisi Bhi (2017), 68,
    159, 208
Exchange Offer, 180

Farooqui, Mahmood, 90

Galgali, Anil, 139
Gandhi (1982), 88, 92
Ganga (2006), 208
Gangotri (2007), 208
Gauri Ammal, Mylapore, 14
Gautamiputra Satakarni (2017),
    208–9
Geet Govind (dance drama), 134,
    135
Gehri Chaal (1973), 45, 70–71,
    72, 85
Ghaav. See *Maahir*
Ghai, Subhash, 117, 214
Ghatge, Vijayendra, 65, 88, 91
Ghosh, Rituparno, 56, 122
Ghosh, Sujoy, 207
Girija Devi, 146
'*Goon goon kore je mon*', 200, 202
Gopalakrishnan, Guru Natanam,
    14, 16
Goswami, Arnab, 140
Govinda, 104–5, 142
Gowri Amma, 16
Gulzar, 57–64, 65, 67, 87, 102,
    106, 108, 145, 205, 207, 215

Gulzar, Meghna, 145
Gupta, Neena, 119
Gupta, Sunil, 86

Haasan, Kamal, 73, 168
Haath ki Safai (1974), 67, 200
Hariyali Aur Raasta (1962), 16
Hassan, Mehdi, 205
Hema Malini: an accident on
    highway, 194–99; awards
    and honours, 42, 57, 59, 66,
    120–1, 138–39, 169, 171–72;
    birth, 5–6; childhood, 5–17;
    dance, relationship with/
    skills, 1–2, 8, 12–17, 18–20,
    24–25, 36, 52, 55, 59–60, 72,
    85, 98, 105–8, 111, 126, 128–
    30, 131–40, 160; experiments
    with spirituality, 160–68;
    ISKCON, association with,
    162–64, 201, 203; marriage to
    Dharmendra, 78–79, 213; as
    National Film Development
    Corporation (NFDC)
    chairperson, 143–45; political
    journey, 80–81, 141–59;—
    Lok Sabha MP from Mathura,
    151–57, 197, 215;—Rajya
    Sabha member, 146–50, 197;
    taxes and debt, 86–87; work
    for television, 101–4, 105
Hemanter Pakhi (2002), 144
Hey Ram (2000), 168
Himalay Putra (1997), 68, 168
HM Creations, 106
Hulchul, 108
Hum Tere Ashique Hain (1979), 78
Hussain, Imtiaz, 110

Idhu Sathiyam (1963), 15
Indira (1992), 201
Indira Devi, Guru Ma, 14, 112,
    136, 137, 161–62, 173
Issar, Puneet, 128

Jaaneman (1976), 34
'Jab tak hain jaan', 52, 55
Jahan Pyar Mile (1969), 24
Jai Durga (tele-serial), 136
Jai Mata Ki (tele-serial), 128–29
Jain, Ravindra, 23, 134, 204
Jairam, Vani, 63
Jaitley, Arun, 143, 146–47
Jamai Raja (1990), 86, 111
Jameela (2002), 144
Janardan, 210
Jasraj, Pandit, 130, 156, 204
Jawahar Bagh, Mathura incident,
    159
Jaya Prada, 78, 100
Jayalalithaa, J., 3, 70–71
Jeetendra, 45, 46, 47, 56, 57, 58,
    68, 70, 71, 75–78, 79, 83, 84,
    116
Jhansi Ki Rani (tele-serial), 127–28
Jis Desh Mein Ganga Behti Hai
    (1960), 21
Johar, Karan, 55, 207
Johny Mera Naam (1970), 23, 25,
    27, 33–35, 72–73
Joshi, Pandit Bhimsen, 163
Joshila (1973), 34
Just Married (2007), 145
Justice Choudhury (1983), 84
Jyoti (1981), 77, 83–84

Kabhi Haan Kabhi Naa (1994), 12
Kahaami (2012), 207

Kalam, A.P.J. Abdul Kalam, 150, 151

Kalyanji-Anandji, 33

'*Kande mon piyashi*', 202

Kanwar, Raj, 208

Kapadia, Dimple, 37–41, 85, 111

Kapoor, Anil, 104, 18

Kapoor, Raj, 18–24, 34, 38, 49, 72, 73, 82

Kapoor, Randhir, 67, 200

Kapoor, Rishi, 103–4, 206, 208

Kapoor, Shammi, 36

Kapoor, Shashi, 25, 28, 29, 49, 105

Kapoor, Shobha *nee* Sippy, 76–77

Kapur, Aditya Roy, 192

Kapur, Shekhar, 50

Karnad, Girish, 46

Kasauti (1974), 71

Kaul, Mahesh, 20–21, 22, 24

Kaur, Prakash 80, 213, 214

Kaur, Satwant, 213

Kaun Banega Crorepati, 202

Khan, Amjad, 50, 55

Khan, Salim. *See* Salim-Javed

Khan, Shah Rukh, 111–15, 189, 192, 206

Khanna, Akshaye, 68, 168

Khanna, Rajesh, 29, 36–39, 82, 84, 96, 207

Khanna, Vinod, 63–64, 67–68, 117, 118, 141–42, 159, 168

Khanum, Farida, 205

Khushboo (1975), 55, 57–58, 60, 75

Kinara (1977), 58–59

Kishore Kumar, 42, 200, 202

Koi Mere Dil Se Poochhe (2002), 182

Kranti (1981), 65, 66

Krishnamoorthy, Kavita, 130, 134, 202

Kulkarni, N.B., 88

Kutty, Govindan, 130

Kutty, Thankamani, 130

Laga Chunari Mein Daag (2007), 208

Lakhandri, Bhushan, 132–33, 136, 137, 166, 185

Lal Pathar (1971), 35–36, 69, 108

Laxmikant–Pyarelal, 63, 205

Maahir (1996), 105

Madhoo (cousin), 108, 122–26

Madhumati (1958), 25

Magunira Shagada (2002), 144

Mahabharat (tele-serial), 170

Mahadevan, Anant Narayan, 107–8, 111

Mahajan, Pramod, 146, 149

Mahal (1969), 33

Mahalaxmi (dance drama), 131, 134, 135

Mahisasurmardini Durga (dance show), 130

Majumdar, Sushil, 35

Malik, Ravi, 129

Mangeshkar, Lata, 56, 59, 63, 90, 147, 200, 205–6

Mani Ratnam, 122, 207

Manoj Kumar, 65, 66

Marg (1988), 67–68, 104

Mausam Ki Tarah, 108

Mazumdar, Deepak, 135, 138

Meena Kumari, 42

Meera (1979), 61–64, 87

Meera (dance drama), 133, 134, 136, 137
Mehbooba (1976), 38, 39
Mehra, F.C., 69
Mehra, Prakash, 67, 200
Mehta, Lalitbhai, 147
Meri Awaaz Suno (1982), 93
Meri Saheli, 129, 143
Mishra, Sajan, 204
Mishra, Sudhir, 145
Mitra, Shibu, 84
Modi, Narendra, 192, 203
Modi, Sohrab, 91
Mohabbat Ke Dushman (1988), 67
Mohammed, Khalid, 111
Mohini (telefilm), 121–22, 124–25
Mukherjee, Hrishikesh, 108, 207, 209
Mukherji, Rani, 164, 184, 206, 207
Mukherji, Subodh, 28, 29, 212
Mukhopadhyay, Bandana, 130
Mukhopadhyay, Deepankar, 144
Muktakashi Rangmanch, Mathura, 156
Mumtaz, 42, 75
My Fair Lady (1974), 78

Naam Gum Jayega (tele-serial), 59, 127
'*Naam gum jayega*', 59
Nagin (1954), 16, 25
Naidu, M. Venkaiah, 149, 150
Nair, Shivam, 180
Nandy, Pritish, 145
Naqvi, Mukhtar Abbas, 149
Nargis (unreleased), 111
Naseeb (1981), 72, 85
Naseer (fight master), 91

Nastik (1983), 83–84
Natya Vihar Kala Kendra, Mumbai, 17, 133–37, 140
New Woman, 143
Nrithyodaya School, 19
Nritya Yatra, 105–6
Noopur (tele-serial), 106–8, 111

'*O ghaata savri*', 29
'*O mere raja*', 34

Paap Ka Ant (1989), 38, 105
Padukone, Deepika, 182, 207
Pai, Madhav, 21
Pakeezah (1972), 42, 88, 90
'*Palna jhule Nand Gopal*', 204
Pandava Vanavasam (1965), 15
Panja, Ajit Kumar, 105–6
Parampara, 138–39
Parveen Babi, 46, 65, 88, 91
Pathak, Bindheshwar, 154
Pather Panchali, 144
Patil, Smita, 118–19
Patthar Aur Payal (1974), 67
People for Ethical Treatment of Animals India (PETA), 166
Pillai, Arunachalam, 14
Pillai, Guru Kittapa, 16, 138
Pillai, Thiruvalaputhur Swaminatha, 14
Poole, Stanley Lane, 91
Pramanik, 194, 197
Pran, 73, 84
Prem Nagar (1974), 37, 38, 82, 96
Premji, 63, 64
Pritish Nandy Communications (PNC), 145

Qaidi (1984), 84
Queen (2014), 207

Raaj Kumar, 35, 36, 69–70, 93
Rabbit Hole, 188
Radha Krishna (dance drama),
    134, 137, 163
Raghavan, Mohan (cousin), 123,
    178
Raghavan, Prabha (cousin), 113,
    123, 159, 178
Raghavan, Shanta (aunt), 30, 90,
    122, 123, 178
Raghunathan, G., 122
Raghunathan, P., 104
Rajadhyaksha, Gautam, 145
Rajarajeswari, Guru, 125
Rajdhani Films, 87
Rajendran, C.V., 56
Rajinikanth, 73
Rakhee, 28, 35, 36, 42
Ralhan, Shyam, 84, 86
Ramachandran, M.G. (MGR), 20
Ramakrishnan, Malayattoor,
    Yakshi, 121
Ramayana (dance drama), 134, 137
Ramayana (tele-serial), 133
Ramkali (1985), 84
Ramma, P., 138
Ranaut, Kangana, 207
Rangoli, 129
'Ranjish hi sahi, dil hi dukhane ke
    liye aa', 205
Rao, Kamalakara Kameshwara, 15
Rao, N.T. Rama, 208, 209
Rao, Rajkummar, 208
Ravi Shankar, Sri Sri, 160, 162
Ray, Pratibha, *Yajnaseni*, 132

Ray, Satyajit, 20, 144
Razia Sultan (1983), 62, 87–93,
    149
Reddy, Vijay, 105
Rehman, Waheeda, 46, 170
Rekha, 46, 85, 100, 104, 148–49,
    169, 171, 207, 208
Reshma (stunt double), 52
Rihaee (1990), 118–21, 169
Robi O Radha (dance drama), 130
Roja (1992), 122, 124
Roy, Bimal, 1, 32
Roy, Dilip Kumar, 161, 162
Roy, Nirupa, 29
Roy, Prannoy, 169
Roy, Reena, 143
Rukmini Parinay (dance drama),
    134

'*Sa re ga ma*', 29
Sachche Ka Bolbala (1989), 34
Sadiyan, 208
Sagar, Prem, 78, 136
Sagar, Ramanand, 48, 133, 136
Sahni, Balraj, 73
Saira Banu, 28, 66, 111, 170
'*Sajna o sajna*', 29
Salim-Javed, 43, 51, 55
Samanta, Shakti, 207
Sangam (1964), 18
Sanjeev Kumar, 43–46, 50, 55, 63,
    74–75, 79
Sanyasi (1974), 55, 66
Sapno Ka Saudagar (1968), 22,
    23–24, 27, 28, 35, 141, 212
Sarkar, Pradeep, 208
Sathe, V.P., 107
Satte Pe Satta (1982), 71

Satyam, Guru Vempatti Chinna,
    14, 16, 209
Savitri (dance drama), 134
Scindia, Rajmata Vijaya Raje, 68
Second Lady, The, 92
Seeta Aur Geeta (1972), 42–46, 49,
    50, 149, 169, 176, 212
Sen, Arabind, 71
Sen, Asit, 32
Sen, Mrinal, 144
Sen, Shambhu, 60
Sen, Suchitra, 55, 59, 127
Sengupta, Rituparna, 121–22
Shah, Naseeruddin, 118–19
Shaikh, Farooq, 217
Shankar-Jaikishan, 21, 205
Shankar, Pandit Ravi, 63
Shanthi, A.B. (Nirmala, Usha
    Kumari), 71
Sharafat (1970), 24, 27, 32
Sharara (1984), 92–93, 104, 116
Shareef Budmaash (1973), 34
Sharma, Kawal, 127
Sharma, Lakshmi, 21
Sharma, Shivkumar, 194–95, 198,
    204
Sharmilee (1971), 28
Shashikala, 83
Sheshadri, Meenakshi, 104, 164
Shimla Mirchi (2015), 208
Shinde, Gauri, 207
Shinde, M.S., 55
Sholay (1975), 46, 49, 50–56, 58,
    71, 123, 169
Shourie, Sattee, 126
Shri Krishna Vijayam (1971), 209
Shriya, 209
'Singara', 15, 16

Singh, Amrita, 111
Singh, Bhupinder, 59, 60
Singh, Dara, 147
Singh, Gagan, 204
Singh, Gulbahar, 68
Singh, Maya, 146
Sinha, Luv and Kush, 69, 180–81
Sinha, Shatrughan, 68–69, 71, 93,
    180, 181
Sippy, G.P., 55
Sippy, Ramesh, 36, 42–46, 50–55,
    58, 59, 207, 208
Sircar, Shoojit, 183, 192, 207
Sitapur ki Geeta (1987), 84–85, 86
Songati (tele-serial), 129
Sonie, Bhappi, 32
Sood, Sonu, 156
Soundarya Lahari (album), 201,
    202, 203
Sridevi, 85, 100, 207
Sridhar, C.V., 1–4, 18–21, 45,
    70–71
Streep, Meryl, 206, 207
Subbulakshmi, M.S., 19
Subhash, B., 85, 86
Subrahmanyam, K., 18, 19–20
Subrahmanyam, Padma, 19–20
Sujata (1960), 1
Sulabh Sauchalay, 154
Supriyo, Babul, 202
Surdas Prabhu, 163–64, 165
Swachh Bharat campaign, 154
Swami (1977), 59
Swami Vivekananda (1998), 116
Swaraj, Sushma, 146, 147
Swayamsiddha, 83

Tagore, Rabindranath,
    Bahnusingher Padabali, 130

Tagore, Sharmila, 60, 61
Takhtani, Bharat (son-in-law), 164,
    180–81, 184, 192, 195–96,
    210, 212
Tandon, Lekh, 126
Tehzeeb, 172
Tell Me O Kkhuda (2011), 115, 125
Terah Panne (tele-serial), 101–2, 105
Tere Mere Sapne (1971), 34
36 Chowringhee Lane (1981), 29
Tiladaanam (2002), 144
Tipu Sultan, 107
Trishul (1978), 46
Tulsi Ramanayan, 138
Tum Haseen Main Jawan (1970),
    24, 32, 68

Umbartha (tele-serial), 129
Usgaonkar, Varsha, 128
Uttam Kumar, 35

Vaastupurush (2002), 144
Vajpayee, Atal Biahri, 149
Vaswani, Vivek, 111
Veenira Aadai, 70
Veer Zara (2004), 206

Verma, Vrindavan Lal, *Jhansi Ki
    Rani*, 128
Vishnu, 21
Vivek Prakash, 204, 205
Vohraa, Darien (grandson), 183,
    189, 191, 193, 194, 204, 210,
    216
Vohraa, Vaibhav (son-in-law), 165,
    191, 192, 193, 210
Vrindavan widows, 157–59
Vyjayanthimala, 12–13, 16, 18, 20,
    25, 46, 69, 126, 164

Wadkar, Suresh, 201
Walia, Sonu, 111
Wallace, Irving, 92
Women of India – Urvashi, 107,
    108, 125, 128

Yadav, Laloo Prasad, 146
Yashoda Krishna (dance drama),
    134
Yug (teleserial), 126, 129

Zameer, 170
Zinta, Preity, 143, 206